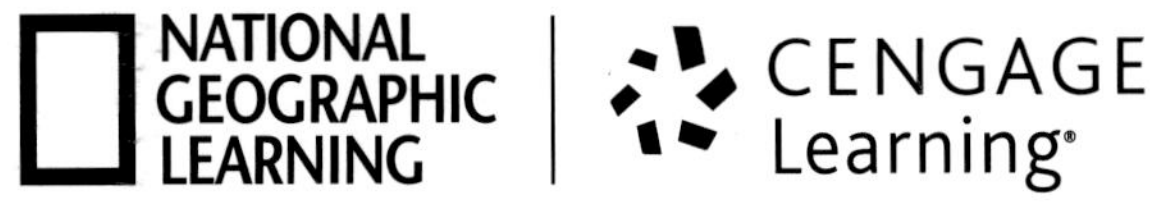

Life

ADVANCED

TEACHER'S BOOK

David A. Hill

Life Advanced Teacher's Book

David A. Hill

Publisher: Gavin McLean

Publishing Consultant: Karen Spiller

Development Editor: Clare Shaw

Strategic Marketing Manager: Charlotte Ellis

Project Editor: Amy Borthwick

Production Controller: Elaine Willis

National Geographic Liaison: Anna Kistin

Art Director: Natasa Arsenidou

Cover design: Vasiliki Christoforidou

Text design: Vasiliki Christoforidou

Compositor: QBS Learning

Audio: Prolingua Productions

ISBN: 978-1-133-31577-3

National Geographic Learning
Cheriton House, North Way, Andover, Hampshire, SP10 5BE
United Kingdom

Cengage Learning is a leading provider of customized learning solutions with office locations around the globe, including Singapore, the United Kingdom, Australia, Mexico, Brazil and Japan. Locate your local office at: **international.cengage.com/region**

Cengage Learning products are represented in Canada by Nelson Education, Ltd.

Visit National Geographic Learning at **ngl.cengage.com**

Visit our corporate website at **cengage.com**

Visit the Life website at **ngl.cengage.com/life**

CREDITS
Although every effort has been made to contact copyright holders before publication, this has not always been possible. If notified, the publisher will undertake to rectify any errors or omissions at the earliest opportunity.

Photos
The publisher would like to thank the following sources for permission to reproduce their copyright protected photographs.
Cover: Bruce Dale/National Geographic Image Collection
Inside: 12 (Rebecca Hale/National Geographic Image Collection), 15 (Angela Bousman/National Geographic Image Collection), 16 (Lawrence Smith/National Geographic Image Collection).

Printed in China by RR Donnelley
Print Number: 03 Print Year: 2016

Contents

Contents

Contents

Contents

Introduction

National Geographic

National Geographic was founded in 1888 and defines its mission as 'to inspire people to care about the planet'. The *National Geographic Society* is one of the world's largest non-profit scientific and educational organisations. It reaches more than 325 million people in more than 30 languages through its magazines, books, TV channels, interactive media, maps, films and music. Proceeds from these activities have funded more than 9,000 scientific, conservation and educational projects around the world. *LIFE* is published in partnership with *National Geographic*, using *National Geographic*'s content and values to 'inspire people to learn English'.

National Geographic topics

The topics are paramount and are the starting point for the lessons. These topics have been selected for their intrinsic interest and ability to fascinate students – and teachers. Once the material has been gathered from the *National Geographic* archives, the language objectives have been matched to the content and then organised into a tried and tested syllabus. The richness of the listening and reading texts and video means that students are so engaged in learning about the content, and expressing their own opinions, that language learning has to take place in order for students to satisfy their curiosity and then react personally to what they have learnt. This element of transfer from the topics to students' own realities and experiences converts the input into a vehicle for language practice and production which fits the recognised frameworks for language learning and can be mapped to the CEFR scales. (Full mapping documents are available separately.)

People and places

LIFE takes students around the globe, investigating the origins of ancient civilisations, showing the drama of natural forces at work and exploring some of the world's most beautiful places. These uplifting tales of adventure and discovery are told through eyewitness accounts and first-class reportage, with superb photos, maps and videos. For example, Unit 2 of the Advanced level tells the story of the lives of the sea gypsies of Myanmar, and Unit 8 includes an article about computer hackers who work for the benefit of society.

Science and technology

Students learn about significant scientific discoveries and breakthroughs, both historic and current. These stories are related by journalists or told by the scientists and explorers themselves through interviews or first person accounts. Students see the impact of the discoveries on our lifestyles and cultures. Because the material comes from a huge archive that has been developed and designed to appeal to the millions of individuals who make up *National Geographic*'s audience, it reflects the broadest possible range of topics. For example, Unit 4 of the Advanced level examines how the ancient art of origami is being used in a range of technological applications from medicine to space travel.

History

History can be a dry topic, especially if it's overloaded with facts and dates. However, the *National Geographic* treatment of historical events brings them to life and there is often a human dimension and universal themes that keep the events relevant to students and to our time. History – or the re-telling of historical events – can also be influenced by a culture or nation's perception of the events. *National Geographic*'s non-judgmental and culture-neutral accounts allow students to look behind the superficial events and gain a deeper understanding of our ancestors. For example, Unit 7 of the Advanced level includes a description of the two sides of the Mongolian General, Genghis Khan and also tells the story of an amazing 16th-century sea voyage that ended in disaster.

Animals

The animal kingdom is exceptionally generative in terms of interesting topics. *LIFE* provides astonishing photos that give a unique insight into the hidden lives of known and lesser-known animals, offering rare glimpses of mammals, birds, bugs and reptiles in their daily struggle for survival. It also informs and surprises with accounts of animals now extinct, species still evolving and endangered species which are literally fighting for their existence. For example, Unit 10 of the Advanced level presents an article about how ants have organised themselves socially to become one of the most successful species on Earth.

Environment

It isn't always possible to find clarity in texts on the environment and climate change, or trust that they are true and not driven by a political agenda. *National Geographic*'s objective journalism, supported by easy-to-understand visuals, presents the issues in an accessible way. The articles are written by experts in their fields. It's often true that those who have the deepest understanding of issues are also able to express the ideas in the simplest way. High-quality thinking and expertise are not synonymous with complicated concepts expressed through complicated language – usually quite the reverse is true. For example, Unit 12 of the Advanced level examines the environmental issues around the extraction of oil from Canada's oil sands in Alberta.

National Geographic photography

We live in a world where images are used more than ever to reinforce, and at times replace, the spoken and written word. To present discourse without them is both unrealistic and unhelpful. Our memories work in pictures, our experiences and the things we learn about the world are stored using them. Raising awareness of this can help students to remember language more easily. All too often photos in books are cosmetic and without impact. *National Geographic* has great photography and powerful images at its core, so it seems natural that photographs in *LIFE* should serve as the starting point for each unit. The photographs in each spread are also integral to the written and recorded content and every opportunity has been taken to use photographs to stimulate learning.

There are photographs which:

- tell a story by themselves
- support understanding of a text and make it memorable
- provoke debate
- stimulate critical thinking by asking you to examine detail OR think about what is NOT shown OR by questioning the photographer's motives
- mean little without a caption or accompanying explanation
- raise questions about the ethics of journalism and photojournalism
- are accompanied by a memorable quotation
- help to remember a lexical set
- help to learn functional language (e.g. how something works)
- lend themselves to practice of a specific grammar point (e.g. significant historical events)

As a first exercise when handing out the new book to your students, why not ask them to flick through the book, select their favourite photograph, and then explain to the class what it is they like about it. You will find specific suggestions in the teacher's notes for using the photographs featured within each unit, but two important things to note are:

- pictures of people or animals capture a moment, so ask students to speculate on the events that led up to this moment and those that followed it
- pictures of places aim to capture their essence, so feed students the vocabulary they need to describe the details that together convey this (the light, the colours, the landscape, the buildings)

National Geographic video

At the back of the Student's Book is a DVD with twelve different *National Geographic* videos on a whole range of subjects. Each video is connected with the topic of a corresponding unit and can be used in conjunction with the video lesson pages in the unit. Typically, a video lesson is divided into three parts:

Before you watch

This section leads students in to the topic of the video and engages them in a pre-watching task.

While you watch

These exercises provide detailed comprehension of the video itself, both in terms of what a student sees and what they hear.

After you watch

This section allows students to respond to the video as a whole and take part in a productive speaking task using language and contexts from the video.

The videos are designed to form part of your lessons. However, if you don't have time in class to watch them all, you can ask students to watch the videos and complete many of the exercises on the page in the Student's Book. This can form a useful part of their self-study. Students can also watch the videos again after seeing them in class. This is useful for review and students can focus on parts of the audio that particularly interest them.

For further variation with the videos, here are some more ideas you can use and develop:

- Play the video with the sound down. Students predict what the narrator or people are saying. Then play with the sound up and compare.
- Play the sound only with no video. Students predict where the video takes place and what is happening on the screen. Then play with the screen on and compare.
- Show the first part of the video, pause it, and then ask students what they think happens next.
- Give students a copy of the audioscript for the video and ask them to imagine they are the director. What will they need to film and show on the screen? Afterwards, they present their 'screenplay' and finally watch the original.
- Write a short text on the same topic as the one in the video. However, don't include the same amount of information and leave some facts out. Students read the text and then watch the video. They make notes on any new information and rewrite the text so it includes the new details.
- With monolingual groups, choose part of the video with someone talking. Ask students to listen and write down what they say. Then, in groups, ask them to create subtitles in their own language for that part of the video. Each group presents their subtitles and the class compares how similar they are.

National Geographic and critical thinking

There is a graded critical-thinking syllabus in *LIFE* that starts with the Elementary level and runs through all the later levels. The critical-thinking activities appear in the c spreads in each unit. The syllabus covers areas such as reading between the lines, differentiating between opinion and fact, evaluating the reliability of source material, assessing the relevance of information, identifying the techniques used by an author to persuade the reader, weighing up evidence, etc. These activities require students to engage with the reading texts at a deeper level and to show real understanding – not just reading comprehension. This training – in evaluating texts, assessing the validity and strength of arguments and developing an awareness of authorial techniques – is clearly a valuable skill for those students learning English for academic purposes (EAP), where reflective learning is essential. However, it is also very much part of the *National Geographic* spirit which encourages people to question assumptions and develop their own well-informed and reasoned opinions. In this sense it adds another dimension to the experience of learning English through *National Geographic* material.

LIFE methodology

Treatment of grammar

Target grammar is presented through texts in the first two spreads of each unit. These texts are authentic reading and listening texts, adapted for level as necessary, which use the target language in natural and appropriate linguistic contexts. Such texts not only aid comprehension, but present good models for the learner's own language production through a variety of 'voices' and genres. The main input alternates between reading and listening on these first two spreads. Where a presentation is a listening text, written examples of the grammar structures are given on the page, for example in content comprehension tasks, so that visual support is also provided.

The primary focus is on the topic content before the learner's attention is drawn to the target grammar structures. Learners are first directed to *notice* this language by various means, such as using highlighting within the text, extracting sample sentences or having learners locate examples themselves.

A variety of task formats are used to lead learners to *analyse* the form, meaning and use of the grammar structures, as appropriate. Such an approach can be highly motivational by actively engaging learners in the lesson and allowing them to share and discuss their interpretation of the new language. After this stage, clear paradigms or examples of form and use are given on the page in a simple *summary* box. This supports the learners and is a 'check point' for the teacher and learners alike as it summarises the information learners will have arrived at through completing the discovery tasks. A cross-reference is provided to more detailed information and additional exercises at the back of the book. These are suitable for use both in class and for self-study, according to the needs of the learners.

The grammar *practice* tasks within the unit are linked to the presentation text and topic and are thus content-rich in the same way. They move from more supported exercises through to more challenging tasks. Depending on the level, they have a differing emphasis on form and use. The practice tasks give learners an opportunity to *personalise* the structures and practise them in the context of their own experiences and situations. This *anchors* the new language in existing frameworks and leads to a clearer understanding of the usage of this new or revised language. Equally, the practice exercises incorporate a real reason to use the target structure whether by devices such as quizzes, games, etc. or by genuine exchange of information between students.

A final task on each spread allows the learners to create their own output and is structured so that learners have the opportunity to use the target grammar as well as other target language, for example, vocabulary, in a meaningful context. This final task has a variety of formats such as discussions, personal narratives, task-based activities (ranking, etc.) and the emphasis from the learner's perspective is on *content and fluency* rather than grammatical accuracy.

Aside from the two main grammar input spreads, the target grammar is also recycled in the subsequent spreads of each unit and beyond.

Treatment of vocabulary

LIFE teaches vocabulary in a range of different ways. This eclectic approach takes account of recent research, but doesn't abandon tried and tested methods. There is further practice of all of this vocabulary input (apart from words occurring in glossaries) in the Workbook.

1 Lexical sets

Some of the benefits generally associated with teaching words in lexical sets are:

- learning words in a set requires less effort
- retrieving related words from memory is easier
- seeing how knowledge can be organised can be helpful to learners
- it mirrors how such information is stored in the brain
- the meaning of words can be made clearer by comparing and contrasting them to similar words in the set

Each unit usually has two or more lexical sets. The lexical sets also cover commonly confused words. There is evidence to suggest that once students have learnt one or more of the words that belong to a group of commonly confused words (e.g. *job* and *work*), it is useful to compare and contrast these words directly to clarify the differences (or similarities) in meaning. *LIFE* focuses on these groups of words as and when they come up.

2 Word focus

The *Word focus* sections take high-frequency words and give examples of the different meanings they can have according to the contexts in which they appear and the different words they collocate with. At higher levels there is increased exposure to idioms and colloquial usage. The Workbook expands the range of phrases and expressions generated by these key words and provides further practice.

3 Wordbuilding

The independent wordbuilding syllabus offers students another opportunity to expand their vocabulary. The *Wordbuilding* boxes in the units focus on areas such as prefixes, suffixes, collocations, parts of speech (e.g. noun→adjective), compound nouns, phrasal verbs, and highlight examples from the reading or listening texts. The box gives a brief explanation and some examples. There is an activity for further practice and a reference to an activity in the Workbook which introduces more words that belong to the same morphological area.

4 Glossaries

Where certain words are important to the meaning of a text, but are above the level of the student, they are glossed. Students aren't expected to learn these words, but the short and simple definitions prevent them from being a barrier to understanding.

Learning skills

There is a comprehensive learning skills syllabus in the Workbook. This covers traditional learning skills, such as recording new vocabulary, using a dictionary, remembering new vocabulary, planning study time, assessing your own progress, etc.

Assessment

Students and teachers can assess progress in the following ways:

- Each unit in the Student's Book finishes with a one-page review where students do the exercises and complete a number of 'can-do' statements linked to the objectives of the unit.
- There are photocopiable tests in the Teacher's Book.
- There is a *Check!* section at the end of each unit in the Workbook for students to check what they have learnt (general knowledge as well as language).
- There are IELTS practice tests at the end of the Workbooks. These have been graded to the level of the course, but follow the format of the test. These allow students to benchmark their progress against the course objectives, whilst becoming familiar with a global test format.

Components

- Student's Book + DVD
- Workbook + audio
- Teacher's Book and class audio

Overview of a Student's Book unit

Opener: a one-page introduction to the unit that gets students interested in the topic

a and b: double-page lessons that teach grammar and vocabulary through reading and listening texts

c: a double-page lesson that focuses on reading comprehension

d: a one-page lesson that teaches a speaking skill and functional/situational language

e: a one-page lesson that teaches a writing skill and the features of a text type

f: a double-page lesson of video comprehension exercises

Review: a one-page lesson of practice activities and 'can-do' check statements

Lesson type b

Grammar and vocabulary

This double-page spread is a grammar and vocabulary lesson: Lesson 4b Fold everything.

The primary focus is on the topic content before the learner's attention is drawn to the target grammar structures.

The main target grammar is presented through texts in the first two spreads of each unit. These texts are authentic or realistic reading and listening texts, adapted for level as necessary, which use the target language in natural and appropriate linguistic contexts. Such texts not only aid comprehension, but present good models for the learner's own language production through a variety of 'voices' and genres. The main input is via both reading and listening on these first two spreads.

reading **origami engineering** • idioms **partitives** • language focus **probability** • speaking **origami ideas**

4b Fold everything

Reading

1 Look at the picture of a horse made using origami, the traditional Japanese art of paper folding. Answer the questions.

1 Do you do any kind of hand crafts? What are they?
2 Have you ever tried origami? What did you make?

2 Work in pairs. What are the basic principles of origami? Are these sentences true (T) or false (F)? Read the first paragraph of the article and check your answers.

1 You need more than one piece of paper.
2 The paper should be square.
3 You mustn't use scissors.
4 Sometimes you need to use glue.

3 Read the rest of the article and find the following.

1 two things used in space exploration that are folded using origami techniques
2 two origami-inspired devices that help to save lives
3 a use of origami that seems like a fantasy
4 a use of origami that can make machines more powerful

Fold EVERYTHING

Almost certainly you have at one time in your life practised origami, even if it was just making a paper aeroplane. Perhaps it was something more sophisticated like a paper crane. The chances are that as you did it, you reflected on how ingenious this traditional Japanese art is. Animals, boxes, flowers, boats – all can be created from a single square or rectangular sheet of paper simply by folding it – no cutting, no pasting.

But did you ever stop to think how the same techniques might be applied to engineer equipment that could be of real practical use? In fact, origami-inspired creations have already flown in space; in 1995, Japanese engineers launched a satellite with solar panels that folded like a map. And very soon origami engineering may well be seen in a host of other applications.

'It's now mathematically proven that you can pretty much fold anything,' says physicist Robert J. Lang, who quit his engineering job in California eight years ago to fold things full-time. Lang, an origami enthusiast since the age of six, advised a well-known car manufacturer on the best way to fold an airbag into a dashboard. He is currently working on a space telescope lens that, if all goes to plan, should be able to unfold to the size of a football pitch.

At the other end of the scale, researchers are also working on tiny folding devices that could lead to breakthroughs in medicine and computing.These include origami stents that are inserted into arteries and open up to keep the blood flowing. Computers of the future are likely to contain tiny, folded motors or capacitors, which will mean faster processing and better memory storage.

There's no doubt that saving space has become important in our world, as the search for ever smaller electronic components shows. But origami also meets the demand for things which need to be small when transported and large when they arrive, like the everyday umbrella.

Applications for origami engineering go further than many of us might imagine. 'Some day,' says MIT's* Erik Demaine, 'we'll build reconfigurable robots that can fold on their own from one thing into another,' like Transformers. Too much like science fiction to be true? Maybe; though you certainly wouldn't bet against it.

* *MIT = Massachusetts Institute of Technology*

crane (n) /kreɪn/ a large bird with long legs
ingenious (adj) /ɪn'dʒiːnɪəs/ very clever
stent (n) /stent/ a thin rod used in medicine to support a cavity in the body

48

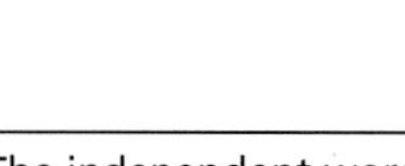

The independent wordbuilding syllabus offers students another opportunity to expand their vocabulary. The *Wordbuilding* boxes in the units focus on areas such as prefixes, suffixes, collocations, parts of speech (e.g. noun > adjective), compound nouns, phrasal verbs, and highlight examples from the reading or listening texts. The box gives a brief explanation and some examples. There is an activity for further practice and a reference to an activity in the Workbook which introduces more words that belong to the same morphological area.

4 Work in pairs. Explain the following terms and expressions from the article.

1 How is a paper crane 'more sophisticated' than an aeroplane? (para 1)
2 What is meant by 'applications'? (para 2)
3 What 'plan' is referred to in the phrase 'if all goes to plan'? (para 3)
4 What scale is referred to in the phrase 'At the other end of the scale'? (para 4)
5 What does 'it' mean in the phrase 'you wouldn't bet against it'? (para 6)

WORDBUILDING past participles as adjectives

We often use past participles as adjectives.
*a **well-known** car manufacturer, tiny **folded** motors*
In a few cases, the adjective form is different from the past participle.
*It has been **proved**. A proven **method**.*

For further information and practice, see Workbook page 35.

Idioms partitives

5 Compare these two expressions. Which expression means 'some' or 'a piece of' and which means 'a small piece'?

1 **a sheet** of paper
2 **a scrap** of paper

6 Look at the partitive expressions in bold and say which mean 'some' and which 'a small piece or amount'.

1 I'm really thirsty. I haven't had **a drop** of water all day.
2 It was **a stroke** of luck getting those tickets. They were the last two available.
3 There's not **a shred** of evidence to suggest that there is life on other planets.
4 The latest figures offer **a glimmer** of hope that the recession is coming to an end.
5 She had **a flash** of inspiration. Why not use the principles of origami to make foldable furniture?
6 There was **a hint** of disappointment in his voice, but he took the news very well.

Language focus probability

7 Work in pairs. How many examples of the following can you find in the article? Compare your answers with your partner.

1 phrases that say something is possible
2 phrases that say something is probable
3 phrases that say something is more or less sure

Example:
1 *Perhaps it was … (paragraph 1)*

8 Look at the sentences and say whether they use a verb, an adverb, an adjective or a noun phrase to express probability. Is there any difference in meaning or register between them?

1 He probably won't come with us.
2 It's unlikely that he'll come with us.
3 He may (well) not come with us.
4 The chances are that he won't come with us.

PROBABILITY

Modal verbs
may/could/might; should
Origami may (well) be the answer.
The telescope should help us to explore the universe.

Adverbs
perhaps; maybe; probably; almost certainly
Perhaps one day they will invent foldable robots.

The adjective (un)likely
It's (un)likely that this technology will be used in computers.
This technology is (un)likely to be used in computers.

Noun phrases
The likelihood is; The chances are; There is a good chance
The chances are that it will be used in robot design.

Note: *should* is not used for the probability of something bad happening.

For further information and practice, see page 161.

9 Look at the language box. Then rewrite the sentences in the text using the words given.

The grocery shopping bag of the future [1] *will perhaps be made of steel* (could). The folding steel bag, invented by Dr Zhong You from Oxford University, [2] *will probably inspire other packaging solutions too* (likely to). Flat-pack boxes used by industry these days have to be fastened at the bottom. But with Dr You's origami design [3] *you can make boxes with a fixed base* (possible). [4] *This is likely to save industry a lot of time and money* (should).

Dr You thinks that if this process works for steel, [5] *it will probably work for a range of other materials* (the chances). Origami engineers hope that [6] *one day perhaps it will be possible to build houses from flat-pack materials* (might). In ten years' time, [7] *it's very possible that we will be folding away our kitchen counters or table* (may well). [8] *The likelihood is that we won't have foldable TVs or cars* (unlikely), but who knows?

Speaking

10 Work in pairs. Think of three more ideas for how origami methods could be used to help save space in the modern home. Then present your ideas to another pair.

Clear paradigms or examples of form and use are given on the page in a simple *summary* box. This supports the learners and is a 'check point' for the teacher and learners alike as it summarises the information learners will have arrived at through completing the discovery tasks. A cross-reference is provided to more detailed information and additional exercises at the back of the book. These are suitable both for use in class and self-study, according to the needs of the learners.

The grammar practice tasks within the unit are linked to the presentation text and topic and are thus content-rich in the same way. They move from more supported exercises through to more challenging tasks.

A variety of task formats are used to lead learners to *analyse* the form, meaning and use of the grammar structures, as appropriate.

A final task on each spread allows the learners to create their own output and is structured so that learners have the opportunity to use the target grammar as well as other target language, for example vocabulary, in a meaningful context. This final task has a variety of formats such as discussions, personal narratives, task-based activities (ranking, etc.) and the emphasis from the learner's perspective is on content and fluency rather than grammatical accuracy.

Lesson type c

Reading

This page is the first page of a double-page reading lesson. The reading text is always on the right-hand page, and the activities on the left.

The mini contents section at the beginning of every lesson sets clear targets.

The *Word focus* sections take high-frequency words and give examples of the different meanings they can have according to the contexts in which they appear and the different words they collocate with.

Critical-thinking activities require students to engage with the reading texts at a deeper level, and require them to show real understanding – not just reading comprehension. This training – in evaluating texts, assessing the validity and strength of arguments and developing an awareness of authorial techniques – is clearly a valuable skill for those students learning English for academic purposes (EAP) where reflective learning is essential. Moreover, it is also very much part of the *National Geographic* spirit which encourages people to question assumptions, and develop their own well-informed and reasoned opinions.

reading **a social entrepreneur** • critical thinking **finding counter arguments** • word focus ***give*** • speaking **being on the spot**

4c The shoe giver

Reading

1 Read the definition of *social entrepreneurship* and say which of the examples (a–c) fit the definition and why. How would you describe the other operations?

Social entrepreneurship is the art of creating a socially responsible business that aims to generate profit while solving social and environmental problems.

a An organisation which collects food near its sell-by date from supermarkets and distributes it free to homeless people.
b An organisation which sells gardening services to companies. The people it employs are all long-term unemployed people who get training, work experience and a small salary.
c An organisation that collects old clothes that people are throwing out and recycles the material to make new clothes which it sells.

2 Read the article on page 51. In what ways does TOMS fit the definition of social entrepreneurship given in Exercise 1? Why? / Why not?

3 Read the article again. Are the sentences true (T) or false (F)?

1 Mycoskie's early career was characterised by establishing and then selling companies.
2 Mycoskie immediately saw the Argentinian children's shoe problem as another business challenge.
3 The main advantage of the one-for-one scheme is that each child is given one pair of shoes.
4 Podioconiosis is a disease that affects children in developed countries as much as in developing countries.
5 The author suggests that, in business, energy and enthusiasm are as important as knowledge.
6 Any business could profit from making a similar one-for-one offer to its customers.

Critical thinking **finding counter arguments**

4 The author presents a positive picture of TOMS, but there are suggestions that there are also arguments against the initiative. Find possible criticisms in the text in these areas.

a the price and quality of the product
b buying shoes as a way of giving to charity
c the business model

5 Work in pairs. Compare your answers from Exercise 4. Then write some questions for Blake Mycoskie that would challenge him on these points.

Word focus ***give***

6 Work in pairs. Find these expressions with *give* in the article and discuss what they mean.

give it a break give it some thought

7 Complete the expressions with *give* using these words. Discuss what each expression means.

best break go go ahead thought time

1 There's no need to tell me your answer now. **Give it some** ________ and then let me know.
2 Don't worry if you don't win: just **give it your** ________.
3 I wasn't actually expecting him to like our business proposal, but he **gave us the** ________.
4 **Give him a** ________. He's only been doing the job two months. He can't be expected to know everything.
5 It's difficult to be in a new environment, but **give it some** ________ and you'll feel more at home.
6 The only way to find out if you can mend it yourself is to **give it a** ________.

8 Match these expressions with a similar expression from Exercise 7.

a chance consideration the green light
a try a while your all

Speaking

9 Work in pairs. You are going to act out an interview between a journalist for an ecology magazine and Blake Mycoskie. Take turns to play the roles of interviewer (the journalist) and interviewee (Blake Mycoskie). Think about the questions that were raised about the shoe-giving initiative in Exercise 5.

Student A: You are the journalist. Focus on the possible problems with the one-for-one shoe giving business and ask questions that test Mycoskie to defend it.

Student B: You are Blake Mycoskie. Defend your business and its philosophy.

50

Lesson type d

Real life

This page is the one-page functional lesson from Unit 7.

real life **asking for confirmation and clarification** • speaking skill **prefacing a question and seeking clarification** • pronunciation **intonation in questions**

7d I blame the weather

Real life asking for confirmation and clarification

1 Work in pairs. Discuss the questions.

1 What was the last lecture or talk you attended?
2 Why did you go?
3 What did you find out?

2 Quickly read the abstract of a history lecture. Then cover the text and answer the questions.

1 What will the lecture be about?
2 What general question will it try to address?

LET'S TALK ABOUT THE WEATHER

2.00 p.m. Forth Lecture Hall

Abstract: Weather affects events. Think how your own plans can be changed by snow or even just by a little rain. Then extend this to a larger scale, and you can imagine how more dramatic changes in the climate might have helped to shape human history. For example, how did a drought in Africa contribute to the decline of the Roman Empire? How did a cold spell in Europe lead to persecutions in the 17th century?

This lecture examines the connection between climate changes and specific events in world history and asks whether we pay too little attention to the environment in our studies of the past.

3 2.4 You are going to hear four people asking questions after the lecture. Put the number of the questioner next to the topic they ask about.

a the meaning of the term 'Little Ice Age' ☐
b the connection between cold weather and punishment ☐
c the connection between the weather and the rat population ☐
d the connection between the weather and the fail of the Roman Empire ☐

4 Speaking skill prefacing a question and seeking clarification

2.4 Work in pairs. Look at the box. The questioners prefaced each question with a comment. Listen again and tick (✓) the phrases they use to preface each question. What is the purpose of these phrases?

▶ PREFACING A QUESTION AND SEEKING CLARIFICATION

Prefacing a question
If I understood correctly, you said that …
I'd just like to make sure I understand what you said about …
I'd like to pick up on one thing you said about …
The logical conclusion of your argument is that …
You mentioned …
Perhaps I missed something, but …

Seeking clarification
Am I right in thinking that [1] ________ ?
Can you expand a bit more on that?
[2] ________ . Is that what you're saying?
Can you explain what you meant by [3] ________ ?
How do [4] ________ fit in with ________ ?

5 2.4 Complete the questions used to seek clarification in the box (1–4). Then listen again and check your answers.

6 Pronunciation intonation in questions

a 2.5 Work in pairs. Listen to the questions. Does the intonation rise or fall in each one? What rule do they follow about *wh-* and *yes/no* questions?

1 Am I right in thinking that the drought was the cause?
2 Would you go along with that?
3 Can you explain what you meant by that?
4 How do punishments fit in with the Little Ice Age?
5 And what's your own opinion?

b Practise reading the questions in Exercise 6a with the correct intonation.

7 Work in pairs. You are each going to give a short talk about a historical event which was affected by weather. Look at the notes and prepare your talk. Then ask and answer questions. Remember to preface each question with a comment.

Student A: Turn to page 155.

Student B: Turn to page 156.

88 TALK ABOUT ▶ STORIES FROM HISTORY ▶ SOCIAL HISTORY ▶ HISTORICAL IRONY ▶ CONFIRMATION AND CLARIFICATION
WRITE ▶ DESCRIBING A PAST EVENT

The d lessons have clear 'Real life' functional aims.

A specific speaking skill is highlighted in every d lesson.

The pronunciation syllabus covers sounds and spelling; connected speech; stress and intonation.

Lesson type e

Writing

This page is the one-page writing lesson from Unit 7.

Every e lesson has a specific text type.

A different writing skill is presented and practised in every e lesson.

Every writing lesson includes a model.

7e Krakatoa

Writing describing a past event

1 Look at the photo and caption. What kind of island is this? Do you know any others like it?

2 Work in pairs. Read the short historical account about Krakatoa and answer the questions. Then discuss your answers with your partner.

1 What historical point is the writer trying to make?
2 What evidence does she give to support this?

In 1883, the volcano on the island of Krakatoa erupted with such force that the explosion could be heard 160 km away, sending ash as high as 6 km into the atmosphere. Until then, few people had ever heard of Krakatoa. It was just a small island passed by ships who navigated the straits between Java and Sumatra.

The major eruption took place on Monday 27th August, causing the deaths of tens of thousands of people on neighbouring islands, and destroying two-thirds of Krakatoa itself. But the lasting climatic effects were just as dramatic. In the preceding months the volcano had already been active, discharging so much ash into the sky that it blocked out the sun for miles around. However, the ash that entered the upper atmosphere after the main eruption was blown right around the globe on the trade winds. The following year, climatologists recorded a 1.2° C drop in global temperatures, which did not return to normal levels until some years later.

Unusual global weather patterns seem to have continued in the years following the eruption of Krakatoa. Nebraska, in the USA, suffered an extraordinary winter in 1888, when temperatures dropped 18 degrees in three minutes and up to 125 cm of snow fell in 36 hours – unheard of in those days, when 60 cm was the average for a whole year. Proving a direct connection between these events and the eruption is, of course, impossible, but the evidence is quite compelling.

Krakatoa erupting, Indonesia

3 Writing skill sequencing events

a Work in pairs. How does the writer sequence the different events surrounding the eruption of Krakatoa? Put these events in the order they appear in the text.

a events following the eruption of 1883
b the events leading up to the eruption of 1883
c the eruption itself

b Read the account again and find time phrases about the past which correspond to each of the present time phrases (a–d).

Present	Past
a up to now	1 ________
b in recent months	2 ________
c next year	3 ________
d nowadays	4 ________

c Complete the sentences with the correct time phrases. Use the words given.

Viewed from the present	Viewed from a point in the past
some days ago	They had met 1 ________ . (earlier)
tomorrow	There were further eruptions 2 ________ . (following)
at the moment	No one was living on Krakatoa 3 ________ . (time)
yesterday	Loud noises were heard 4 ________ . (previous)
from now on	Krakatoa became famous 5 ________ . (then)

4 Write about an event that happened in your town or region. Use the ideas below to help you. Describe the events leading up to the main event, the main event and the aftermath. Write 200–250 words.

- an extreme weather event
- the visit of an important person
- a sporting event or festival
- a special music event or festival

5 Exchange accounts with your partner. Use these questions to check your accounts.

- Is the sequence of events clear?
- Are the facts presented objectively?
- Are arguments supported by clear evidence?
- Have the correct time phrases been used?

Students always finish with a productive task.

Students are encouraged to take part in peer correction.

Unit 1 Lessons for life

Lead-in

Personal response

Ask students to say what they know about life in the desert. Try to elicit information about how people survive there, what they do and what problems they face. If any students have experience of being in a desert, invite them to tell the class about it. Then ask specifically if they know anything about the Tuareg.

1 Ask students to work in pairs to talk about the photo, and discuss what the Tuareg proverbs say about their views on life. When they have discussed their ideas with another pair, elicit ideas from the class, and open up the discussion to everyone.

2 Ask students to read through the three questions to focus their listening. Play the recording once and ask students to answer. They can then check with a partner. Play the recording once more to check, correct and complete. Elicit the answers.

ANSWERS

1 Speaker 1: You can't change other people.
Speaker 2: You shouldn't get angry over little things, or react too quickly and emotionally.
2 Speaker 1: He followed this advice with a work colleague and now they have a better working relationship.
Speaker 2: She had a disagreement with a friend and they ended up not speaking.
3 Speaker 2: It is always possible to reach agreement.

Audioscript [1.1]

Speaker 1

I think the most valuable lesson anyone has ever taught me was when I was about 25. I was getting really frustrated with a guy I was working with. We'd set up our own web design business and Giles – that was the name of my business partner – would always get lost in little details and take ages making a first design to show the customer. And my dad said, 'Look, you can't change other people; you can only change the way you behave towards them.' So I accepted that was just Giles's way – that he loved the little details – and I tried to think of it as a positive thing and we've got on so much better ever since, and worked much more effectively. So that's become a sort of guiding principle for me in life – not to try to change others – and I have to say, it's stood me in very good stead.

Speaker 2

Here's a good rule of thumb: 'Don't come to blows over small things.' But it's a lot easier said than done. The number of times I've sent off an angry email without thinking about the consequences, or got upset because something wasn't done the way I wanted it to be done, you'd think I'd have learned my lesson. The other day my friend, John, asked for my help writing a job application, and I told him the letter he had written was much too informal. He didn't agree and I ended up getting really frustrated and shouting at him. He didn't talk to me for days afterwards. I feel really ashamed when I think about it. Now I always make a point of not reacting too quickly to things I disagree with.

Background note

The Tuareg are a Berber people traditionally living a nomadic lifestyle across the Sahara Desert in north Africa; they are the main people found living across Mali, Niger, Algeria, Morocco, Libya and Burkina Faso. The language they speak is called Tamasheq. Their life is based upon trading, and they are famously connected with the great camel trade routes across the Sahara. They also herd cattle and are involved in agriculture.

3 [1.1] Ask students to complete the sentences individually, then check with a partner. Play the recording again for them to check, complete and correct their answers. Elicit answers from the whole class.

ANSWERS

1 valuable
2 guiding
3 stood, stead
4 thumb
5 said, done
6 point

4 Ask students to consider a time when they learned an important lesson; suggest that they make a few brief notes to answer the questions. Then ask them to share their experience with a partner, and ask and answer questions about it. Elicit some experiences from those who wish to share them with the class.

1a Learning from the past

Lead-in

Personal response

Ask students as a whole class to discuss whether they think people ever learn from the past. Ask them to give examples which show that people do or do not do so. If the general conclusion is that people do not learn much from the past, you might try to elicit why this happens (e.g. if we learn from the past that war is terrible, why do we keep having wars?).

Reading

1 Ask students to read and discuss the Eleanor Roosevelt quotation in pairs. Elicit their responses to it as a whole class.

2 Ask students to read the three types of lesson and remember them as they read the article, in order to match the people with the lessons they taught. Draw students' attention to the two vocabulary glosses at the bottom of the article. Elicit answers from the whole class.

ANSWERS

1 c 2 a

Extra activity

Ask students what they know about Confucius and Nelson Mandela. Try to initiate a discussion about the importance of what they did and said for humankind.

Background notes

Confucius (551–479 BC) was a Chinese thinker and social philosopher. His teachings emphasised morality, correct social relationships, justice and sincerity.

Nelson Mandela (b. 1918) is a South African politician who was imprisoned for 27 years by the white regime, but then fought for reconciliation and became the first fully democratically elected president from 1994–1999.

3 Ask students to read through the sentences, then read the article and decide whether the sentences are true or false. They can then check with a partner before you elicit the answers from the whole class. Have students read out the statement before they say whether they think it is true or false.

ANSWERS

1 T 2 T 3 F 4 T 5 F 6 T

4 Ask students to find the expressions individually, then check them with a partner. Elicit the phrases, and discuss their use with the class. Read the description of noun formation and the examples in the *Wordbuilding* box. Ask students if they can give some more examples. Point out what happens to adjectives like *happy* in this process (the *-y* is changed to *-i* before the suffix is added: *happiness*). If you feel it is necessary, look at the further information on Workbook page 11 with the class.

ANSWERS

1 point the way
2 sums up the government's philosophy
3 strive for
4 follow the example set by
5 heed this warning

Language focus time phrases

5 Ask students to work individually to find the verbs which are used with the phrases and identify their tenses. They can check their answers with a partner. Elicit answers from the whole class. Read through the language focus box about time phrases with the class, and discuss the contents. If you feel it is necessary, look at the further information and do the practice on page 157 with the class.

ANSWERS

1 has become (present perfect simple)
2 have been saying (present perfect continuous)
3 focused (past simple)
4 had not been (past perfect)
5 is … developing (present continuous)
6 sums up (present simple)
7 he was living (past continuous)
8 will have to (future simple)

Grammar notes

The time phrases we most frequently use with particular tenses support the meaning of that tense, so *every day, each week, on Mondays* emphasise the 'routine' sense of the present simple, and thus would be inappropriate for the present continuous with its 'at the moment' reference, or the past simple with its 'completed past action' sense. This is true of all the time phrases and their related tenses referred to in the language focus box.

6 Ask students to work in pairs. They should use the information about time phrases from the language focus box to help them complete the sentences with the phrases in the box. Note that in some cases more than one answer is correct. Elicit the answers from the whole class and discuss what alternatives are possible.

ANSWERS

1 50 years ago
2 nowadays / at the moment
3 in the coming years
4 over the last 25 years
5 for some time
6 often
7 at the moment
8 at the time
9 ever
10 before that

7 Ask students to write personal sentences individually, then share them with a partner.

8 Ask students to pass on some of the information they have heard to a new partner. If it is appropriate, elicit some examples from the whole class.

Extra activity

Play a fast response game with the class, where you give a time phrase to a student and they have to respond immediately with a personal sentence using that phrase, and using the correct tense, as in the following example.

Teacher: *Maria: last week*.

Maria: *I went to Rome last week*.

Teacher: *Mikel: since*.

Mikel: *I've been studying English since I was fifteen*.

Try to keep the pace going, to make it more like real-life conversation.

Speaking

9 Ask students to match the expressions in pairs, then check with another pair. Elicit the answers and discuss their ideas with the whole class.

ANSWERS

1 b 2 c 3 e 4 a 5 d

10 Organise the class into groups of four or five students. Read through the instructions with the class, then ask students to write their favourite English saying, or one from their mother tongue translated into English, on a piece of paper. In their groups they should put all the pieces of paper in a pile on the table. Students take turns to take a paper, read the saying and discuss the meaning, then guess who wrote it.

1b Who do you think you are?

Lead-in

Personal response

Ask students to work with a partner and answer the question *Who are you?* in five different ways. Give them an example, by having different students ask you the question, e.g. Student 1: *Who are you?* Teacher: *I'm an English teacher*. Student 2: *Who are you?* Teacher: *I'm Donald's daughter*. Student 3: *Who are you?* Teacher: *I'm a bicycle rider*. Discuss the activity and its outcomes with the class.

Listening

1 Ask students to work with a partner, look at the photo and discuss the two questions. Elicit ideas from the whole class.

SAMPLE ANSWERS

1 No, he didn't. He wants us to look at his portrait and not at him. Perhaps he doesn't want us to compare the real man with the portrait, which shows how he would like us to see him.
2 The portrait shows him as a dramatic and romantic figure with his black hat and cloak. He probably looks more attractive in the portrait.

2 Ask students, individually, to decide which factors they think are most important in defining who they are (point out that they shouldn't tick the items as they will need to do this in Exercise 3). Suggest they can add other factors if they feel something important is not covered. Ask them to then discuss their ideas with a partner. Elicit answers from the whole class and have an open discussion.

Extra activity

You could try and do a whole-class ranking activity, in which the class discusses all the factors and comes to a group decision about importance, with you listing them on the board from most important at the top to least important at the bottom.

3 [1.2] Ask students to listen to the sociologist and tick the factors in Exercise 2 as they are mentioned. They should also decide which factor she feels is most important. Students can check their answers with a partner. If it seems necessary, play the recording again for them to check before you elicit answers from the whole class.

ANSWERS

The sociologist mentions b, c, e, f, g.
She thinks the most important factor is your life experiences.

Audioscript [1.2]

So let's start by considering these descriptions of people: 'Oh, John – he's a family man'; 'Sarah's an anthropologist – she's spent most of her life studying apes in Africa'; 'Frank's a keen coin collector – he's been collecting coins since he was a boy'; 'Jack is one of life's drifters – he will have been just about everywhere by the time he's 60'; 'Anne's a committed animal rights campaigner – that came as a shock to her friends because she had never even owned a pet before she joined the Animal Defence League!'

We define each person by a different criterion: their interests; their profession; their outlook on life; or by their values – like the importance of family for John – and their beliefs. So which of these things is it that really defines a person?

What if we asked the same question about a six-year-old child? Well, you'd actually say that what defined them first and foremost are the common factors that make them a child – being curious about the world, often playful, a bit vulnerable maybe. In ten years, that child will have become a teenager and teenagers, of course, share certain defining characteristics too. They tend to be quite self-centred and moody. Often they're angry at the world. And because they're not sure of what their identity is, they define themselves by what they are not and by the things they dislike. 'But Mum, I don't want to go to technical college. I hate maths.'

Now let's look again at the adults we described at first. John, our family man, has a job as a carpet salesman, which is OK. It's a job and it keeps him and his family comfortable. He had had an opportunity to run his own business at one point, but he decided job security was more important. His real passion is his family and spending time with his two boys. Sarah, the anthropologist, on the other hand, lives for her work. She's visited Central Africa many times to study Bonobo apes and is fascinated by their social behaviour. Jack – 'the drifter' – has been doing bits and pieces of carpentry and building work. He loves travelling and experiencing different environments, so he picks up work as and when he can. He fell in love when he was 25, but the relationship ended and he hasn't committed to anyone else since.

So, we can see that what defines each of these people in the end is their life experiences. It could be within their job or interests or relationships that these occurred, but it is the experiences themselves that shape each of us as individuals. So when someone asks you, 'What do you do', they are …

4 [1.2] Ask students to read through the multiple-choice options carefully. Play the recording again while they listen and choose the correct options. They can then check with a partner. If it seems necessary, play the recording again for them to check before you elicit answers from the whole class.

ANSWERS

1 a 2 c 3 c 4 b 5 b 6 a

Extra activity

Ask students to look at the audioscript on page 174 of the Student's Book and find words with the following meanings:

devoted to his wife and children; enthusiastic; a person who moves from place to place; very involved; defenceless; bad-tempered and depressed

(Answers: *a family man, keen, a drifter, committed, vulnerable, moody*)

Idioms irreversible word pairs

5 Ask students to underline the correct word pairs individually, then check with a partner. Discuss the meanings with the class (in brackets in the answer key).

ANSWERS

1 first and foremost (=the most important thing)
2 as and when (=when it is possible)
3 bits and pieces (=various different things)

Extra activity

Ask students individually to write three sentences about themselves, using one of the three expressions in Exercise 5 in each one. They should then share them with a partner. Elicit some of their sentences in a whole-class setting.

6 Ask students to match the words in the box with the irreversible pairs in bold in the sentences. They can then check with a partner. Elicit answers from the whole class.

ANSWERS

1 odds and ends – small things; by and large – in general
2 law and order – control of crime; peace and quiet – a state of calm
3 ifs and buts – objections; in this day and age – nowadays
4 rough and ready – basic; heart and soul – all one's efforts

Pronunciation linking in idiomatic phrases

7a [1.3] Read the instructions about what to listen for to the class, then play the recording while they listen and follow. Have students practise the weak /ən/ sound individually and chorally. Play the recording again, pausing after each word pair for students to repeat chorally and individually.

Audioscript [1.3]

1 odds and ends — by and large
2 law and order — peace and quiet
3 ifs and buts — in this day and age
4 rough and ready — heart and soul

7b Ask students to work in pairs to read the sentences from Exercise 6, and check and help each other with the pronunciation.

Language focus the perfect aspect

8 Ask students to match the sentences to the times individually, then check their answers with a partner. Elicit answers from the whole class.

ANSWERS
1 d 2 a 3 b 4 c

9 Read through the box about the perfect aspect with the class, and discuss it with them, making sure they understand the concept of the speaker's perspective on time. Ask students to look at the pairs of sentences in the exercise with a partner and try to understand the difference in meaning. Elicit suggestions from the whole class and talk about them.

ANSWERS
1a I'm talking about completed actions (i.e. travelling) at indefinite times in a period of time which continued up to now. The reference point is now because the period of time is still continuing: the actions may be continued or repeated again.
1b I'm talking about completed actions at a definite, finished time in the past ('in my 20s').
2a I'm looking back from now at an action that started in the past and is still continuing (i.e. I'm still wondering).
2b This is an action that is happening now.
3a I'm looking back from a point in the future ('this time next year') at a completed action ('I will have retired').
3b I'm making a prediction about the future.
4a I'm looking back from a point in the past ('When I left school') to an earlier action ('I had decided').
4b I'm talking about two events which happened one after another at a specified time in the past ('When I left school', 'I decided to be').

10 [1.4] Ask students to underline the correct tenses in the sentences individually, then check with a partner. Play the recording for students to check, and discuss the answers with students as necessary.

ANSWERS
1 spends
2 had just left; was wondering
3 will settle; will have done
4 have written; am working
5 had been joking

Audioscript [1.4]

1 Oscar's a dreamer. Each evening he spends hours reading astronomy magazines, hoping to become an astronaut one day.

2 Kate's a worrier. When I first met her, she had just left her job and was wondering what to do with her life.

3 Ben's a free spirit. I imagine he will settle down one day. But he will have done a lot more than the rest of us by then.

4 I like to think of myself as a doer. I have written eight books so far and now I am working on my ninth.

5 Harry's a joker. For a long time he'd been joking about joining the army, so his friends were shocked to hear he actually had.

Speaking

Extra activity

Read through the words in the box in Exercise 11 for pronunciation, and ask students to repeat them chorally and individually. Ensure they pronounce the *-er* endings as a schwa /ə/.

a chatterbox	*a free spirit*
a control freak	*a go-getter*
a doer	*a joker*
a dreamer	*a planner*
a drifter	*an outgoing type*
a fighter	*a worrier*

11 Ask students to discuss the meanings of the expressions in pairs. Elicit ideas and discuss them as a class.

ANSWERS

a chatterbox – someone who talks a lot, in a lively way

a control freak – someone who wants to control everything and make all the decisions

a doer – someone who is energetic and achieves a lot

a dreamer – someone who seems to be in another world and not driven to achieve things

a drifter – someone who likes to try different things and places, often someone easy-going who goes where life takes them

a fighter – someone who is determined and will overcome difficulties to achieve things

a free spirit – someone who doesn't like to be tied down by other people or by routines

a go-getter – someone dynamic who is determined to achieve what they want

a joker – someone who likes to be funny and play jokes on people

a planner – someone who plans ahead instead of taking decisions quickly

an outgoing type – someone sociable and lively who likes to be with other people

a worrier – someone who worries a lot and often thinks bad things will happen

12 Read the instructions and the examples with the class, then ask them to think about three people (e.g. themselves, a friend, a relation, a colleague) and describe their character to a partner.

Elicit some examples from the whole class.

Extra activity

Ask students to write a detailed paragraph about someone they know, using as many of the expressions (and others) as are appropriate.

1c Immortal words

Lead-in

Personal response
Ask students if they can quote any famous words that someone said, and get them to tell the rest of the class. Find out why they know the quotation and how they learnt it.

Reading

1 You will be able to treat this activity differently depending on whether you are teaching a monolingual or multilingual mother-tongue class, and if the former, whether you share the mother tongue with your students. In this latter situation, you will be able to focus on questions 1 and 2 with great clarity. In the other situations, you will have to rely on what students tell you. Elicit answers to all four questions from the whole class.

2 Ask students to read through the article quickly and answer the question.

ANSWER

The author mentions several answers given by other people: Shakespeare was a great storyteller and he wrote beautiful poetry. His stories contain strong characters who say things about life that we can all identify with, expressed in a way that makes them more memorable.

Background notes

William Shakespeare (1564–1616) was born in Stratford-on-Avon, south of Birmingham. He lived and worked under Queen Elizabeth I during a time of wealth and prosperity, and in the reign of the increasingly problematic King James I. He worked as a dramatist and actor in London, but kept his family in Stratford. His company built its own open-air theatre in 1599 (The Globe), and they regularly played elsewhere, including the court. However, control was kept on what plays were like, and no religious or political issues could be discussed, nor could contemporary people be mentioned.

3 Ask students to read the questions, and then read the article again to find the answers. They should do this individually, then check with a partner. Elicit answers from the whole class.

ANSWERS

1 vibrant
2 Shakespeare wrote about characters with strong personalities.
3 succinctly and poetically
4 'coined the terms'
5 Its meaning has changed slightly.
6 the beauty of Shakespeare's language and the fact that the words are still relevant today

4 Ask students to read the eight phrases after paragraph 3 in the article, and match them with the definitions a–h in this exercise.

ANSWERS

a seen better days
b wear my heart upon my sleeve
c the world is (my) oyster
d neither here nor there
e foregone conclusion
f a sorry sight
g at one fell swoop
h full circle

Vocabulary notes

The following words and expressions from the text may be unfamiliar:

a *rival* = a person who is as good as you and competes with you

to endure = to last for a long time

vibrant = full of energy

the human condition = what it is like to be a woman or man

succinctly = in a few words

sanctimonious = acting as if you are morally superior

Critical thinking developing an argument

5 Ask students to find what reasons other writers give for Shakespeare's popularity by scanning the text again (see answers to Exercise 6)

6 Ask students to work in pairs to discuss what the author thinks about the comments of the other writers listed in Exercise 5. Elicit suggestions from the class.

ANSWERS

a Some scholars say Shakespeare lived during a period where there was a lot of cultural activity in England and this enabled him to write a huge volume of work.
The author says: 'This last explanation seems rather unsatisfactory.'

b Harold Bloom argues that Shakespeare wrote about strong, lifelike characters, which hadn't been done before. The author says this is 'a more interesting answer' but that it is put forward 'a little over-enthusiastically'.

c Michael Macrone does not give reasons for Shakespeare's popularity. He talks about the influence his language has had on language today and points out that we still use many expressions which were coined by Shakespeare.
The author says: 'light-hearted book', which suggests it is funny but not very important.

d Ben Jonson described Shakespeare as a writer 'not of an age, but for all time'.
The author says: 'Ben Jonson generously called his rival …' 'And so it has proved to be'. He admires Ben Jonson for being so positive about someone who was a rival. Time has shown that he was right.

7 Ask students to work in pairs to discuss the author's own conclusion. Elicit answers from the whole class.

ANSWER

The author's conclusion is that it is the 'humanity and enduring relevance of their message' that has ensured the lasting popularity of Shakespeare's language. He agrees most with Ben Jonson because his conclusion is based on what Ben Jonson said.

Word focus *life*

8 Ask students to find the expressions in the article.

ANSWERS

1 lifelike (para 2)
2 bring (them) to life (para 5)

9 Ask students to discuss the meaning of the *life* expressions. Elicit answers from the whole class.

ANSWERS

1 It's what always happens to me.
2 a big personality
3 something we must accept
4 every kind of social background
5 having a great time
6 something one couldn't have managed without

10 Read the instructions and the example to the class. Ask them to get into groups of four to tell each other similar examples using the expressions from Exercise 9.

Speaking

11 Read through the instructions with the whole class, then divide them up into groups of six divided into two threes (Group A and Group B). They should follow the instructions, reading the words on their pages only, and play the game. Circulate and help as necessary.

Homework

If students have direct experience of Shakespeare's plays (e.g. reading, studying, watching or acting in the plays), ask them to write 100–150 words about that experience. If they have no Shakespeare experience, ask them to choose another playwright, or any writer, to write about.

1d Tell me about yourself

Lead-in

Personal response

Draw on the board the logos of Mercedes (circle with three lines from the centre), Citroen (two ^ signs one above the other) and Audi (four interlocking circles). Ask students to say what they stand for. Elicit any other car logos they can name, and if they can draw them, invite them to the board to do so. Ask if anyone has a car, and what its logo is.

Real life presenting yourself

1 Ask students to read the definition, then discuss the two questions in pairs. Elicit answers from the whole class.

2 Ask students to work in pairs to discuss the meaning of *personal brand*. They should then read the text to check their ideas. Elicit the meaning from the whole class.

ANSWER

Deciding what your best qualities are and publicising them to the world.

3 [1.5] Read through the instructions with the class, then play the recording and elicit answers. Encourage discussion amongst the students.

ANSWERS

Although she is a little nervous, she follows the guidelines quite well. She is herself; she shows she is passionate about taking action and working for some positive good in society; she lists some of her achievements. Overall she gives an image of a sincere and concerned individual.

Audioscript [1.5]

M = manager, K = Katy

M: OK, Katy, so tell me about yourself.

K: OK, so I'm Katy. I'm 24 years old and I'm a very active person. I don't just mean that I play a lot of sports – although I do run and go to the gym several times a week. What I mean is that, um, I'm a person who likes to get involved in things. I've organised a lot of social events in my life and I've been part of a lot of campaigns, um … A recent one was campaigning against the building of a new car park in the centre of my home town. And that was successful actually, we got it stopped or at least delayed so, um … Excuse me, I'll just take a sip of water … Yes, so, as I was saying, I'm a firm believer in taking action. I don't think it's enough to want to change things and to say the right things, I think you have to act – to get out of your chair and do something that makes a difference.

M: And your current situation?

K: Well, I graduated from university two years ago with a degree in journalism, but I haven't been able to find a job that really suited me. To be honest, newspapers aren't an easy world to break into, unless you have the right contacts. So instead, I decided on a fresh approach, which was to seek out companies I admire; basically any company or organisation that's working for some positive good in society. And that's how I found you. And my hope is that when I find the right company, they'll see that I have the right attitude and the right skills, so that we can both benefit from working together, um, yeah …

Speaking skill keeping going

4 [1.5] Read through the phrases in the box for keeping going with the class. Make sure they understand the meanings. Play the recording again for them to listen to what Katy uses. Elicit answers from the whole class.

ANSWERS

Excuse me, I'll just take a sip of water …

Yes, so, as I was saying,

5 Ask students to discuss their strategies, and then elicit ideas from the whole class.

SAMPLE ANSWER

Take a deep breath, ask for clarification or for someone to repeat the question, say something light-hearted about the fact you feel nervous.

Pronunciation content words

6a [1.6] Read through the instructions with the class, and then play the recording for them to mark the changes in rhythm. You may need to play it once or twice more for students to check and complete their answers. Then play it again, pausing at the end of each sentence and after long phrases for students to repeat them chorally and individually.

ANSWERS

OK, so I'm Katy. I'm 24 years old and I'm a very active person. I don't just mean that I play a lot of sports – although I do run and go to the gym several times a week. What I mean is that … I'm a person who likes to get involved in things.

6b Ask students to work in pairs to help each other practise Katy's words with the correct rhythm and stress patterns.

7 Read through the instructions with the whole class. Ask them to read the information about Oxtail Housing, and check that everyone understands the information. Then put students into groups of four. They should have some time to prepare, then take it in turns presenting themselves to the other three. The three should give feedback – positive as well as negative – to each one in turn.

1e A letter of application

Lead-in

Personal response

Ask students to tell the class about any applications they have made for work. Get them to describe the process and say whether they wrote a letter, and if so, what it was like.

Writing a covering letter

1 Read the instructions and the list of elements to be found in the letter with the class, and make sure everything is clear. Ask them to read the letter and find the key elements individually, then check with a partner. Elicit the answers from the whole class.

ANSWERS

1 Trainee Accounts manager
2 in last Tuesday's *Guardian* newspaper
3 a recent graduate
4 My two proudest achievements are … I think I am a suitable candidate as: …
5 contact me at any time by phone or in writing
6 Thank you for considering this application

2 Read the instructions and the statements with the class. Ask students to answer true or false individually, then check with a partner. Elicit answers from the whole class.

ANSWERS

1 F 2 T 3 F 4 T

Writing skill fixed expressions

3 Ask students to read the phrases a–h, and find equivalents in the letter. They should do this individually, then check with a partner. Elicit answers from the class.

ANSWERS

a I am seeking
b please find enclosed
c a suitable candidate
d I am available for
e the requirements you mention
f In response to your advertisement … for a Trainee accounts manager
g do not hesitate to
h The job attracted me

4 Ask students to write a letter of application for the job described in the Oxtail Housing advertisement on the previous page. They should do this individually, then exchange letters with their partner.

5 Ask students to check their partner's letter as described, and then discuss what is done well and what could be improved, and how. Students could then write a second draft based on the feedback.

1f Arctic wisdom

Before you watch

1 Students work in pairs. Ask them to look at the photo and map and say what they can see, then choose the options. Take feedback from the class.

2 Before watching the video, ask students to predict three things the Inuit elders might say about modern life.

While you watch

3 Give students time to read through the words in the glossary. Play the whole of the video for students to check their answers to Exercise 2. They should not try to understand everything at this stage.

4 Give students time to read the questions. Then play the first part of the video (to 02.24). Ask students to answer the questions. Check the answers, and if necessary play that part of the video again.

SAMPLE ANSWERS

1 They have seen a lot of change.
2 Their words, their advice and their knowledge of the past.
3 'Respect your elders.'
4 As nomadic hunters.
5 Orally (nothing was written down).

5 Give students time to read the summary then play the second part of the video (02.25 to 03.39) for them to complete it.

ANSWERS

1 advisors
2 expert
3 survive
4 animal
5 basics
6 changes
7 forget

6 Give students time to read the questions then play the third part of the video (03.40 to 05.50) for them to answer.

ANSWERS

1 The population has grown. There are more younger people and fewer elders because of lower mortality rates and better healthcare.
2 Respect yourself and those around you; high self-esteem; be positive.
3 Because the younger generation don't understand the Inuktitut language.
4 It represents the average age in Iqaluit.
5 It was passed on verbally, through storytelling.
6 Tradition, culture and history; knowing the past.

After you watch

7 Students work in groups to roleplay a village meeting, according to the instructions.

8 Students work in groups to discuss the questions.

Videoscript

Part 1

00.30 Hi, my name is Charlie. Welcome to *explore*. We're in the Arctic.

I've a great job. I travel to different places and try to find positive people doing good things on the planet. Then we help fund some of them. Now we're doing something on the Arctic.

Here's a photograph of the mayor.

00.50 Elisapee Sheutiapik My name is Elisapee Sheutiapik. I'm the mayor of the city of Iqaluit. Iqaluit is the capital of a new territory called Nunavut, which became its own territory in '99.

01.08 Charlie As mayor, what are some of the changes you'd like to implement?

Elisapee Right now, I'm going through a long-term planning and visioning. I understand our elders have always been really good at planning. They've gone through and seen so much change in a very short time. Their words are very important to us. Even at a government level, they have a committee of elders. There's an elders society where they meet every day, and this is also another opportunity for us to go and seek advice.

01.43 Charlie So the phrase 'Respect your elders' is very alive and well in Iqaluit?

Elisapee Oh, very much!

Charlie When we went to the Iqaluit elders centre, it struck me that we were visiting the first settled generation. The parents of these men and women lived as nomadic hunters. Also, up until this generation, all of the Inuit traditions and history were passed down orally. Nothing had been written down, making their knowledge of the past invaluable.

Charlie This is great … great stuff. Great photography!

Part 2

02.25 Has the role of the elder changed from when you were growing up?

Jonah Kelly Yes, I think so. It has changed. Elders would always play advisors to generation to generation. Advisors meaning that no one person makes a decision to survive. Everybody makes the decision to survive. One will be expert on the weather, one will be expert on environment, one will be expert on different kinds of animals.

So in our society today, in our generation today, it's hard to imagine how they were.

03.05 Elisapee Sheutiapik I believe that Inuits are very happy with the very basics and it's about life experience that's brought us to where we are today.

So one thing my mother always said was never forget who you are. She went from living on the land to settling to a community and saw a lot of changes in a short time, but she reminded me that we will probably forever be changing, seeing change, but not to forget who we are.

Part 3

03.40 Another reason this group of elders is so special is the disproportionate age groups of Iqaluit. Factors such as lower infant mortality and improved healthcare have allowed the population to grow, but means more young people and fewer elders. All the more reason to now obtain their advice and unique perspective.

04.00 What is the key to living a happy life?

Woman (words translated) Respect yourself and those around you. It's important to have high self-esteem and encourage yourself and others to be positive.

04.26 Charlie How has life changed today versus when you grew up?

Woman (words translated) It's a challenge to pass on words of wisdom to the youth because of the communication barrier. Some of them may understand basic Inuktitut language, but not enough for me to converse with them.

04.55 Elisapee Sheutiapik We have such a young population that our average age in Iqaluit, for example, is 23 years old.

We had a culture where it was all verbal, and the youth they acknowledge that they have to hear these stories and they think it only helps them understand where their ancestors came from.

05.30 Charlie Tradition, culture, history. The future can only be improved by knowing the past. Only two per cent of the entire population of Iqaluit is aged 65 or older. Responsibility now lies with today's generation to record and pass on the wisdom of the ages.

Unit 1 Review

Grammar

1 Ask students to read the article and answer the questions.

ANSWERS
A griot is a storyteller.
It's important to take time to share stories with friends.

2 Ask students to read the article again and complete it with the correct verb forms.

ANSWERS
1 visited
2 think
3 hasn't always been
4 was
5 was sitting
6 had already gathered
7 sing
8 have learned
9 listened
10 had told
11 quoted
12 will stay

3 Students work in pairs to discuss their stories.

Vocabulary

4 Ask students to complete the expressions.

ANSWERS
1 larger
2 walks
3 time
4 done
5 thumb
6 small

5 Students work in pairs to put the word pairs in order.

ANSWERS
1 heart and soul
2 by and large
3 first and foremost
4 peace and quiet
5 day and age

6 Ask students to write sentences using two word pairs.

Real life

7 Students complete the phrases for keeping going.

ANSWERS
b As c sip d 've lost e Let

8 Ask students to match the underlined phrases with phrases from Exercise 7.

ANSWERS
1 b 2 e 3 d 4 a 5 c

9 Students work in pairs to practise presenting themselves.

Speaking

10 Students work in pairs to discuss an interview.

Unit 2 More than a job

Lead-in

Personal response

Ask students to tell a partner what their ideal job would be, and why. Elicit some examples from the whole class.

1 [1.7] Ask students to discuss the photo and caption with a partner. Elicit some responses from the whole class.

ANSWER

He is hunting with a golden eagle.

Audioscript [1.7]

The animal herders of western Mongolia have been called the last nomads. The horses, goats and cattle that they move from pasture to pasture on horseback are their livelihood. From them, they get their food, clothing and money to buy other goods.

Among these nomadic peoples are Kazakhs. Increasingly, many of these are trying to make a better living by seeking jobs in the city, but there are others who try to maintain the traditional nomadic way of life, living in tents by summer and in small houses during the cold winters. Among their customs, the most unusual, perhaps, is hunting with eagles, an art practised since the days of Genghis Khan.

For many hunters these days, eagle hunting is less a job and more a sophisticated sport. An eagle hunter spends ten years with each bird, training it – a task which requires great skill and patience – and sharing the meat of the animals which it kills, usually fox. At the end of the ten years, the hunter must part company with the eagle, because at this age, eagles are ready to start having chicks.

In the past, the skins of the foxes and other animals were traditionally sold to clothes makers. Winters are cold in Mongolia, and wearing fur is the best way to keep warm. These skins still provide some extra income to Kazakh nomads, but it isn't only for the money that they hunt with eagles: they want to keep alive this ancient tradition.

2 [1.7] Ask students to read through the questions to focus their listening, then play the recording again for them to answer individually. They should check with a partner. Then play the recording once more for them to check, complete and correct their answers. Elicit answers from the whole class.

ANSWERS

1 They keep animals (horses, goats and cattle) for food, clothing and money.
2 They have jobs in the city.
3 Living in tents in the summer and small houses in the winter.
4 It's classed as a sport these days.
5 It takes great patience to train an eagle.
6 Hunting for fox skins to sell for clothing.

Extra activity

Ask students what they think about the Kazakh way of life. Do they agree that it is important to keep ancient traditions alive? Does it matter if eagle hunting has become a sport rather than a way of life? Is it inevitable that the traditional way of life is disappearing?

3 Ask students to discuss the differences in meaning with a partner. You may wish to make this into a dictionary exercise if you feel it would be too difficult for your students otherwise. Elicit answers for whole-class discussion.

ANSWERS

1 a way of life: how you live day by day
a livelihood: what you depend on for your income / survival (e.g. coal for a mining community)
2 a career: a profession that you follow through your life, progressing from job to job
a vocation: a job which you feel you are naturally and strongly called to do (e.g. teaching, nursing)
3 a profession: a job that involves long training and high qualifications (e.g. dentist, lawyer)
a trade: a job requiring skilled manual labour (e.g. carpenter, builder, etc.)
4 an occupation: a job
a living: the way that you earn the money to live
5 a job: an occupation or profession
a task: a specific job to be done (e.g. painting a room, writing a report)

4 Ask students to work together in groups of four to make a list of examples of each type of work. Elicit answers from the whole class, and make a master list on the board.

SAMPLE ANSWERS

a farmer, vet, butcher, pet shop owner
b blacksmith, watch repairer, tailor
c surgery, teaching, training animals

2a Sea gypsies of Myanmar

Lead-in

Personal response
Ask students what they know about gypsies in general and what their way of life is like.

Reading

1 Ask students to discuss the title, picture and questions with a partner. Elicit answers from the whole class. Then ask them to read the article to check their ideas. Elicit the answers from the text, and discuss them.

ANSWERS
1 People with no fixed home, who live at sea.
2 They gather and sell food and shells from the sea and beaches.
3 They can dive over twenty metres without breathing equipment; they have underwater vision; they can read changes at sea; it has been said that they can tell when a tsunami is approaching.

Background notes

Myanmar is the modern name for Burma, the largest country in southeast Asia, which has a population of over 60 million. One third of the country has a coastline, running for 1,930 km along the Bay of Bengal in the north and the Andaman Sea in the south. It is in the extreme south that the Mergui Archipelago lies. The group of 800 islands of very variable size has remained relatively untouched by modern life. They are a haven for wildlife, both in the rainforests and other habitats on the islands, and in the sea. Environmentalists are concerned that diving and other types of tourism have been starting to threaten the area.

2 Ask students to read through the six questions to focus their reading. Then ask them to scan the text to find the answers. You could set a time limit of four minutes for this, to encourage students to scan rather than read through the text.

ANSWERS
1 The Moken are nervous of strangers because people often cause them trouble.
2 The *kabang* are small, wooden boats.
3 They travel by boat, they collect only what they need to live from the sea and beaches, and have very few possessions.
4 Because of the monsoon rains.
5 It is getting smaller.
6 If they move permanently to the land, they could lose their unique understanding of the sea.

3 Ask students to work in groups of four to discuss the questions. Then open up the discussion to the whole class.

SAMPLE ANSWERS
Advantages: freedom, independence, continuing traditions, living close to nature and to the sea
Disadvantages: insecurity, no access to health care and other amenities

Vocabulary notes

At this level, phrasal verbs are an essential element for language development, enabling the understanding and production of natural English. Phrasal verbs can be difficult for students because one root verb has many possible meanings when used with different prepositions, e.g. *get up* (get out of bed), *get ahead* (improve one's career or work), *get on with* (like and enjoy being with someone), *get down to* (start working hard), etc. Students have no option but to learn and practise the different meanings, preferably in the context of full examples.

Vocabulary phrasal verb *get*

4 Ask students to choose the correct meaning of the phrasal verbs with *get* individually, then check with a partner. Elicit answers from the whole class.

ANSWERS
1 c 2 f 3 a 4 d 5 e 6 b

5 Ask students to work in pairs to make their own sentences using the phrasal verbs with *get*. Elicit some examples from the whole class.

Vocabulary notes

Common collocations with the *get* phrasal verbs are:

get down to work / one's studies / business

get ahead at school / in one's job / on the career ladder

You need to point out to students that not all verb + preposition constructions are phrasal verbs, and that sometimes the same verb + preposition can have a literal and an idiomatic meaning:

I opened the door and ***looked into*** *the room.*

When I told them about it, the police ***looked into*** *the matter.*

In the first sentence *look into* means a literal physical action; in the second sentence it has a figurative, idiomatic use meaning *investigated*.

Language focus the continuous aspect

6 Ask students to work with a partner to match the sentences with the description of use. Elicit answers from the whole class. Discuss the uses as necessary and clear up any misunderstandings.

ANSWERS
1 b 2 c 3 a 4 e 5 d 6 f

7 Ask students to work in pairs to talk about the different meanings of the sentences. Elicit answers and encourage discussion from the class.

ANSWERS

1 a I am living on a houseboat at the moment.
b I always live on a houseboat.
2 a They arrived and interrupted us in the process of eating.
b They arrived and then we ate.
3 a She started writing in the past and continued writing until now.
b She finished writing the travel book at an unknown time in the past.
4 a They travelled for days up to a point in the past.
b They travelled 300 km at a time in the past before the point focused on.
5 a At a time in the future (eight o'clock) I will be in the process of making my supper.
b At eight o'clock I will start making my supper.

8 Read through the box about the continuous aspect with the class and discuss the contents as necessary. Ask students to choose the correct verb form in the text individually, then check with a partner. Elicit the answers from the class as complete sentences.

ANSWERS

1 learn
2 have developed
3 discovered
4 are being lost
5 had already moved
6 arrived
7 was receding
8 have they been waiting
9 do not wish
10 will still be leading

Speaking

9 Make sure students are familiar with all the jobs in the box. Ask them to get into groups of four to decide which are more than just a job, and discuss why.

SAMPLE ANSWERS

Farmers have to work very long hours, they usually live in the same place as they work, and will get up in the middle of the night if necessary. Their work is affected by the weather and the seasons.

Fishermen / women sometimes have to go away for days fishing, they live on their boats and work long hours, their work is governed by the weather and conditions at sea.

Lorry drivers spend long periods of time away from home, when they sleep and live on their lorry.

Coal miners work long hours in very difficult conditions underground, and their job is dangerous.

10 Ask students to work individually to think of another job that is a way of life. They should then discuss their suggestion with the rest of the group. Elicit ideas from the whole class and open up a discussion.

Homework

Ask students to write 100–150 words about a 'way of life' job that interests them.

2b Smokejumpers

Lead-in

Personal response

Ask students to list the three public services which one can call for assistance (police, fire, ambulance). Ask them to talk about their experience and opinions of the three services and the people who work for them.

Listening

1 Ask students to work in pairs and answer the questions about fire. Elicit answers from the whole class, and discuss them.

ANSWERS

1 a forest fire; they are started by lightning or by people dropping cigarettes or having barbecues or campfires; they can be stopped by dropping water on them from planes
2 A 'fireman' is male; a 'firefighter' can be male or female.
3 Possible answers: you need to be physically and mentally strong, practical, brave, be able to make quick decisions, well trained, disciplined.

2 [1.8] Ask students to read the sentences. Then play the recording and ask them to mark the sentences true (T) or false (F). They can then check with a partner. Elicit answers from the whole class. If there are problems, play the recording again to check.

ANSWERS

1 T 2 F 3 F 4 F

Audioscript [1.8]

P = presenter, **K** = Kerry

P: We'd all like to jump into a fire, right? Er … I don't think so, but that was how smokejumper Kerry Franklin explained her career choice to me earlier when I interviewed her for GBC. For those of you who don't know, smokejumpers are firefighters who are dropped into remote and inaccessible areas to combat forest fires. Here's what Kerry told me.

K: Women firefighters are well suited to this kind of work. Weighing on average around 70–80 kilos, we're the right weight for it. If you're a lot heavier than that, you descend too fast and hit the ground hard, risking serious injury. And if you're a lot lighter and there's a strong wind, it can take your parachute and leave you a long way from your intended landing point.

P: You mean like in the centre of the fire itself?

K: Yeah, that's been known to happen. But we wear a lot of protective gear. Of course, we're aware of our personal safety, but it's not the first thing on our minds – in this kind of job you can't wrap people in cotton wool.

P: No, I imagine not. So, having landed near the fire, what do you do then? I mean, not having a fire engine or a fire hydrant nearby, you can't exactly start fighting the fire in the conventional way, can you?

K: You see, we're like the initial line of attack. We get dropped in with tools – chainsaws, axes, chemicals for fighting fires – we get water pumps too, portable ones. But first we need to assess how bad the fire is, how we think it's going to develop and get that news back to base. If it's cooking pretty good, we've got to look for a way to try and contain it. Usually that means finding a natural firebreak.

P: What's that?

K: It's something like a road, or an area of rock, or thinner vegetation that the fire's going to have to cross before it continues on its path of destruction. So having located a firebreak, we do our best to make sure it's going to be effective, getting anything that could burn easily out of the way, sometimes using controlled burning to burn back to the main fire as it approaches the break.

P: And what's it like being a woman in this world, because firefighting is traditionally a male-dominated domain?

K: Fire doesn't distinguish between men and women, nor do the trainers at smokejumping school for that matter – you either make the grade or you don't. Having faced the same challenges together in training, those who make it have a natural respect for each other. Sure, doing my training I met a few guys who had a different attitude, but I haven't met any who didn't just end up thinking a smokejumper is a smokejumper.

Vocabulary notes

Introduce students to the following words:

arson = the act of illegally and deliberately setting fire to something

pyromaniac = a person who enjoys, or is obsessed with, fire

lightning strike = when lightning hits an object and starts a fire

spark = a tiny glowing particle which is thrown from a fire

deliberately lit = lit with the aim of causing a fire

3 [1.8] Ask students to read through the options for answers to focus their listening, then play the recording again. They should check with a partner and, if necessary, listen to the recording once more to check their answers. Elicit answers from the whole class.

ANSWERS

1 a 2 c 3 a 4 b 5 b

4 Ask students to discuss the statement and the questions with a partner. Elicit the answers and continue the discussion with the whole class.

ANSWERS

She is committed to doing a good job, she thinks it doesn't matter whether you are male or female.

In this context, the expression 'you either make the grade or you don't' means you can either do the job well or you can't, regardless of your gender.

Extra activity

Ask students to talk about their feelings about a firefighter's life, and discuss the job and what it entails.

Language focus present and perfect participles

5 Read the instructions and example with the class. Ask students to complete the other changes individually, then check with a partner. Elicit answers from the whole class.

ANSWERS

2 with the result that you risk
3 Because you don't have
4 After we locate
5 and in order to do this we use
6 Because we have faced

6 Read through the information in the language focus box with the class and make sure they understand the contents. If you feel they need further explanation and practice, refer to page 159.

Ask students to rewrite the sentences individually, then check with a partner. Elicit answers from the whole class and discuss them.

ANSWERS

1 Having failed the course twice, I decided not to try again.
2 I burnt my hand trying to put the fire out.
3 Working in forestry, I know the dangers of forest fires very well.
4 Remaining calm, he got everyone out of the building.
5 Looking back on it, I can see that it was a mistake to leave him in charge.
6 I called the fire brigade, thinking it was the best thing to do.
7 Having landed, the smokejumpers search for the equipment that has been dropped.
8 The smokejumpers work closely together, keeping in radio contact.

7 Ask students to work in pairs and find the sentences where the speaker has not followed rule 2. Elicit answers from the whole class. Ask students to explain the actual meaning of these incorrect sentences.

ANSWERS

Sentences 2 and 3 do not follow the rule.

Sentence 2 means that the waiter ate the person's main course, then offered to bring dessert.

Sentence 3 means that the dog was waiting for the taxi, and came and sat next to the person while it was waiting.

Grammar note

The subject of a participial clause has to be the same as the subject of the main clause, or the sentence produced can be confusing or amusing. The incorrect sentences in Exercise 7 have an amusing meaning, but often when people make this type of mistake the sentence is just confusing and difficult for the listener to follow.

Extra activity

Ask students to think of another funny sentence which does not follow rule 2 in the box, so that the real meaning is humorous. They could perhaps modify the correct sentences in Exercise 7 to do this.

8 Ask students to complete the four sentences individually. Ask them to get into groups of four and read their sentences to each other, one by one, then discuss them, and decide which is the best ending for each of the four sentences. Elicit the 'best' sentences from each group round the whole class.

Idioms health and safety

9 Ask students to discuss the meaning of Kerry's idiom in pairs, then elicit ideas from the whole class.

ANSWER

To wrap people in cotton wool means to protect people too much, by not letting them get into dangerous situations, or hear unpleasant things. It is often used about people's treatment of children.

10 [1.9] Ask students to complete the idioms with the words from the box individually, then check with a partner. Then play the recording for them to check. Invite the whole class to discuss meanings.

ANSWERS

1 nature
2 side
3 danger
4 net
5 precaution
6 book
7 corners

11 Ask students to talk to their partner about a job where health and safety is very important, using as many of the idioms as possible. Elicit some answers from the class.

ANSWERS

Possible jobs might include construction, healthcare / nursing, chemical laboratories, electricians, factory jobs involving heavy machinery.

Speaking

12 Read through the instructions and rules with the class and make sure they understand everything. Ask them to get into groups of four to discuss and write down their ideas. Elicit answers from the whole class and discuss them.

2c Daring, defiant and free

Lead-in

Personal response

Ask students as a whole class to talk about sports and similar activities they have taken part in. Ask if they were ever dangerous, or if anyone got hurt, and if so, how? Have they ever done a dangerous activity? Discuss their reasons for and feelings about doing such activities.

Reading

1 Continuing from the lead-in, ask students to think of other sports and activities which they consider to be dangerous and discuss why people do them.

SAMPLE ANSWERS

motor racing, surfing, rugby, boxing

2 Ask students to look at the photo of the free climber and answer the two questions, as a whole class. Elicit different responses. Then ask students to read the text to check their answers.

ANSWERS

1 He's hanging on by his fingertips, with his feet resting on small footholds.
2 A professional photographer who is also a climber takes the photos.

3 Ask students to read the sentences to focus their reading, then read the article again and answer. They can check with a partner. Elicit the answers from the whole class as complete sentences.

ANSWERS

1 became paralysed
2 chalk and rock shoes
3 mentally exhausted
4 blown away or amazed
5 to be a reliable member of the climbing team
6 a story

4 Ask students to read the phrases, and then find the words and expressions in the text. They should do this individually, then check with a partner. Elicit answers from the whole class.

ANSWERS

1 clinging, hanging on
2 in the zone
3 flawlessly
4 vacillate
5 rally
6 dangling

Critical thinking using contrasts

Extra activity

Write the word *image* on the board, and ask students what they understand by it. On the one hand it can mean a picture, real or imagined, on the other hand it can mean the special way something is described in writing. Literature, and especially poetry, relies upon the use of striking, unusual images for much of its impact. The commonest images are similes (e.g. *the moon is like a pale sailing ship*) which say something is 'like' something else, and metaphors (e.g. *the moon is a pale sailing ship*) which simply say something *is* another thing.

5 Ask students to find the images in the text. They should do this individually and not discuss it yet.

ANSWERS

1 sheer, an edge of rock as thin as a coin, glass-slick slab
2 freed of the prison
3 dangling like a spider

Vocabulary notes

The following words and expressions from the text may be unfamiliar:

slick = shiny and slippery

to smear = to spread something carelessly

to forge = to create

blew his mind = amazed him

calligraphy = artistic handwriting

6 Ask students to find the factual information described; they should do this individually, and not discuss it yet.

ANSWERS

1 the shy 23-year-old from the suburbs (Honnold); Chin had a traditional upbringing from his Chinese-American parents in the flat countryside of southern Minnesota
2 'I rallied because there was nothing else I could do,' 'When I started shooting photos I didn't really think too much about it.'

7 Ask students to check their answers to Exercises 5 and 6 with a partner. Elicit the answers from the whole class, and discuss them.

SAMPLE ANSWERS

The contrast makes the two men seem very modest and appealing. At the same time it makes their achievements seem more remarkable and we admire them all the more.

Word focus *foot*

8 Ask students to find the two *foot* words individually, then discuss them with a partner. Elicit ideas from the whole class.

ANSWERS

1 foothold (a place where you can put your foot when climbing)
2 footing (the secure grip with your feet, your balance)

9 Ask students to work in pairs and discuss the meanings of the *foot* words in the six sentences. Elicit answers from the whole class and discuss the meanings and use with them.

ANSWERS

1 get a first job or opportunity in a company which might allow you to move up
2 pay
3 damaged her own interests
4 said the wrong thing (often causing embarrassment)
5 have the same job as someone, or do similar things
6 be firm

Vocabulary notes

Explain to students that the word *foot* has three basic meanings: a part of the body, a unit of measurement and the base of something (e.g. *at the foot of the tree*). Ask them to find two examples of the first two uses in the article.

Also introduce some other expressions with *foot*:

footsteps = the noise the feet make when walking or running

footprints / *footmarks* = the marks left by the feet in mud or snow

footnote = additional information at the bottom of a page

footwear = shoes, sandals, boots, etc.

10 Ask students to ask and answer questions as indicated. Circulate and monitor their conversations. Elicit some questions and answers from the whole class.

Speaking

11 Ask students to work in pairs and do the quiz on page 153. Check first that they understand the meaning of 'comfort zone', i.e. situations where you feel comfortable and not too anxious or stressed. Circulate and monitor their speaking. Elicit some questions and answers from the whole class.

12 Ask students to consider the question and possible answers individually for a few moments; you might suggest they make some notes. Then ask them to get into groups of four to talk about themselves and others in this light. Elicit some ideas from the whole class and open points up to general discussion, if appropriate.

Homework

Ask students to choose one of the items in the quiz that made them feel out of their comfort zone, and write about their feelings, what made them feel uncomfortable and what they could do to overcome them.

2d In my experience

Lead-in

Personal response
Ask students to think about what they consider to be the most important experiences they had in the first 18 years of their life (i.e. until they left school), and why they were important. Ask them to discuss these with a partner and then elicit some experiences from the whole class.

Real life giving a talk

1 Ask students to think about a particular experience or experiences in their life and answer the two questions. They should do this individually before sharing their experience with a partner. Elicit examples from the class.

2 [1.10] Ask students to read through the four questions to focus their listening, then play the recording. Ask them to check their answers with a partner. Elicit answers from the whole class.

ANSWERS

1 The day is for new students to the university.
2 He's a recent graduate.
3 He advises them to get involved in clubs, societies or voluntary groups and develop their interests.
4 He joined the university broadcasting society, did some reporting, then got a holiday job as researcher at a local radio station. It helped him find out what he wanted to do, and make some work contacts.

Audioscript [1.10]

Hello, everyone. I hope you're enjoying your first day. I imagine you're feeling pretty overwhelmed by everything you've had to take in, and I don't want to keep you long. I've been brought back as someone who's been through the system and come out the other side, and so the university asked me to talk to you as one of you and to give you a student's side of the story.

So with that in mind, I'd just like to say one thing really, which is: get involved in something other than your course as soon as you can. You'll be amazed by how quickly time goes here. Before you know it, you'll be in your third year and you'll be thinking, 'What now?' How many of you actually know what you're going to do when you leave? I'm sure there will be some people who know what career they'd like to embark on, but there will be an awful lot of you – and I was definitely one of those – who don't.

That's where university clubs, societies and volunteer groups come in. I remember when I first came here to study history, I had no idea of what job I'd end up doing. But in my first year, I joined the university broadcasting society. I was interested in reporting, so I used to go out and find interesting stories about university life, and then come back and present them – when they were interesting enough to everyone else, that is. I did that once a week. Then in my second year, I got a holiday job, helping out as a researcher at the local BBC radio station, and really it all led on from there, because first of all I was clear about what I wanted to do – which was to work in broadcasting – and secondly, I had some contacts I could call on, which in this line of work is a key thing.

So that's really my message to you today. Don't delay, get out there, join some clubs and societies and start developing your interests. This university has so many fantastic opportunities to do that and you won't get another chance in life like it. So, thanks for your time. Oh, and do come and chat afterwards if you'd like to … I'll be in the bar.

Speaking skill keeping people's attention

3 [1.10] Read through the instructions and the phrases for keeping people's attention with the class. Play the recording again for them to tick the phrases the speaker used. Ask them to check with a partner before eliciting the answers. If necessary, play the recording again to check.

ANSWERS

I'd just like to say one thing …
So that's really my message to you today.
I remember when I first …
How many of you actually …?

4 Ask students to work in groups and consider the questions about keeping listeners' attention. Elicit suggestions from the whole class, listing them on the board and discussing them with everyone.

SAMPLE ANSWERS

using visuals (e.g. slide presentations)
giving listeners an individual task
making the aims of your talk clear
inviting audience comment
Techniques will vary according to the age of the audience, their relationship to the speaker, the amount of time available, etc.

Pronunciation checking specific words

5a [1.11] Ask students to work in pairs to read the extract and discuss how they think the underlined words should be pronounced. They can then listen and check.

5b Ask students to work in groups and practise saying the paragraph, focusing on correct pronunciation. Circulate and monitor their speaking.

6 Read through the instructions and suggestions with the class. Ask them to prepare a talk, as indicated. They could then give their talks in small groups, and take feedback from others in the group.

2e Your first day

Lead-in

Personal response

Ask students to work in groups of four and tell the others about one of their first days (e.g. at primary or secondary school, at university, at a new job, or in other situations).

Writing taking notes

1 [1.12] Read through the instructions with the class, then ask students to read the notes made, and identify what they have to listen for. Play the recording and elicit the answers from the whole class.

ANSWERS

2 p.m. (not 3 p.m.)

Room number 301

Audioscript [1.12]

Hello, everyone. First of all, can I extend a warm welcome from me and all the staff. My name's Sarah Curtain, and I'm the principal here at King's College. I'm very happy to see, once again, such a large and diverse range of nationalities at the college. This year we have over 60 different nationalities, speaking 33 different languages. It's that diversity and international perspective that makes King's College a unique place to study.

I'm afraid I have to mention a few administrative matters first, but then I'll give you some more general advice about how to make the most of your time here.

So, immediately after this session, there will be coffee in the student's union where you can meet and chat to staff and other students. That's from 11 to 12.30 p.m.

Course registration takes place on Monday morning. That is compulsory for everyone to attend, and it'll be in the main university hall – this room – between 10 a.m. and 2 p.m. You must attend to officially register for the courses you are going to do this year.

Also during the next week, I'd ask those of you who haven't done so already to bring copies of all your documents to the Admissions Office – Room 301 – so that we can keep them on file. So that's all official documents – secondary education certificates, student visas, bank account details – to Room 301 by the end of next week. This applies to all overseas students, that is everyone except those from the UK and the European Union. Even if you don't think you have all of these, please come and see us anyway – that's very important.

Now, as for your orientation here at King's College, …

2 Ask students to discuss what information was given but not noted, in pairs. Elicit suggestions and write them on the board, but do not say what is correct.

3 [1.12] Play the recording for students to check. Ask the whole class to answer why they think this information was omitted.

ANSWERS

She told the students her name and role. (My name's Sarah Curtain and I'm the principal here at King's College.)

She gave information about the diversity of the student body. (This year we have over 60 different nationalities, speaking 33 different languages.)

She told students about an informal meeting after the talk. (… coffee in the student's union where you can meet and chat to staff and other students. That's from 11 to 12.30 p.m.)

This information was general information, not practical information that needed to be noted down. The meeting which was mentioned was straight after the talk, so there was no need to note the information.

Writing skill abbreviations

4a Ask students to work in pairs and list the abbreviations they find in the notes, saying what they mean.

ANSWERS

a.m. = morning
p.m. = afternoon
reg = registration
uni = university
i.e. = that is
UK = United Kingdom
EU = European Union
docs = documents
incl. = including
OS sts = overseas students
approx. = approximately
hrs = hours
p.w. = per week
e.g. = for example
sthg = something
NB = note
etc. = etcetera

4b Ask students to compare their answers with another pair and match the abbreviations with the six meanings.

ANSWERS

a incl.
b approx.
c e.g.
d i.e.
e NB
f etc.

4c Ask students to read and discuss where abbreviations could be used, then elicit answers from the whole class.

ANSWERS

2 and 4

4d Ask students to write the memo in note form individually, then compare and discuss it with a partner. Elicit suggestions from the whole class and produce a version on the board.

> SAMPLE ANSWER
>
> NB the mtg with Ellis & Co will be tomorrow, Tues 12th May, 3.00 p.m. Pls send any info you have about them, incl. financial details, names of directors, etc.

5 [1.13] Ask students to listen to the talk and take notes. Play the recording.

Audioscript [1.13]

OK, everyone, I'd just like to say a few words about reading – something you're going to be doing a lot of here. At the end of this session, I'll give you your reading list for this particular course. Your other tutors will do the same. There'll be 30 or so books on each list, but please don't think that means you have to read every page of every book. There are three or four key books highlighted at the top of each list, which we do recommend that you read in full, but the others will mainly be for reference – that's to say, there'll be one or two chapters in them that are relevant to a particular essay or piece of work.

So, most importantly, when I give you the list, please don't go out to the nearest bookshop and buy them all. If you do that, you'll leave yourself no money for food or anything else. All these books are, in principle, available in the library – some may be out on loan, of course, when you want them. You'll probably want to buy some of the more important ones. My advice to you is first to look at one of the internet booksellers and see if you can pick up any second-hand, or at least cheaper copies there. There's also a second-hand section in the main university bookshop, where you might find what you're looking for.

What about strategies for reading? As I said at the beginning, you'll have a big volume of reading to do, so it's important that you get faster at it. Is there a secret to that? Well, I'm afraid the answer is not really. What I would say though is that the more you read, the faster you will get. So don't worry too much if it seems like it's taking ages at first – everyone feels that …

6 Ask students to exchange notes with their partner and check each other's notes for the points indicated. They should give feedback to their partner. Elicit what notes should have been made from the whole class, and compile a class version on the board as a model.

2f Climbing Yosemite

Before you watch

1 Students work in groups. Ask them to look at the photo and say what they can see, then discuss the question.

2 Ask students to read the adjectives and discuss in pairs which words describe the activity. They can use a dictionary to check meaning.

While you watch

3 Give students time to read through the words in the glossary. Play the first part of the video (to 01.04) for students to answer the question. Take feedback from the class and ask if they were surprised by the use of the adjectives.

> ANSWERS
>
> The adjectives he uses are: *cerebral, difficult, rewarding, scary, slow.*

4 Give students time to read the sentences. Then play the second part of the video (01.05 to end). Ask students to decide if the sentences are true or false.

> ANSWERS
>
> 1 T 2 F 3 T 4 F

5 Give students time to read the notes, then play the second part of the video again (01.05 to end) for them to complete them.

> ANSWERS
>
> 1 ski
> 2 professional
> 3 year, climb
> 4 car, roofs
> 5 community
> 6 good
> 7 ranges
> 8 500, continue

6 Ask students to work in pairs to discuss what the quotes refer to and what Chin meant by them.

> ANSWERS
>
> 1 refers to looking for a job: he wasn't really interested in it.
> 2 refers to wanting to do climbing: he had to try it in order to move on and do something more serious.
> 3 He had to do what he wanted rather than what others wanted.
> 4 refers to his paid work: he was doing whatever different jobs were available.
> 5 He was committed to his activities and to doing them as well as he could.

After you watch

7 Students work in pairs to roleplay an interview between a journalist and an adventure photographer, according to the instructions.

8 Students work in groups to ask and answer the questions.

Videoscript

Part 1

00.05 Ultimately, like, the process of climbing is very rewarding to people.

It's very difficult physically, but it's also a very kind of cerebral sport. It's slow and methodical, and you have to think.

00.30 You can't move very well when you're scared. You have to be able to control that fear and maintain your breathing because there's very real consequences when you make mistakes.

You can make a wrong move when you're free soloing, and you fall hundreds or thousands of feet and die.

01.05 In college I found … I skied on the ski team and then I … found climbing, and so after college, you know, I went to the Bay area and I was looking for a job … trying to … you know, thinking that I would find something in the professional realm.

But then, it just didn't … I couldn't get myself excited about it and so I kind of made up my mind … I had this great idea. And I was like: 'Hey, Mom, Dad, I'm going to take a year off. I'm just going to get it out of my system. I'm going to climb and ski full-time. Don't freak out – it's really temporary. I just, I got to do it for me.'

01.51 So essentially their worst nightmare was realised when probably close to seven years later I was still living in the back of my car, just doing odds and ends for jobs, shovelling roofs and waiting tables. But really, you know, in love with what I was doing and where I was spending my time. I would wake up in the back of my Subaru in Yosemite or in the Eastern Sierras or in the Tetons, and I would just think, like, you know, there's no other place that I would rather be. I just felt so fortunate and every day I would, you know, I knew that since I wasn't doing anything else, I was going to throw myself at climbing and skiing and really kind of taking myself as far as I could in that realm.

02.44 So Yosemite was a very, kind of, influential home for me. I spent a lot of time there over the course of seven years. Made a lot of friends. I felt like I found my community there.

People that were really passionate about what they were doing and every day, you know, you'd go out and climb and … I mean, really living the good life.

03.13 After spending a lot of time there, you know, my aspirations changed, and I really wanted to go and take what I learned in Yosemite to some of the greater ranges of the world.

And it was in Yosemite that I picked up a camera for the first time.

I took a photo with a friend's camera who wanted to be a photographer. I took a photo with it and he eventually tried to sell his photos, and a client bought one photo and it happened to be the one that I took.

03.41 So, and they paid me and at the time, you know, I could live on nothing forever, basically, and they paid five hundred dollars for this photo. Of course, now I know for the usages that they used it for, they should have paid me like many thousands of dollars, but at the time I didn't know and I was like: 'If I take one photo a month, I could do this forever,' you know, and I was like: 'OK, this is awesome' so …

04.12 I wish, I, you know, I'm sure some photographers probably cringe and they're like: 'God, he has no sense of creativity or the tradition of photography,' but that was really how I started. I didn't really have a sense of, like, wanting to be an artist or photographer in any other way than to continue what I was doing.

04.29 So I took, you know, a camera and I started to head out into the world and really, you know, Yosemite is a special place for me because it launched me into this career. And, you know, over the course of the next ten, eleven, twelve years I … travelled the world and really got to shoot on some really insane assignments with some amazing people and some amazing locations.

Unit 2 Review

Grammar

1 Ask students to read the article and complete it with the correct verb forms.

ANSWERS

1 believes
2 was working
3 travels
4 testing
5 Working
6 has been doing
7 has tested
8 Creating
9 understanding
10 takes
11 has succeeded
12 Having beaten
13 am having
14 have
15 will still be doing

2 Ask students to read the article and answer the questions.

ANSWERS

1 travelling round the world testing water slides and pools
2 because the company needed someone to control quality in their selection of 'splash resorts'
3 the paperwork

3 Students work in pairs to discuss their dream job.

Vocabulary

4 Ask students to complete the questions with the correct prepositions.

ANSWERS

1 by
2 in
3 through
4 in
5 on
6 on

5 Students work in pairs to ask and answer the questions from Exercise 4.

Real life

6 Ask students to read the extract and choose the correct phrases to complete it.

ANSWERS

1 d 2 a 3 c 4 b

7 Students work in groups to give their speeches.

Speaking

8 Students work in pairs to discuss a person they admire.

Unit 3 Four walls

Lead-in

Personal response

Ask students to tell the rest of the class about a building they have seen that really impressed them for some reason. Encourage them to say what it is made of, when it was built, what is is / was used for, why they went there and what they did there. Encourage the others to ask questions.

1 [1.14] Ask students to discuss the photo, caption and questions in pairs. Elicit answers from the whole class, without saying what is correct. Play the recording for them to check. Elicit comments from the class.

ANSWERS

1 It's an Old-West-style shop. It reminds the second speaker of a building from a western film.
2 It's used as a visitor attraction and in film sets.

Audioscript [1.14]

A: I love this picture. The mountain behind and the colours of the rock are absolutely wonderful, but there's something about the simplicity of the building that sets it all off. A plain, wooden, Old-West-style shop – nothing fancy about it. It blends in very naturally with its surroundings.

B: It looks like something from the set of a western film – like those buildings you see cowboys tying up their horses in front of.

A: Funny you should say that. This one's near a place called Kanab in Utah, also known as Little Hollywood because of all the westerns that get filmed around there. This one's been well preserved so visitors can get an idea of what buildings were like in those days. It's also used by film-makers. What's interesting too is the false front on the building. A lot of buildings had those in the Old West, although this one's not particularly spectacular. They were usually bigger, and more ornate – and every building along the main street would have one, disguising a more modest structure behind it. So as you walked down the street, you got the impression that the town was much grander than it actually was – which was the intention, of course.

Background notes

The Grand Staircase-Escalante National Monument is an area of 7,571 square kilometres of land in southern Utah which was designated as a US National Monument in 1996. It consists of three distinct areas: a series of tilted terraces called the Grand Staircase (the highest part), the Kaiparowits Plateau, and an area of deep intricate gorges called the Canyons of Escalante. The whole area is very desolate and inhospitable, though fascinating. Pueblo people first inhabited the area in AD500, but the first whites did not settle there until 1866. It is noted for its fossil remains, particularly some important 75-million-year-old dinosaur finds.

2 [1.14] Ask students to read the sentences and focus on the words in bold. Play the recording for them to write what the speaker actually said. Elicit answers from the whole class.

Play the recording again to check, if necessary.

ANSWERS

1 plain wooden
2 blends in
3 false
4 ornate, modest

3 Ask students to classify the words in the box with a partner. Elicit answers from the whole class. You may wish to write the table on the board and complete it as they give the answers.

ANSWERS

material: brick, concrete, glass, steel, wooden
period / style: 1960s, colonial, futuristic, modern, traditional
impression: characterless, elegant, imposing, plain, striking
type: cottage, office block, shack, tower, warehouse

Extra activity

Ask students to work in pairs to add other words under each of the four headings (e.g. materials: stone, mud, rushes; period / style: gothic, art nouveau, classical; impression: run-down, dull, colourful; type: detached house, school, public building).

Elicit answers from the whole class, and expand the lists.

Vocabulary notes

Check some noun-adjective collocations with students:

an elegant colonial mansion

a futuristic modern office block

Remind students of the word order for adjectives:

other	colour	origin / place	material	purpose	
a new	blue	Italian	cotton	dancing	dress

4 Ask students to think of a building and describe it using the words in this section. Do an example with them first (e.g. *I love the Tate Modern building in London. It's a big, imposing, concrete power plant, built in the 1930s I think, which has now been converted into an art gallery*). You could ask students to bring in a picture of the building which they are going to describe and show it to their partner when they have finished describing it. The partner can say whether the building in the picture is close to what they understood from the description or not.

Homework

Students can write their description of a building and attach a picture.

3a Compact spaces

Lead-in

Personal response

Ask students to tell the class about the smallest space they have ever been in. Where was it? What was it used for? Why were they there? What was it like? How did they feel?

Listening

1 Ask students to work in pairs and ask and answer the three questions. Elicit some answers from the whole class.

2 [1.15] Ask students to look at the two photos and talk about them with a partner. Elicit some ideas from the class about what they can see and where the photos were taken. Ask students to read the two questions to focus their listening. Play the recording, then elicit answers from the whole class.

ANSWERS

1 Photo A is a Dolgan home, in Russia. Photo B is a small apartment in Hong Kong.
2 The Dolgan home uses natural materials, has only the basic necessities and can be easily moved. The Hong Kong apartment is only 32 square metres, but can be transformed into 24 different rooms by using sliding walls.

Audioscript [1.15]

P = presenter, **J** = Jonas Wilfstrand

P: Welcome to *Grand Architecture*. We're changing focus completely today and looking at small homes. I'm very pleased to welcome Swedish architect, Jonas Wilfstrand, who specialises in the design of compact living spaces. I've been looking at some of these on your website, and I must say some of them are absolutely stunning. I really liked the timber and glass vacation house with the built-in sauna. Is this a trend we're seeing, Jonas, for smaller homes?

J: I don't think it's really a trend in the sense that lots of people are wanting smaller homes, but I think there is definitely more interest in them. In a lot of places, dwellings are small from necessity – people are either incredibly short of space or they simply can't afford a bigger house.

P: And where have you taken your inspiration from? Where did you look for ideas?

J: Well, there were two homes in particular that got me interested in this. One was the houses of the Dolgan people in central north Russia, who live a lot of the year in freezing temperatures, as low as minus 40 degrees. Their houses are shaped a bit like a sugar cube and extremely basic – just a single room with two or three beds, a table and a stove. They're constructed from wooden frames and reindeer skins, which is a great insulator. The Dolgan are nomadic people who tend reindeer and when it's time to find new feeding grounds, they move house, quite literally. Their houses are on sled runners and they get pulled along by the reindeer to the next stop.

P: Why did these Dolgan houses impress you so much?

J: Well, several reasons: their mobility, the way the Dolgan use only readily available materials, and the fact that they're just so simple. They were what got me thinking about the whole concept of more compact living.

P: And you mentioned another home that inspired you?

J: Ah yes, that's not at all simple. It's the apartment of an architect in Hong Kong. As you probably know, space is at a premium in Hong Kong. It's a really overcrowded city. Gary Chang lives in a tall apartment block in a flat that's only 32 square metres. And he used sliding walls – partitions – within the flat to be able to transform it into a living room, a kitchen, a library, a bedroom; in fact, he claims he can have 24 different rooms in all. He entirely rethought the way we arrange living space – I thought it was wonderfully innovative. There are some great photos of it on his website. Here's one …

P: It looks distinctly cramped to me, but very stylish …

3 [1.15] Ask students to underline the best options in each sentence, then check with a partner. Play the recording again for them to check, then elicit the answers from the whole class.

ANSWERS

1 the efficient use of space
2 are curious about
3 one room
4 their animals
5 move
6 has mixed feelings about

4 Ask the class to discuss the questions in open class.

Background notes

Gary Chang was born in Hong Kong in 1962, graduated in architecture from Hong Kong University in 1987, and set up his own company, EDGE, in 1994. He has specialised in designing interiors for everything from flats to shops, hotels, restaurants, offices, boats and planes. He had his first solo exhibition in Hong Kong in 2000, the year he also exhibited at the Venice Biennale.

Language focus intensifying adverbs

5 Read the instructions and the example with the class. Elicit from them what is meant by *an intensifying adverb* (an adverb which adds strength to the meaning of another word). Ask students to do the exercise individually, then check with a partner. Elicit answers from the whole class and discuss each one thoroughly to aid understanding.

ANSWERS

The intensifying adverb is in **bold** and the word it intensifies is underlined.

1 *changing focus* ***completely*** (verb)
2 ***very*** *pleased* (adjective)
3 ***absolutely*** *stunning* (adjective)
4 ***incredibly*** *short* (adjective); ***simply*** *can't* (verb)
5 ***quite*** *literally* (adverb)
6 ***just so*** *simple* (adjective)
7 ***really*** *overcrowded* (adjective)
8 ***entirely*** *rethought* (verb)

6 Ask the whole class to discuss and answer these questions. Make sure students understand the concept of 'gradable' and 'ungradable'.

ANSWERS

gradable: *short* ungradable: *stunning*

7 Ask students to work in pairs and decide which words are gradable and ungradable. Elicit answers.

ANSWERS

gradable: *difficult, innovative, plain, simple, strong*
ungradable: *brilliant, filthy, freezing, huge, perfect*

8 Read through the box about intensifying adverbs with the class and discuss anything which is not clear. Ask them to choose the correct adverb individually, then check with a partner. Elicit the answers from the whole class.

ANSWERS

1 so
2 extremely
3 quite
4 completely
5 utterly
6 absolutely
7 really
8 very

Vocabulary notes

Note that when using intensifying words, they are often placed early in the sentence to add emphasis, e.g. *it was a* ***desperately*** *unlucky decision*, rather than *the decision was* ***desperately*** *unlucky.*

These intensifying words should not be used in normal everyday situations, or they can sound out of place and ridiculous: *she made some* ***wildly*** *nice toast for breakfast.*

Pronunciation stress in intensifying adverbs

9a [1.16] Ask students to read through the six sentences first, then play the recording while they underline the stressed syllables.

ANSWERS

1 You're absolutely right.
2 That's really kind of you.
3 I'd be very grateful.
4 It's completely out of the question.
5 Yes, I'm quite certain.
6 That's so typical.

9b Ask students to write some (perhaps four) two-line conversations using the expressions in 9a, and practise saying them. They should then perform them for another pair and check each other's pronunciation.

Vocabulary adverb and adjective collocations

10 Ask the class to discuss the questions about the meaning of *distinctly* in this example.

ANSWER

very

11 Ask students to decide individually in which two cases the adverb does not mean *very* or *absolutely*. They should then check with a partner, before you elicit the answers from the class.

ANSWERS

mildly and *vaguely* are the two adverbs which do not mean *very* or *absolutely*.

12 Ask pairs to think of examples which illustrate the descriptions. They should then share their ideas with another pair. Elicit examples from the whole class.

SAMPLE ANSWERS

1 paint drying, water boiling
2 that you will win the lottery next week
3 that Marilyn Monroe was a woman
4 a cyclist crashing when in the lead in a race
5 asking to be allowed time for lunch each day

Speaking

13 Ask students to work in pairs to discuss the rooms in the box. Elicit some answers from the whole class.

ANSWERS

1 conservatory: a glass extension
2 a courtyard: an open area surrounded by buildings
3 a games room: a room for games like table tennis
4 a garage / workshop: a place to keep a car and / or do DIY
5 a gym: a room with equipment for exercising
6 a home cinema: a room for watching films on a large screen
7 a roof garden: a garden planted on a flat roof
8 a sauna: a small steam room
9 a veranda: an open, roofed area on one side of a house
10 a walk-in wardrobe: a small room for clothes

14 Ask students to think about their ideal home individually, then get into groups of four to ask and answer questions.

Homework

Ask students to write up their description of their ideal house and its rooms and fittings in 100–150 words.

3b Old new towns

Lead-in

Personal response

Ask students to tell a partner about a town, village or city which they like very much, explaining why they like it. Elicit some responses from the whole class.

Vocabulary towns

1 Ask students to work in pairs to match the words in A and B, then match the collocations to the definitions.

Ask them to check with another pair, then elicit answers from the whole class.

ANSWERS

1 historic city *or* town
2 market town
3 housing estate
4 vibrant city *or* metropolis
5 dormitory town
6 sleepy village *or* neighbourhood
7 leafy suburb
8 sprawling suburb *or* estate

2 Ask students to work out a description of one or more places they have lived. Suggest they make some notes to help them. They should then tell a partner. Elicit some examples from the whole class.

Extra activity

Ask students to write up their description from Exercise 2 into a detailed descriptive paragraph. Alternatively, ask students to think of two very different places they know (e.g. an industrial city and a rural village, or two parts of the same city – one commercial, one residential), and, using the terms from Exercise 1, write a text comparing and contrasting the two places (in 100–125 words).

Reading

3 Ask the class to discuss the photos and make suggestions about the places they can see. Do not comment on any of their ideas. Ask them to read the article to find out the correct answers.

ANSWERS

Photo 1 is from Poundbury, Dorset, UK
Photo 2 is from Thames Town, near Shanghai

4 Ask students to read the questions to focus their reading, then read the article again and answer the questions. They can check their answers with a partner before you elicit answers from the whole class.

ANSWERS

1 They are both new towns, modelled on the style and design of old English villages.
2 Poundbury was created as an alternative to modern city living; Thames Town was built as a suburb for rich people in Shanghai.
3 Poundbury – yes; Thames Town – no

Background notes

Poundbury is a new town near Dorchester in south-west England. Work began on building the new town in the mid-1990s, and it is expected to be completed by 2025. It will have 5,000 residents and offer 2,000 jobs. It is designed with a mixture of town houses, cottages, shops and light industry, built with a combination of traditional architecture and modern town planning.

5 Ask students to read the list of things they have to look for, then work with a partner to find them in the text. Elicit answers from the whole class. Point out the phrase *affordable housing* in paragraph 4 of the reading text and read through the *Wordbuilding* box with students. Ensure that they understand the process. If you feel that they need some more explanation or practice, see page 27 in the Workbook.

ANSWERS

1 high-rise apartment blocks, large housing estates, zonal planning
2 quaint cottages, grander houses
3 a pub, a fish and chip shop, a 19th-century church
4 Offices and places of work are near residential areas; there is plenty of communal green space.

6 Ask students to discuss the issue of recreating old towns with a partner. Elicit ideas from the whole class for a wider discussion.

Language focus emphatic structures

7 Ask students to work with a partner, reading the sentences and answering the three questions. Elicit answers from the whole class.

ANSWERS

1 *It was here that he could offer an alternative to 'ugly' high-rise apartment blocks.* This sentence has more emphasis. The word *here* (i.e. Poundbury) is emphasised; the phrase *It was* is added in front of *here*, and placed at the start of the sentence.
2 *What I was trying to do was remind people that it is pointless to throw away the knowledge ...* This sentence has more emphasis. It emphasises the intentions. The start of the sentence is changed to a *what* clause.
3 *Rarely do you find nostalgia taken to such extremes.* This sentence has more emphasis; *rarely* is emphasised by being moved to the start of the sentence.
4 *As far as friendly urban planning goes, Poundbury does seem to work.* This sentence has more emphasis. The auxiliary *does* is added before *have*, which gives it extra force.

8 Read through the language focus box about emphatic structures with the class and discuss the points made; if you feel students need more explanation and practice, see page 160. Ask students to rewrite the sentences with more emphasis. They should do this individually, then check with a partner. Elicit answers from the whole class.

ANSWERS
1 What I love is the human scale of Poundbury.
2 Seldom do you need a car to go shopping.
3 The thing the architects wanted to do was encourage people to mix, so they included communal green spaces in the design of the town.
4 It's in these public spaces that children socialise.
5 What isn't surprising is that Poundbury has cost a lot of money to build.
6 Not once did the developers opt for cheaper materials like concrete when they were building Poundbury.
7 When asked, the developers did admit that they expected Thames Town to be more popular with residents.
8 They do think, however, that the Italian and Austrian towns will be popular.

9 Ask students to work with a partner to decide which sentences do not really require the emphatic structure. Elicit answers from the whole class.

ANSWER
The sentences which shouldn't use an emphatic structure are sentences 1, 3 and 4.

Speaking

10 Ask students to work together in groups of four to discuss the four issues related to town planning. Suggest one of them becomes secretary and keeps notes for the group. Discuss the ideas as a whole class.

Extra activity

Elicit comments from all the groups and open a whole-class discussion of the issues. If everyone is from, or lives in the same place, discuss what town planning choices have been made and what the advantages and disadvantages are for your area.

3c The paper architect

Lead-in

Personal response
Ask the class to say what they know about what an architect does on a day-to-day basis. What skills does an architect need? How and where do they work? If someone in the class is an architect, then let the others give their ideas first, then have the architect tell them about their work.

Reading

1 Ask students to discuss the question about 'the paper architect' in pairs. Elicit answers from the whole class.

ANSWERS
Suggestions might include:
she makes buildings out of paper;
she never built anything, so her buildings are just designs on paper;
she makes paper models of all her buildings first.

2 Ask students to read the three statements to focus their reading. They should then read the article and decide which is the best summary.

ANSWER
c

Vocabulary notes

The following words and expressions from the text may be unfamiliar:

interlocking = connected and linked
to intrigue = to interest greatly
to pin down = to classify, to describe exactly
sought after = requested, wanted (from the verb *to seek*)
to sprout up = to grow very quickly from nothing

3 Ask students to read the eight questions before they reread the text and find the answers. They can check with a partner before you elicit the answers from the whole class.

ANSWERS
1 Because at one time, she designed buildings which weren't actually built.
2 Because it's a male-dominated profession and they find it difficult to be recognised.
3 That she is very independent: she does her own thing in her own way – regardless of what others are doing.
4 They like to play with the traditional shape of buildings and fragment them (break them up).
5 She likes to work on public buildings.
6 To compensate for the lack of internal space.
7 They feel surprised and charmed.
8 By her contemporaries and natural landscapes.

Background notes

Dame Zaha Hadid was born in Baghdad, Iraq in 1950. After studying architecture in Beirut and London, she set up her own practice in London in 1980. She has spent a lot of time teaching at prestigious architectural institutions. In 2004 she was awarded the Pritker Prize for her architecture, and then the Stirling Prize in 2010 for the MAXXI National Museum in Rome, and again in 2012 for the Evelyn Grace Academy in Brixton, London. In 2008, Forbes rated her as the 69th most powerful woman in the world. She was made a CBE in 2002 and a DBE in 2012 for her services to architecture.

Critical thinking fact or opinion

4 Ask students to read the six statements, then work with a partner to find evidence for them in the article. They should check with another pair, then discuss the answers as a class.

ANSWERS

1 *in a profession still dominated by men ... / less than 15% of practising architects are women*
2 *Working in this way, she and her fellow architects have produced various, rather off the wall spaceship-like structures*
3 *this has drawn her increasingly to become interested in public projects*
4 *so that the visitor is surprised and charmed at each turn*
5 *like winding streets* and *It's about promenading*
6 *always ... trying to keep human interests ... at heart. Perhaps we could do with more architects like her.*

5 Ask students to mark the statements as opinion or fact individually, then check with a partner. Elicit answers from the whole class.

ANSWERS

1 F 2 O 3 F 4 O 5 F 6 O

6 Ask students to write a summary about Zaha Hadid and her work.

Extra activity

Ask students to exchange their writing from Exercise 6 with a partner, and check each other's work. They should check for content, organisation and language and then give feedback to each other. They could write a second draft.

Word focus *wall*

7 Ask students to find the two expressions with *wall* in the text and choose the meaning from the options. Elicit the answers from the whole class.

ANSWERS

1 a 2 a

8 Ask students to work with a partner to decide on the meanings of the further six *wall* expressions. Elicit answers from the whole class.

ANSWERS

1 making me mad *or* very irritated
2 the ATM *or* cashpoint
3 went bankrupt *or* closed down
4 there are clear signs that the end (or failure) is near
5 watching without anyone noticing
6 be blocked / unable to make further progress

9 Ask students to think of personal examples for each of the situations, then tell a partner. Elicit a few examples from around the class.

Extra activity

Ask students to write an expanded version of one of the situations they talked about in Exercise 9, using a couple of the expressions with *wall*. They can exchange their writing with a different partner for comment.

Speaking

10 Ask students to think about their feelings related to the five public spaces listed; they may want to make a few notes. Ask them to talk to a partner about them. Elicit some experiences from the whole class.

11 Ask students to work in groups of four to discuss one of the public spaces. You might like to assign a different space to each group to avoid repetition. Ask the groups to appoint a secretary to keep notes on their ideas. They can then present their ideas to the rest of the class. The others should comment on what they hear.

Homework

Ask students to choose a different public space from the one they discussed in their group, and possibly a different one from any of those in Exercise 10. They should then write a detailed description of their ideas of what it should be like, explaining why; they can include plans and diagrams. In the next lesson, they should present their ideas in groups of four.

3d A public project

Lead-in

Personal response
Ask students to think about the place where they live, and say what they think is the best public space there, explaining why. Encourage comment and discussion.

Real life making recommendations

1 Ask students to work in pairs to talk about public works of art in their town. Elicit some examples and opinions from the whole class. Plainly, this activity will be different if all of your class are from the same place, or if there are students from many different places. You might ask them to bring in photos of the works of art they are talking about, particularly if they are all from different places.

2 Ask students to look at the picture in the book and discuss the questions with a partner. Elicit some responses from the whole class.

ANSWERS
1 Students' own answers.
2 It would attract more visitors to the town; it would encourage local people and visitors to use the area as a communal space; bring families to the area; give locals a sense of pride in their town; encourage modern art.

3 [1.17] Read through the instructions and questions with the class to focus their listening. Play the recording and ask them to find the answers. They can check with a partner. Play the recording again for them to check their answers. Elicit answers from the whole class.

ANSWERS
1 An interactive work of art in the shape of a book.
2 He is in favour of it.
3 It's accessible, it reflects the tradition of the city, it's fun, it's interactive, it could become a tourist destination.

Audioscript [1.17]

I have to say, I really like this piece. It has several things to recommend it. First of all, as a work of art, it seems very accessible. What I mean is it's not too intellectual or difficult to understand, like a lot of modern art pieces. So in that way, I think everyone – children and adults – should be able to relate to it. Also, the fact that it's in the shape of an open book will give it popular appeal. It reflects the long tradition of our city as a place of learning very well. It's a clever touch, I think

Thirdly, and I don't think we should underestimate this, it's just good fun. The quotes and jokes that appear on the pages will attract a lot of attention. People will be able to sit on benches and watch as the different messages roll across the screen. So it becomes an interactive work of art and I think this is important, given its central location in the city. And the idea that it could become a tourist destination also really appeals to me.

Well, that more or less sums up my position. What does everyone else think?

Speaking skill making a case

4a [1.17] Ask students to read through the box of expressions for making a case, to focus their listening. Play the recording again for them to complete the sentences, pausing as necessary to allow time for students to write the answers. They should check with a partner. If necessary, play the recording again for them to check, complete and correct their answers. Elicit the answers from the class as complete sentences.

ANSWERS
1 I really like this piece
2 several things
3 very accessible
4 it's not too intellectual or difficult to understand
5 be able to relate to it
6 it is in the shape of an open book
7 it's just good fun
8 its central location in the city
9 it could become a tourist destination

4b Ask students to discuss the two questions in pairs and mark the sentences with P or E as indicated. Elicit answers from the whole class and discuss the responses.

ANSWERS
1 The phrases which are always positive:
It has … to recommend it.
Also, the fact that … will give it popular appeal.
It's a clever touch, I think.
And the idea that … also really appeals to me.
2 The phrases which give extra emphasis are:
I have to say
I don't think we should underestimate this
I think this is important, given …

Pronunciation linking

5a [1.18] Read the instructions and the example with the class and play the example sentence. Elicit from students how the words link. If necessary write the sentence on the board and point out some of the linking sounds, particularly the addition of the linking /w/ sound which is not in the individual words. Ask them to work in pairs to decide on how the sounds link in the other two sentences. Point out that they should listen out for any different linking sounds. Play the recording for them to check. Elicit the answers from the whole class. Check that they have noticed the linking /j/ and /r/ sounds.

ANSWERS
2 'The_/j/_idea that_it could be_/j/_a tourist destination'
3 'The water_/r/_and_the_/j/_area_/r/_in front_of the fountain'

Pronunciation notes

Note that in linked speech the following things happen:

a normally silent final consonants (/r/, /t/, /d/) are pronounced before a vowel at the start of the following word (e.g. *and area*)

b sounds not in the words are added between two vowel sounds (/w/, /j/, /r/, e.g. *too /w/ intellectual, really /j/ appeals, area /r/ in front of*)

c words are run together so that the final consonant of the first word sounds as if it belongs to the next word (e.g. *an elephant* becomes *a nelephant*)

Extra activity

Play the recording a few times for students to listen, then play it again, pausing at suitable points for them to repeat chorally and individually.

5b Ask students to work in pairs and say the sentences to help each other with their pronunciation.

6 Ask students to discuss the proposal guidelines in threes. Elicit answers from the whole class.

ANSWER

The authorities are hoping to commission a piece of art to go in the park in order to attract more visitors.

7 Read through the instructions with the whole class. Ask them to get into groups of three and turn to the appropriate page, then prepare their presentation. Circulate to monitor and help students with their preparation. They then give their presentations and vote on the winning proposal in their groups. Choose some students to give their presentation to the whole class.

3e Old and new

Lead-in

Personal response

Ask the class to express some opinions about contemporary architecture – what do they like and dislike, and why? If they can refer to particular buildings that others know, it could be helpful.

Writing an opinion essay

1 Ask the whole class to answer the questions about the picture.

2 Ask students to read the essay question, then the essay, then answer the two questions. They should check with a partner when they have finished. Elicit answers from the whole class.

ANSWERS

1 The writer's opinion is that modern buildings can be built next to older buildings in a historic area of a city.
2 He gives examples from the town of Tours, where he lives.

3 Ask students to find the examples in the text individually, then compare their findings with a partner. Elicit answers from the whole class.

ANSWERS

1 *Admittedly, there are examples of new buildings which have spoilt the area they are in.*
2 *Although we have to respect people's feelings as fellow users and viewers …*
3 *If we constantly reproduced what was there before, we would all still be living in caves.*

4 Read through the instructions and the four key elements with the class, and ensure they understand them. Ask them to find the examples individually, then discuss their answers with a partner. Elicit answers from the whole class.

ANSWERS

a paragraph 4
b paragraph 2
c paragraph 3
d paragraph 1
The correct order is: d, b, c, a

Writing skill linking devices

5a Read through the instructions and the words in the box with the class, and ensure they understand both. Ask students to answer the four questions individually, then check with a partner. Elicit answers from the whole class.

ANSWERS

a however, but
b admittedly, although, even though
c indeed
d so, thus

5b Ask students to work in pairs to complete the sentences with words from the box in Exercise 5a. Elicit the answers as complete sentences from the whole class.

ANSWERS

1 Indeed
2 even though
3 Admittedly
4 However
5 Thus *or* So

6 Ask students to write the essay as instructed. You may wish them to do this for homework.

7 Ask students to exchange essays with a partner and check one another's writing, commenting as indicated on the three points.

3f Denmark bridge

Before you watch

1 Students work in pairs. Ask them to look at the photo and say what they can see, then discuss the questions. Take feedback from the class.

ANSWERS

1 It's a road and rail bridge connecting Denmark and Sweden.
2 It's very long and built across the sea.
3 Using ferries or planes for transport.

While you watch

2 Ask students to read the questions, then watch the video and find the answers.

ANSWERS

1 The sea is ten miles wide and the weather is bad ('lousy'), there is air and shipping traffic.
2 They built the Øresund Bridge, part bridge and part tunnel.

3 Give students time to read through the table and the words in the glossary. Play the first part of the video (to 01.54) for students to complete the facts. Take feedback from the class.

ANSWERS

1 ten miles
2 lousy (bad)
3 cheaper housing
4 more jobs
5 cars and trains
6 200 feet
7 670 feet

4 Give students time to read the questions. Then play the second part of the video (01.55 to end) for them to answer.

ANSWERS

1 There's an international airport; computer simulation shows that the bridge would obstruct the air traffic.
2 It would block Denmark's shipping traffic.
3 beautiful and (very) expensive
4 They needed dry land for the tunnel to emerge from underwater.
5 They built an island.

5 Give students time to read the notes, then play the video again for them to complete them.

ANSWERS

1 Strait
2 metropolis
3 pact *or* agreement
4 consortium
5 air
6 expensive
7 bridge
8 longest

After you watch

6 Students work in pairs to roleplay a debate according to the instructions.

7 Students work in groups to ask and answer the questions.

Videoscript

Part 1

00.03 What's it take to build one of the world's mega bridges?

00.18 In northern Europe, the Baltic Sea converges with the North Sea at the Øresund Strait. It's ten miles wide with lousy weather. And it's done a great job of keeping Denmark separate from Sweden.

00.36 The Øresund Strait is a frustrating barrier because each shore has something the other needs. Copenhagen, Denmark needs cheaper housing. Malmö, Sweden needs more jobs. Connect the dots and you could unleash an economic powerhouse. A bridge would make them one big metropolis, but it's never been possible. Until now.

01.10 Enter the Øresund Bridge. The world's longest cable-stayed bridge that can carry cars plus the enormous weight of trains.

3,583 feet of road and rail dangling from 160 cables.

01.34 200 feet above the sea, the support towers soar 670 feet, jabbing at clouds and making the Øresund Bridge one of the tallest cement structures in Sweden.

Part 2

01.55 Companies from both countries must form a consortium to build the bridge together. The consortium's first challenge: figuring out how to build a bridge ten miles long. Immediately, they face a dangerous setback.

On the Denmark side, right at the shoreline, is the Copenhagen international airport, Kastrup.

Computer simulations show that building a bridge with high towers would obstruct air traffic … or worse. A low bridge would be safer for air traffic, but it would block Denmark's ship traffic.

02.42 When engineers can't build over the water, they consider building under it, with a tunnel ten miles long.

Peter Lundhus That would be the beautiful solution, building a tunnel from one side to the other, but that would be the expensive solution. So the third solution that we decided was, of course, to build part-bridge and then a tunnel where we were getting close to the airport.

A bridge would have been easier or cheaper, but would not have been a good idea for the aeroplanes.

03.14 Somewhere, they need dry land for the tunnel to emerge from under water. They need an island, so they'll have to build one, from scratch.

Unit 3 Review

Grammar

1 Ask students to look at the photo and discuss it in pairs, then read the text to check.

ANSWER

It's the London Olympics Aquatics Centre.

2 Ask students to read the article and choose the correct options to complete it.

ANSWERS

1 really	3 very	5 quite
2 absolutely	4 really	6 incredibly

3 Students rewrite the sentences to be more emphatic.

ANSWERS

1 … Zaha Hadid's ability to design large public buildings which do work.
2 Rarely do design and function come together as successfully as this.
3 What I like is the way that she has made the roof look like moving water.

Vocabulary

4 Students work in pairs to discuss their favourite sports building.

5 Ask students to complete the definitions.

ANSWERS

1 shack	4 metropolis
2 leafy	5 housing
3 characterless	6 sleepy

6 Students work in pairs to describe places from Exercise 5.

Real life

7 Ask students to read the article and choose the correct options to complete it.

ANSWERS

1 have	3 underestimate	5 appealed
2 recommend	4 think	6 touch

8 Students work in groups to present their proposals.

Speaking

9 Students work in pairs to discuss the buildings in Unit 3.

Unit 4 Innovation

Lead-in

Personal response
Ask the class to say what they think have been the most interesting, the most important or the most useful innovations of the past few years, and why. Encourage students to ask questions and discuss any suggestions.

1 [1.19] Ask students to discuss the picture and its implications for transport. Elicit some responses from the whole class, but do not comment on what is said. Play the recording and ask for students to feedback on what they heard.

SAMPLE ANSWERS

It's like a bicycle railway. The pods are mounted on rails, and are powered by pedalling.

The advantages are that it's green, convenient, cost-competitive and fun.

Audioscript [1.19]

In the late 19th century, someone had the bright idea of mounting a bicycle-like contraption on rails. The idea was to give a smoother ride than could be achieved on conventional bicycles. At the time, no one recognised that a breakthrough had been made, but, more recently, the idea of a pedal-powered monorail has been revived and updated at an amusement park in New Zealand by a company named Shweeb.

Google, always good at spotting a trend, has invested $1 million to support further development of the system for an urban environment. Like the original bicycle railway, the Shweeb system is meant to reduce friction between the wheel and the surface it makes contact with 'by running hard wheels on hard rail', just like a train. But the Shweeb concept also takes the idea one stage further. Drivers lie back in bullet-shaped hanging 'pods' and pedal with their feet forward, as on a reclining bicycle. The pods hang from 20-centimetre-wide rails constructed above street-level pedestrians and traffic.

There's no need to worry about overtaking because two Shweebs travelling in a line are more efficient owing to reduced air resistance.

And is there a real demand for this? Well, both Google and Shweeb are convinced that it fills an important need for transport which is green, convenient, cost-competitive and fun. You could say they've reinvented the wheel!

2 [1.19] Ask students to complete the text individually from memory, then check with a partner. Play the recording again for them to check, complete and correct their answers. Elicit answers from the whole class as complete sentences.

ANSWERS

1 rails
2 smoothly
3 amusement
4 Google
5 pedal
6 above
7 fun

Background note

The Shweeb (which comes from the German verb *schweben* meaning to float or to suspend) is the brainchild of Geoffrey Barnett. When working as an English teacher in Japan, he saw the terrible traffic jams, and dreamed of a way of moving people around the city faster, without building more roads and without pollution. Later he experimented, and came up with the Shweeb, which was built in Rotorua, New Zealand. There are two parallel 200-metre monorails, with pods suspended underneath them. People can pay to ride or race, and it has proved very popular as a leisure activity.

3 Ask students to match the two halves of the collocations, then discuss with a partner what they think each of the expressions means. Elicit the answers from the whole class.

ANSWERS

1 d 2 b 3 f 4 c 5 a 6 e

Extra activity

Write the following phrases up on the board and ask students to match them with the collocations in Exercise 3 to check their understanding (answers are in brackets).

a *identify a new fashion* (3f)
b *create something that already exists* (6e)
c *take a big step forward with a new discovery* (2b)
d *provide something that is lacking* (5a)
e *think of something clever* (1d)
f *develop an idea* (4c)

Point out the play on words in the audioscript, *you could say they've reinvented the wheel.* This phrase is usually used to mean that somebody has wasted time doing something that has already been done, but in this case they have 'reinvented' a wheel that is more useful than the traditional one.

4 Ask students to work in pairs to use the phrases from Exercise 3 to describe an innovation. They should then tell another pair and listen to their description. Elicit some responses from the whole class.

SAMPLE ANSWER

In the 1980s, Sony came up with the idea of the Sony 'Walkman', having spotted a trend for mobile music devices. This was taken a step further with the invention of MP3 players and smartphones that could play music.

Other inventions might include the iPad, the electric toothbrush, air-filled trainers, low-energy light bulbs, etc.

Extra activity

Ask students to write 100–125 words about the Shweeb and what they think about it. In a further lesson, they can exchange their writing and give one another feedback.

4a The mother of invention

Lead-in

Personal response

Ask students to say what the most useful object they possess is and explain why. Ask everyone to discuss the suggestions.

Listening

1 Ask students to discuss the quotation with a partner, then elicit ideas on its meaning from the class and discuss whether it is always true. Ask the class what other things might motivate people to invent things (money, curiosity).

ANSWER

It means that things are invented or created to fill a particular need. Whilst this is often true, sometimes inventions come about by accident. Saccharin and the microwave oven are both examples of inventions which were discovered by accident, not necessity.

2 Ask the class to look at the picture and suggest answers to the questions. Encourage discussion and comment.

SAMPLE ANSWERS

Quirky, eccentric, original, impractical.

3 [1.20] Ask students to read the three statements to focus their listening. Play the recording and ask them to discuss their answer with a partner.

ANSWER

b

Audioscript [1.20]

P = presenter, **M** = Martha Kay

P: It's difficult to imagine what life must have been like before the invention of certain things. If you're in your teens or twenties, you might never have wondered how people searched for information before the Internet existed. The electric light is another thing that we all take for granted. But how do such inventions come about? Is it necessity that drives innovation? Or commercial profit? Or something else? Here to discuss these questions is business historian, Martha Kay. Martha, there are a lot of things around us that we clearly could live without, so the necessity argument is not the whole answer, is it?

M: Hello, Evan. No, of course it isn't. History is littered with inventions that people thought they didn't need at the time. In 1878, a British Parliamentary committee, which had to comment on the usefulness of Alexander Graham Bell's telephone, said '… it is good enough for our transatlantic friends, but unworthy of the attention of practical men.'

P: Yes, well, perhaps they should have been more open-minded. But in 1878 people didn't need to have phones, did they? You could conduct your daily business and daily life perfectly well without one. But now it's become a necessity, a need has been created, if you like.

M: Well, people in the 19th century needed a way to communicate at a distance more effectively; they just hadn't envisaged the telephone. Of course, there are some inventions which fill an urgent need – vaccines against particular diseases come to mind. But most innovations aren't like that. Entrepreneurs have often come up with ideas to make our lives a little more convenient or comfortable and then, over time, we come to rely on them. Television is a case in point. Remote shopping – that's to say mail-order, or these days internet shopping – is another. It was dismissed by *Time* magazine in the 1960s because they said, 'women like to get out of the house and like to be able to change their minds'.

P: I'm sure they did – like to get out of the house, that is. That certainly was a different era …

M: Another form of innovation is to take something that's at first expensive to produce and therefore exclusive to rich people, and make it available to many. There are quite a few things that we now see as everyday necessities that have come to us in this way – where an entrepreneur has found a way to produce something more cheaply, like the mobile phone or the computer. Another example, in the 1890s, the motor car was thought to be a luxury for the wealthy. *Literary Digest* predicted that it would never 'of course, come into common use'.

P: I see, so in that sense what it comes down to is wants rather than needs. But what about all those things that we don't really need. How do you explain …

4 [1.20] Ask students to read through the sentences first, then listen to the recording and choose the correct options. They can check with a partner before you elicit answers from the whole class.

ANSWERS

1 doing research
2 an academic
3 of little use
4 didn't exist before
5 easier
6 going out to shop
7 very expensive at first
8 remain a luxury

5 Ask students to discuss the facts with a partner, then elicit some responses from the whole class.

Vocabulary phrasal verb *come*

6 Ask students to choose the meanings of the expressions individually, then check with a partner.

ANSWERS

1 b 2 a 3 c 4 b 5 a 6 b

7 Ask students to write their three sentences individually, then read them to a partner as indicated. Elicit some of the sentences from the whole class.

Language focus past modals

8 Ask students to match the sentences with the functions of the modal verbs individually, then check with a partner. Elicit answers and discuss them with the whole class.

ANSWERS

1 c 2 a 3 d 4 b

Grammar notes

Remind students that these modals (*might, may, could*) are used to express degrees of certainty, possibility and impossibility.

Ask students what the past form of *must* is (*had to*) and contrast this with *must have* + past participle as used for speculation:

Pete: *I **had to** visit my granny yesterday because she isn't well.* (Pete was obliged to visit her.)

*Pete **must have visited** his granny yesterday. He said she wasn't well.* (This is my speculation about what he did and where he was yesterday.)

9 Read through the language focus box about past modals with the class and discuss the contents. If you feel they need more explanation and practice, turn to page 160. Ask students to work in pairs to complete the sentences, then elicit answers from the whole class.

ANSWERS

1 can't have been *or* couldn't have been
2 didn't need to own
3 had to depend
4 might *or* may have driven
5 needn't have bought *or* didn't need to buy *or* shouldn't have bought
6 must have been
7 needn't have bothered *or* shouldn't have bothered
8 should have been given
9 must have realised *or* might have realised
10 might have come (*would have come* is also possible)

Pronunciation weak forms

10a [1.21] Make sure students understand the term *weak form*, and then ask them to circle them in the six sentences. They should do this individually, then check with a partner. Elicit suggestions from the whole class and play the recording for them to check.

ANSWERS

1 You should have told me.
2 Did you have to wait?
3 He must have forgotten.
4 You needn't have worried.
5 She may have left already.
6 I didn't need to be there.

Pronunciation note

Point out to students that as well as not stressing the weak forms, the value of the sounds also change: *have* no longer has its full sound value, but becomes /əv/.

10b [1.22] Ask students to listen and underline the stressed words in the paired sentences. Elicit the answers, then discuss the difference in meaning the different stress gives. Play the recording for students to repeat.

ANSWERS

1a You might have told me.
In this sentence, the speaker can't remember if they were told about something or not.
1b You might have told me.
In this sentence, the speaker wasn't told and wishes they had been.
2a You shouldn't have waited.
In this sentence, the speaker is saying that the other person needn't have waited when they did.
2b Flowers? Oh, you shouldn't have.
In this sentence, the speaker is expressing appreciation at having been given flowers.

11 Ask students to discuss the problems in groups of four. One should be a secretary and note their group's ideas. Elicit responses from the whole class and invite students to engage in a wider discussion.

SAMPLE ANSWERS

They had to rely on their own body clocks.
They must have put their cash in some kind of safe box.
They might have sung songs or told stories.
They must have used herbal medicines.
They must have needed help from neighbours.
They might have had a fire burning all the time.
They must have had skills to recognise broken bones.

Speaking

12 Ask students to think of two inventions individually, then discuss them with their partner and others. Elicit comments and responses from the whole class at the end.

Homework

Students can write a paragraph about each of the two inventions they chose in Exercise 12.

4b Fold everything

Lead-in

Personal response

Ask the class if anyone knows how to make a paper aeroplane. If someone does, give everyone a sheet of A4 paper and ask the person (or people, with the class divided into groups, if there are several) to show others how to do it. If different students produce different models, compare them and see which flies better. Discuss the process and how easy / difficult it was.

Reading

1 Ask the class to look at the picture and answer the questions, then discuss the answers.

Background notes

Origami is a Japanese word coming from *ori* (folding) and *kami* (paper). The art of paper folding started in China in the 1st or 2nd century AD. Paper was a very rare and expensive commodity, and so origami was only practised by the rich and powerful. It came to Japan around the 6th century AD, and remained an activity for the privileged few, very often used for special ceremonies by Samurai and priests. In 1797, however, a book called *How to fold 1,000 cranes* was published, which was the first time origami instructions were written down. In 1845 another book came out called *Window on midwinter* which had instructions for 150 origami models, many of which are still popular today (e.g. the frog).

2 Ask students to discuss origami using the statements given, then read the first paragraph of the text to check their answers. Elicit ideas from the whole class.

ANSWERS

1 F ('it can be created from a single sheet of paper')
2 F ('from a single square or rectangular sheet of paper')
3 T ('no cutting')
4 F ('no glue')

3 Ask students to read the four things to focus their reading, then read the rest of the article to find the answers. They can check with a partner before you elicit the answers from the whole class.

ANSWERS

1 solar panels and telescope lens
2 airbags (in cars) and stents (used in arteries)
3 robots
4 tiny folded motors or capacitors

4 Ask students to work in pairs to explain the phrases from the text. Elicit answers from the whole class.

ANSWERS

1 'More sophisticated' means a paper crane is more complex to make than a paper aeroplane.
2 It means different uses.
3 The plan is that the folded space telescope will unfold to the size of a football pitch.
4 It refers to very small objects (as opposed to very large things).
5 'It' means people building reconfigurable robots.

Idioms partitives

5 Ask the class to answer the questions, and discuss the differences.

ANSWERS

1 'some' or 'a piece of paper'
2 'a small piece of paper'

6 Ask students to decide on the meaning of the words in bold individually, then check with a partner. Elicit the answers from the whole class.

ANSWERS

1 a drop = a small amount
2 a stroke of = some
3 a shred = a small amount
4 a glimmer = a small amount
5 a flash = some
6 a hint = a small amount

Language focus probability

7 Read the instructions and the example with the class, then ask students to work in pairs to find more examples in the text as indicated. Elicit answers from the whole class.

ANSWERS

1 Perhaps it was (para 1); might be applied (para 2); could be (para 2); could lead to (para 4); might imagine (para 6); Maybe (para 6)
2 The chances are (para 1); may well be (para 2); are likely to (para 4)
3 Almost certainly (para 1); can (para 3); should be able (para 3); There's no doubt that (para 4)

8 Ask the class to say what each of the four sentences uses to indicate probability.

ANSWERS

1 *probably* = adverb
2 *unlikely* = adjective
3 *may not come* = verb
4 *The chances are that* = noun phrase

Meaning: The meaning of each sentence is very similar.

Register: *Probably*, *It's unlikely that* and *The chances are* are more informal, and *He may not* is more formal.

9 Read through the language focus box about probability with the class and then ask them to rewrite the sentences using the words given. They should do this individually, then check with a partner. Elicit the answers as complete sentences from the whole class.

ANSWERS

1 could be made of steel
2 is likely to inspire other packaging solutions too
3 it is possible to make boxes with a fixed base
4 This should save industry a lot of time and money
5 the chances are that it will work for a range of other materials
6 one day it might be possible to build houses from flat-pack materials
7 we may well be folding away our kitchen counters or table
8 It's unlikely that we will have foldable TVs or cars

Grammar notes

Point out to students that, although there are many different ways to express probability in English, with the exception of one or two phrases (e.g. *The likelihood is …*), there is little to distinguish between them in terms of either meaning or register.

Although most of these expressions of probability will already be familiar to students from a receptive point of view, there is often a tendency even with advanced students to rely on *perhaps* and *maybe* too much, so try to encourage active use of the whole range.

Point out to students that *should have* + past participle is used for belated advice rather than possibility (*They should have been more careful, and then it wouldn't have happened.*)

Also stress to students that we do not say *Yes, we should lose* when the team we support are playing badly, but *We'll probably lose*. On the other hand we do say *We should win* when we think that is the likely result.

Speaking

10 Ask students to think of three more ideas for using origami in the home. They could discuss these in pairs, then write down their ideas using expressions of probability. They can exchange these with another pair.

4c The shoe giver

Lead-in

Using words

Ask students to discuss the difference between an *entrepreneur* and a *businessman* with a partner. Elicit ideas from the class and try to agree on a definition (e.g. a businessman is somebody that works in business and often for a company in a managerial position. An entrepreneur is somebody that creates business and sets up their own companies, often by having creative commercial ideas).

Reading

1 Ask students to read the definition and choose which organisations fit it individually, then check with a partner. They should then describe the other organisations and explain why they do not fit the definition. Elicit answers from the whole class.

ANSWERS

a is a charity, not a business (it doesn't sell anything or make a profit)
b fits the definition, because it is a business, selling services for profit, but it also performs a social function by employing long-term unemployed people.
c also fits the definition: it is a business that sells clothes, but it also helps an environmental problem by recycling clothes.

2 Ask students to read the article and answer the questions. Elicit answers from the whole class.

ANSWER

It fits the definition because it aims to make a profit and also solves a social problem by providing shoes for poor children, but the text also says that the company 'does not yet make a profit'.

Background note

Blake Mycoskie was born in 1976. He has started six different companies: a door-to-door laundry service, media billboards, Reality 24/7 TV channel, DriversEdDirect (a driving school), Closer Marketing Group (a marketing company) and TOMS, his shoe company.

3 Ask students to read the six sentences to focus their reading, then read the article again to decide if they are true or false. They should check their answers with a partner. Elicit answers from the whole class.

ANSWERS

1 T
2 F ('after giving it some thought')
3 F ('One pair of shoes per child would not make that much difference' and 'That way he could guarantee a continual supply.')
4 F ('in parts of France and Hawaii, where people wear shoes and are not affected')
5 T ('The vital element that Mycoskie added was his own passion.')
6 F ('one-for-one is not an offer that you can just add to your existing business model')

Vocabulary notes

The following words and expressions from the text may be unfamiliar:

serial = one after another

a laundry service = a company washing bedclothes and clothes

burned out = exhausted, and without ideas and energy

canvas = a strong material made of cotton, jute or hemp

to thrive = to be successful, grow healthily

Critical thinking finding counter arguments

4 Ask students to find criticisms in the text in the three areas given. They should do this individually.

ANSWERS

a price: customers pay $50 for a $30 pair of shoes; quality: 'a poor job of making shoes'
b 'the money spent by customers might otherwise have been used to make direct charitable donations'
c 'it doesn't yet make a profit'

5 Ask students to check their answers to Exercise 4 with a partner. Elicit answers from the whole class. Then ask them to work together to make questions as indicated.

SAMPLE ANSWERS

1 Why should I buy these shoes? Are they really worth the money?
2 Do you think it's right that people should pay 70% more than the shoe is worth? Why don't they just give the extra money directly to charity?
3 How can this be a good model if it isn't even making a profit yet?

Extra activity

Ask students to work in groups of four and discuss the TOMS idea, saying what they think of it as a way of helping poor people. Elicit ideas from all the groups and discuss them as a class. Broaden the discussion if appropriate to the issues of philanthropy and corporate responsibility. Are businesses like TOMS just exploiting consumers' wishes to do good? Do all companies have social responsibilities, e.g. to the local community, to less privileged social groups, to the natural environment?

Word focus *give*

6 Ask students to find the expressions with *give* in the article and say what they mean.

ANSWERS

give it a break: stop doing something for a while

give it some thought: think about an idea

7 Ask students to complete the sentences individually, then check their answers with a partner. Elicit the answers from the whole class as complete sentences.

ANSWERS

1 thought (think about it, usually over some time, e.g. a few days)
2 best (do it as well as you can – *give it your best shot* is also common)
3 go ahead (authorise something, decide to commit to something)
4 break (don't be too hard on someone)
5 time (wait, be patient)
6 go (try, make an attempt at something even if you aren't very confident)

8 Ask students to match the expressions individually, then check with a partner. Elicit the answers from the whole class.

ANSWERS

a chance = a break (sentence 4)

consideration = thought (sentence 1)

the green light = the go ahead (sentence 3)

a try = a go (sentence 6)

a while = some time (sentence 5)

your all = your best (sentence 2)

Speaking

9 Read through the instructions with the class, and give them time to prepare what they want to say. Suggest it would be a good idea to make a few notes. Then ask the pairs to do the roleplay. Circulate and monitor their interviews. You may wish to ask one or two pairs to perform their roleplay for the others.

4d An elevator pitch

Lead-in

Personal response
Ask students about their experience of people trying to sell them things (e.g. cold calls on the phone, people at the front door); ask them to say what sort of things sales people do and how they react to them.

Real life making a short pitch

1 Ask students to discuss Franklin Roosevelt's advice together. Elicit some responses about its meaning from the whole class.

ANSWER
It means you should be serious about and believe in what you have to say and keep your talk as short and to the point as possible.

2 Read the instructions with the class, then ask them to read the text and summarise it to a partner. Elicit suggestions from the whole class.

SAMPLE ANSWER
An elevator pitch is where you have a very limited time (i.e. the time spent in an elevator) to persuade someone that your idea or product is worth considering.

Vocabulary notes

There are a number of expressions around the verb *to pitch*. The original meaning of the word is connected to throwing, and by connotation, also to the distance thrown, e.g. *a cricket pitch* is the length which the ball is *pitched*.

The expressions *to make a pitch* and *to pitch for* are figurative, meaning to throw or thrust what one wants to say at the listener. It is used in business, and also in politics, and has to do with making a clear statement.

We also use the expression *to pitch something at the right level* in teaching, meaning to present the information with the appropriate level of challenge and support for the learners it is aimed at.

This is also connected to the musical concept of *the pitch* of a voice or a note, meaning how high or low it is.

3 Ask students to discuss the questions in pairs. Elicit some ideas from the whole class.

SAMPLE ANSWERS
1 They may want to gain experience in a certain job / sector; they may want to help their community or a certain charity.
2 Work in a charity shop; work with children, the elderly or people with disabilities; help to provide food for homeless people; work in the community, e.g. clearing litter, raising money for local facilities, providing transport / doing shopping for elderly neighbours, etc.

4 [1.23] Ask students to read the questions to focus their listening. Play the recording for them to answer. Ask them to check with a partner. If necessary, play the recording again. Elicit the answers from the whole class.

ANSWERS
1 It's a new smartphone app called 'Volunteer Planner' which allows interactive communication between organisations who need volunteers and people who want to do voluntary work.
2 It solves the communication problems so that more people will actually volunteer.
3 Volunteer Planner; volunteer / voluntary; help; it allows; more people / a few people

Audioscript [1.23]

We have an idea to encourage volunteering. It's a new phone app called Volunteer Planner. What is it? It's an interactive diary that links volunteers to organisations looking for voluntary help. Why is it necessary? Because there are a lot of people out there who'd like to give their time to help others in the community – helping the disabled or the elderly. But they never come forward because their time's limited and it's too complicated to organise. So what does Volunteer Planner do exactly? The app allows organisations to show when they need voluntary help; it allows the volunteer to communicate their availability; and it allows both parties to make changes to the schedule in real time. What's our ambition for Volunteer Planner? Ultimately, it means more people giving a little of their time rather than a few people giving a lot. So it encourages and spreads the practice of volunteering.

Speaking skill using rhetorical questions

5 [1.23] Read through the box about using rhetorical questions with the class, and ensure that they understand the concept of rhetorical questions. Read the instructions, and then play the recording for them to tick what they hear. They can check with a partner. Elicit the answers from the whole class.

ANSWERS
The phrases used are:
What is it? (It's an interactive diary that links volunteers to organisations looking for voluntary help.)
Why is it necessary? (Because there are a lot of people out there who would like to give their time to help others in the community.)
What does ... do exactly? (The app allows organisations to show when they need voluntary help.)
What's our ambition for ...? (Ultimately, it means more people giving a little of their time rather than a few people giving a lot.)

Pronunciation long and short vowels

6a [1.24] Read the rubric with the class, then play the recording for them to listen to the rhetorical questions in the box. Ask students to decide if the underlined syllables in the words in the box have a long or short vowel sound. Check the answers as a class. Then play the recording again, pausing after each question for students to repeat it chorally and individually. Then ask students to practise the questions with their partner.

ANSWERS

Short vowels: *is, necessary, what, expensive, ambition*

Long vowels: *work, do, achieve*

6b Ask students to look at the pairs of words and think about how they are pronounced, then underline the long vowel sound in one of the two words.

ANSWERS

1 loop
2 scheme
3 father
4 training
5 both
6 internal
7 forward

7 Read through the instructions with the class. Ask students to get into threes, decide who is A, B and C, and look at the appropriate pages. Ask them to study what they have to do, and practise it to themselves a little, thinking of the best phrases to use. Then ask the groups to make their pitches to each other, and decide which was the best and why, and how they might improve.

4e Volunteer planner

Lead-in

Personal response

Ask students to tell a partner how something works (e.g. a bicycle, a CD player, a ball-point pen). Elicit a few descriptions from the whole class.

Writing describing how things work

1 Ask students to read the questions to focus their reading, then read and find the answers.

ANSWERS

1 It's an overview for potential users or investors.
2 factual

2 Elicit answers to the questions from the class, and discuss which are the most important features.

ANSWER

It has sub-headings, bullet points and short, straightforward sentences.

Writing skill punctuation

3a Ask the whole class to say where they find examples of the punctuation in the text.

ANSWERS

a in the first paragraph and to introduce the bullet points.
b in the first and last paragraphs.
c Dashes could be used in place of brackets in the third bullet point.

3b Ask students to match the punctuation and uses individually, then check with a partner. Elicit answers from the whole class.

ANSWERS

1 semi-colon 2 colon 3 dash 4 colon 5 semi-colon

3c Ask students to punctuate the extract individually, then check with a partner. Elicit answers from the class.

ANSWERS

The three good reasons to use the volunteer planner are: to help you to plan your volunteering; to help the organisation; and – this is our sincere hope – to increase the number of volunteers.

4 Read through the instructions with the whole class and make sure they understand what to use, and how to organise their writing.

5 Ask students to exchange their writing with a partner and check for the criteria listed. They should give each other feedback on their writing.

4f Ethical ocean

Before you watch

1 Students work in pairs. Ask them to look at the photo and say what they can see, then discuss the question. Take feedback from the class.

> ANSWER
> A social entrepreneur creates a business which is socially responsible. So the business aims to generate a profit while solving social and / or environmental problems.

2 Ask students to discuss ideas with their partner.

While you watch

3 Give students time to read the words in the glossary. Play the video for students to check their answers to Exercise 2. Take feedback from the class.

> ANSWER
> *Ethical Ocean* provides a marketplace for ethical goods.

4 Give students time to read the sentences. Then play the first part of the video (to 01.22) for them to choose the correct options.

> ANSWERS
> 1 Canada
> 2 without borders
> 3 wells
> 4 engineers
> 5 a lack of business ability

5 Give students time to read the table then play the second part of the video (01.23 to 02.06) for them to complete the information.

> ANSWERS
> 1 marketplace
> 2 stop
> 3 organic, animal, free
> 4 shoes, cleaning

6 Give students time to look at the words, then play the third part of the video (02.07 to 03.12) for them to summarise the information.

> ANSWERS
> 1 Companies list their products and say which category they fall into. They then have to provide certification that guarantees the ethical credentials of the product.
> 2 The companies write the story about their product(s) and say why it's ethical.
> 3 Consumers can vote for products, write comments and start conversations. In this way, the website is self-regulating.

7 Give students time to read the questions, then play the fourth part of the video (03.13 to end) for them to answer.

> ANSWERS
> 1 Women's clothing and accessories.
> 2 Earth Berries
> 3 You can use them again and again, you save money, they are natural.

8 Students work in groups to discuss the social enterprise idea.

After you watch

9 Students work in pairs to discuss which ethical criteria are relevant to which product.

> SAMPLE ANSWERS
> a furniture, stationery
> b car, electronic equipment, toys
> c fruit and vegetables, cosmetics
> d clothes
> e fruit and vegetables, toys, clothing
> f fruit and vegetables
> g stationery, toys, electronic equipment

10 Students work in pairs to roleplay a product pitch according to the instructions.

Videoscript

Part 1

00.08 In the heart of Oxford, at Oxford University's Saïd Business School is the Skoll Centre for Social Entrepreneurship. Each year, this institute awards scholarships to passionate individuals committed to the cause of social enterprise. David Damberger is one of these.

Paul Dummett David, I know you have quite a lot of experience in this field. I was just wondering how you … and I've seen also you have some background in engineering, which struck me as a little strange, perhaps. Can you just tell me how you got into this field?

00.43 David Damberger As an engineer back in Canada, I was a part of starting Engineers Without Borders and what we did is we … thought at the time that some of the issues dealing with poverty in Africa and South Asia … all that was needed to help solve those was a bunch of engineers to go there and help improve wells or improve bridges.

And so we did that and – very naively – and then realised that that actually wasn't the problem. The lack of technology … there was technology. There were bridges, there were wells and there was engineers, local engineers that were able to solve those problems. But what we did realise is that some of the problems were surrounding the businesses that were there. And so actually we started working with some of the businesses to help improve their ability.

Part 2

01.23 Paul Dummett OK. And you've since moved into more of a business field with a company called Ethical Ocean, which as I understand it is a kind of e-marketplace for ethical goods. Could you just pitch that to me as if I were a potential investor?

David Damberger So, Ethical Ocean is a one-stop shop – shopping mall – where everything you can buy is ethical. And so, ethical has a number of different categories: there's organic, there's fair trade, there's animal-friendly, there's sweat shop labour-free.

And so you can go onto the site and purchase clothing, you can purchase shoes, you can purchase home cleaning products – a whole range of products – but guaranteeing that every single product on the site is ethical.

Part 3

02.07 Paul Dummett So what kind of criteria do you apply to participating companies? How do you decide which suppliers you allow onto this e-marketplace?

David Damberger This is a great question because what is ethical to one person might not be ethical to another person. So what we do is the companies that sell on the site have to list what their product is and what category it fits under, so whether it's an organic product or a fairtrade product. And then they have to list the certification that said … that guarantees that the product is that.

The second thing we do is we let the companies write the story about the product to try and explain to the customers why it's more ethical and what makes it better than a traditional product.

And the third thing we do is we let consumers on the site vote whether they agree with the claims made by the company, whether they think it's ethical or not, and write comments and start a conversation because, as we know, it's …

02.59 Paul Dummett So it's kind of self-regulating in a way.

David Damberger It is self-regulating. Exactly.

Paul Dummett Yeah. You don't have to keep going back and checking the company's credentials, and so on.

David Damberger No, only if the company is … we see a bunch of people claiming that it's not ethical, then we will take it off the site and do an investigation.

Part 4

03.13 Paul Dummett So what are the most successful products, then?

David Damberger So a lot of the products are actually women's clothing and women's accessories. But some of the most popular, one of the most popular ones is something called Earth Berries and these come from a tree called, believe it or not, a soapberry tree. And basically, they replace laundry detergent. And so they're just a bunch of these berries off a tree that are very natural, and you put them in a bag and you throw them in your laundry without having to put any detergent in it, and it cleans your clothes. And basically you can get …

03.42 Narrator You use them once, or?

David Damberger No, you can use them, I think, about a hundred times before they wear out their regular life. They're about twenty pounds. And so you save a ton of money. I think it's about, you know, five pence per wash for this detergent, for the replacement for the detergent, so they're one of the most popular cleaning products.

Narrator Presumably, you've done comparisons with biological products or …

David Damberger Yeah. Exactly, yeah.

Unit 4 Review

Grammar

1 Ask students to read the article and complete it.

ANSWERS

1 likelihood	5 likely	9 unlikely
2 chances	6 probably	10 need
3 might	7 should	
4 must	8 could	

2 Ask students to read the article again and answer the questions.

ANSWERS

1 There is always a catch.
2 Reorganising the energy network so we can produce our own electricity.
3 fairly pessimistic

3 Ask students to discuss the questions about energy.

Vocabulary

4 Ask students to complete the sentences.

ANSWERS

1 thought, up	3 across, stroke	5 about, fulfill
2 shred, go	4 flash, breakthrough	

5 Students work in pairs to discuss their experiences.

Real life

6 Students complete the product pitches with rhetorical questions.

ANSWERS

1 What is it?
2 Why do we need it?
3 How does it work?
4 How much will it cost?
5 How will we do that?

7 Students think of a product and present it to their partner, using rhetorical questions.

Speaking

8 Students work in pairs to discuss a device or gadget.

Unit 5 The writer's journey

Lead-in

Personal response

Ask students to tell a partner about a journey they went on once. It can be any journey, even a simple bus ride for two stops, or a long-haul flight across the world. Ask them to share some impressions and feelings about the experience.

1 Ask students to work in pairs to discuss the photo of Paris, and Paris in general. Elicit some responses from the whole class. If you have students who are from France, or Paris, or who have been there, get them to give further information.

ANSWER

The photo was taken in Paris, looking towards the Eiffel Tower. Paris is a city known for its romantic character, its cafés and landmarks such as the Eiffel Tower, the Arc de Triomphe, and wide boulevards such as the Champs Elysées.

2 [1.25] Ask students to discuss the two questions with a partner, then play the recording and ask them to discuss the differences between their own ideas and what the speaker says. Elicit some responses from the class.

ANSWERS

1 How we are feeling when we arrive; who we meet; and what preconceptions we have about a place.
2 Someone who can write about a place and its people so that you feel you know them.

Audioscript [1.25]

Three people visit the same place and each one leaves with a different story. One remembers a romantic evening in a cosy restaurant and a long walk through a beautifully lit city by night; another remembers an argument with an officious museum curator about the closing time of an art gallery; another remembers sitting and watching the world go by on a lazy, hot afternoon in an elegant park.

Our travel experiences are influenced by so many different factors: the circumstances and state of mind in which we arrive; the people we happen to meet – an affable fellow traveller or a wary local; the preconceptions that we bring to each place we visit. The gift of a good travel writer is to capture the essence of a place in a way that we can all identify with, so that it's instantly recognisable not just superficially – in its grand architecture or lively cafés – but in the way that a particular place feels and thinks. Because the best travel writers aren't really writing about travel, they're writing about how people have shaped places and how places have shaped people.

3 [1.25] Ask students to classify the adjectives individually. Play the recording again for them to decide how the speaker uses them. Ask them to check with a partner. Play the recording again, if necessary, then elicit answers from the whole class.

ANSWERS

People: officious, lazy, affable, wary
Places: cosy, grand
Both: romantic, elegant, lively
romantic evening
cosy restaurant
officious museum curator
lazy (hot) afternoon
elegant park
affable (fellow) traveller
wary local
grand architecture
lively cafés

4 Ask students to think about a place they know and like very much, and work out a description of it using some of the adjectives from Exercise 3. Ask them to get into groups of four and tell each other about their place. Elicit some examples from the whole class. If you feel that students need further help with this, you could write the following example on the board:

I love Valencia in Spain. It's a great mixture of old and new, with grand architecture in the centre and amazing new buildings by the seafront. It's got a relaxed, confident feel and the people are very affable.

Extra activity

Ask students to write up their description from Exercise 4 into a 100–120 word essay. They can exchange this with a partner for comment in a later lesson.

5a Where the Indus is young

Lead-in

Personal response

Ask students to tell a partner about a distant place they would like to travel to, saying why it attracts them and what they would do there. Elicit some responses from the whole class.

Listening

1 Ask students to discuss the two questions in groups of four. Elicit or explain the meaning of 'travelogue' – a non-fictional account of a foreign place or a journey. Elicit answers from the whole class and invite comments.

2 [1.26] Ask students to read the table to focus their listening. Play the recording and ask students to complete the table, then check with a partner.

ANSWERS

1 Type of book: novel / travelogue
2 Setting (time and place): the 1970s, along the Indus River valley (in Baltistan) into the Himalayas
3 Subject of book: the description of the journey the author took with her six-year-old daughter along the Indus River valley into the Himalayas
4 Adjectives used to describe it: *wonderful, amazing, gripping*

Audioscript [1.26]

P = presenter, **S** = Sophie

P: … to places you and I would probably never think of visiting. And Sophie, what's your book?

S: My choice is *Where the Indus is young* by the Irish writer, Dervla Murphy. It's about a trip that she took with her daughter up the Indus River valley – a region called Baltistan – into the heart of the Himalayas when the girl was only six years old. This was in the 1970s.

P: And why have you chosen this one particularly?

S: Well, travelling in this region is dangerous enough at the best of times, but to do so with a six-year-old girl is just incredible. They encounter raging rivers, falling rocks, steep rocky ascents. Murphy herself says in the book that the extremeness of the landscape in this region cannot be exaggerated. In fact, Rachel – that's her daughter's name – became the hero for me, because where many kids would be complaining constantly, she never does. Her mother takes advantage of this, and so keeps pressing on, along narrow paths next to deep ravines. I'd like to read a short extract if I may, where they're coming down a track on horseback next to the side of a mountain:

*We found ourselves looking into a ravine so profound that one's first reaction was incredulity. The shadowy chasm was very narrow and perhaps half a mile long. It lay between the brown mountain we now stood on and the white mountain ahead, and at a conservative estimate it was 1,500 feet deep, with absolutely sheer sides. This scene was the very quintessence of Himalayan drama – vast, beautiful, cruel – belonging to a landscape that has no time for the paltry endeavours of men.**

P: I've heard critics say that Murphy can be political. Would you agree with that?

S: Well, perhaps. She does mention a few times in this book and in others, how unspoiled places like this are being ruined by 'technological progress' and western ideas. An example of the former is when she talks about modern transport bringing diseases to areas that hadn't suffered these before. Other writers, of course, have said the same thing … and I'm always a bit suspicious of people who want to enjoy unspoilt parts of the world and then return home to the comforts of their own western lives. But you can't say that the point of this book is to a put across a political message. It's not. It's just a wonderful description of an amazing journey, and the ability of a young child to overcome fear and a completely different environment. I found it absolutely gripping.

3 [1.26] Ask students to read the options to focus their listening. Play the recording for them to answer. They can check with a partner before you elicit the answers from the whole class. Read the *Wordbuilding* box about *-ing* adjectives with the students. If necessary, look at the information on page 43 of the Workbook and do the exercises there.

ANSWERS

1 b 2 b 3 a 4 a 5 b 6 b

4 Ask students to discuss the issue of taking a young child on a dangerous trip with a partner. Elicit responses from the whole class.

Vocabulary roads and ways

5 Ask students to find the words in the audioscript on page 177, and then discuss the meanings with a partner. Elicit the answers from the class and discuss the differences in meaning (see vocabulary notes).

ANSWERS

ascent = the way up (a hill or mountain)
path = a narrow way that you can walk along
track = a rough road

1 up = *ascent*; down = *descent*
2 a *path* is not for cars (a *track* is a rough but wide way that could be used by cars or farm vehicles)
3 *course* describes the route of a river (*way* is a general word meaning either the physical road / path, etc., or 'how to get somewhere')
4 *trail* is only an overland way (*route* is the detailed description of how to get from A to B, and could include sea crossings)
5 *street* is only in a city, town or village
6 American English = *highway*; British English = *motorway*

Vocabulary notes

course = the route of a river or other waterway

a highway (US) / *motorway* (Brit) = a wide road carrying fast traffic in several lanes.

a road = a way that carries traffic through a town or between towns; it can be outside a town or inside a town

a street = a small road in a city or town. It is especially used for small shopping areas in the centre of a city, or residential streets where there is not much through traffic.

a trail = an overland way; it often refers to a very old established long-distance path or track across the countryside (particularly in North and South America), or it can be a long-distance path for walkers.

Language focus substitution

6 Ask students to look at the highlighted words in the audioscript on page 177, and work with a partner to decide on the substitutions. Elicit answers from the whole class.

ANSWERS

a the daughter
b the story *or* the trip
c book *or* story
d to travel in this region
e complains
f the fact that her daughter never complains
g that Murphy can be political
h other books
i 'technological progress'
j that remote places are being spoilt by progress
k not the point

Grammar note

Elicit ideas from students about why substitution is used in spoken and written texts (e.g. to avoid repeating the same word, to be more concise, to sound more natural, to add interest, to produce a better style).

7 Read the language focus box about substitution with the class and check that they understand it; if necessary, look at the explanations on page 162 and do the exercises there. Ask students to substitute the underlined words in the text with the ones in the box. They should do this individually, then check with a partner. Elicit answers from the whole class as complete sentences.

ANSWERS

1 doesn't	4 others	7 –
2 this	5 a lot	8 to do so
3 a trip	6 it	9 one

Pronunciation intonation in short responses

8a Ask students to work in pairs to complete the six responses with one word. Elicit answers from the whole class, but do not say if they are correct.

SAMPLE ANSWERS

1 that	3 so	5 some
2 did	4 it	6 one

8b [1.27] Play the recording for students to check their answers, then again for students to listen to the pronunciation, then a final time, pausing after each response for them to repeat it chorally and individually. They could then practise further with a partner, helping each other with the pronunciation.

Audioscript [1.27]

1 **A:** You have to be careful not to get ripped off in the local markets.
B: Yes, I know that.

2 **A:** Would you like to drive?
B: No, I'd rather you did.

3 **A:** Did he take warm clothes with him?
B: I hope so.

4 **A:** Do you mind travelling alone?
B: No, I actually prefer it.

5 **A:** Are there many good guidebooks about this region?
B: Well, there are some.

6 **A:** Have you got an up-to-date map of Russia?
B: No, but I've got an old one.

Vocabulary and speaking a good read

9 Ask students to rewrite the sentences using a noun, then check with a partner. Elicit answers from the whole class as complete sentences.

ANSWERS

1 setting	3 appeal	5 story
2 description	4 comment	6 theme

10 Ask students to work in groups of three, and select one of the three roles. They will need to choose a book and prepare what they have to say. Circulate and monitor their speaking.

Homework

Ask students to write a full book review of the book they chose for the role play.

5b The adventures of Hergé

Lead-in

Personal response

Write *Tintin* on the board and ask students to say anything they know about Tintin.

Reading

1 Ask students to discuss the two questions with a partner. Elicit answers from the whole class.

2 Ask students to read the questions to focus their reading, then read the article to find the answers. They can check with a partner before you elicit answers from the whole class.

ANSWERS

1 It's a book-length comic which has a single, continuous story or narrative.
2 Because they were about places that people had never been to or perhaps would never go to.
3 His technical drawing skills and his careful research.

Background notes

Georges Prosper Remi (1907–1983), known to the world by his pen-name Hergé, was a Belgian comic artist and story-writer. He is best known for the 23 *Tintin* books which were published between 1929 and 1983, first as black-and-white newspaper strips, but later as colour books. They tell the adventures of the young reporter and his dog, Snowy, in many different countries.

Hergé also wrote various other series of popular comic strips, such as Quick & Flupke (1930–40) about some Brussels street urchins, and Jo, Zette & Jocko (1936–57). Tintin has maintained its popularity, and in 2011 Steven Spielberg directed a Tintin adventure called *The Secret of the Unicorn.*

3 Ask students to read the questions to focus their reading, then find the answers from the article. They should check with a partner before you elicit the answers from the whole class.

ANSWERS

1 T (*Cartoons suit the way we like information to be presented these days*)
2 F (*but appeared soon after in book form*)
3 T (*Hergé also steers a fine line between serious topics and humour*)
4 T (*Written in 1953, sixteen years before the first moon landing; to understand what a place was like without ever having travelled there*)

4 Ask students to discuss the questions with their partners, and then elicit responses from the whole class.

SAMPLE ANSWER

They might be successful because of Hergé's skill as a graphic artist; because he takes people to places they have never been or may never go to; because he combines serious topics with humour; because of his skill and instinct as a storyteller.

Idioms rhyming expressions

5 Read through the instructions and ask the whole class to find the answers.

ANSWERS

a fine line (a point where it is difficult to see the difference between two things)

fair share (the right amount due to a person when something is divided up)

6 Ask students to discuss the expressions with a partner. Elicit answers from the whole class.

ANSWERS

ill will = bad feeling towards another person

nitty-gritty = the heart of the matter, the essential point

no-go = out of bounds; you can't go there

real deal = a genuine and excellent example

tell-tale = which gives the answer, revealing the truth

wishy-washy = not definite, lacking in strength or clarity, indecisive

The expressions which truly rhyme are: *fair share, fine line, ill will, nitty-gritty, no-go, real deal*

7 Ask students to complete the sentences with the expressions from Exercise 6 individually, then check with a partner. Elicit answers from the whole class.

ANSWERS

1 ill will
2 tell-tale
3 no-go
4 wishy-washy
5 nitty-gritty
6 real deal

Language focus nominalisation

8 Ask students to read through the pairs of sentences and then answer the four questions below individually. They can check their ideas with a partner. Elicit answers from the whole class.

ANSWERS

a 1 adjective 2 verb 3 preposition
b a preposition
c No, there is no difference in meaning, but the b sentence in each pair is more emphatic.
d Sentence b

9 Read through the language focus box about nominalisation with the class. Refer to page 163 if necessary for further information and practice. Ask students to find the examples in the text, then check with a partner. Elicit answers from the whole class. Note that in examples 4 and 5 the noun in the article (*attempt, nature*) is not directly related to the verb or adjective in the sentence.

ANSWERS

1 the worldwide popularity
2 The creation of the Belgian cartoonist, Hergé
3 One of the main attractions for readers
4 an attempt at a military coup
5 the nature of space travel

Grammar notes

Make sure students understand the function and purpose of nominalisation:

a to produce a more formal / academic style

b to be more impersonal (because you can cut out the subject of the verb)

c to be more concise

Nominalisation also allows students a different way of saying the same thing, so that within any given text they can use a range of structures, adding interest for the reader and a change of tone / style, e.g.

The quality of the drawing is excellent, which is why many people enjoy the books.

The excellent quality of the drawing is one reason why many people enjoy the books.

10 Ask students to rewrite the sentences using nominalisation. They should do this individually, then check with a partner. Elicit answers from the whole class as complete sentences.

ANSWERS

1 One of Hergé's inspirations was Chinese drawings.
2 He admired the simplicity of these drawings.
3 In later life, Hergé became an enthusiastic collector of modern art.
4 He had a particular interest in pop art.
5 Despite references to the politics of the time, the books do not contain a political message.
6 A museum in Belgium recognises all Hergé's achievements.

Speaking and writing speech bubbles

11 Ask students to work in pairs and write the speech bubbles for the cartoon on page 156. They should then compare their ideas with another pair. Elicit some sequences from around the class and discuss them.

Homework

Ask students to write 100–150 words about one cartoon; either a book or a film. They should describe the drawing, style and content in detail.

5c In Patagonia

Lead-in

Personal response

Ask students to say what they know about the geography of Argentina, describing what the different areas are like as much as possible.

Reading and speaking

1 Read through the instructions with the whole class. Ask students to get in pairs and do their A and B tasks, then exchange information with their books closed. Elicit some information from the students which they didn't know before.

2 Ask students to read the three statements to focus their reading, then read the extract from Chatwin's *In Patagonia* and decide which sentence is true. Elicit answers from the whole class.

ANSWER

c

Background notes

Bruce Chatwin (1940–89) was a British-born writer of novels and non-fiction. After school at Marlborough College, he later became Sotheby's expert on Impressionist Art and a Director of the company, and a writer for *The Sunday Times Magazine*. However, in 1974 he spent six months in Patagonia, and the resulting book *In Patagonia* (1977) established his reputation as a writer. Other travels produced other books, e.g. Benin: *The Viceroy of Ouidah*, a novel about the slave trade; Australia: *Songlines* (1987) a mixture of fact and fiction about Aborigines; Welsh Borders: *On The Black Hill* and Prague: *Utz* (1988). He died in 1989.

3 Ask students to correct the underlined words in the extracts individually, then check with a partner. Elicit the answers from the whole class.

ANSWERS

1 forty
2 toads
3 Shelves
4 almonds
5 dam, built
6 two books of

Vocabulary notes

The following words and expressions from the text may be unfamiliar:

an alexandrine = a line of poetry with six iambic feet

to clatter = to make a loud rattling noise by knocking things together

to grip = to hold tightly

a packing case = a wooden chest made for packing tea or other products

a plank = a long flat narrow piece of wood

to be littered with = to be covered with things in no particular order

thistledown = the floating seeds of the thistle flower

Critical thinking analysing descriptive language

4 Ask students to read the text to find the adjectives that describe the four things listed. They should do this individually, then check with a partner. Elicit the answers from the whole class.

ANSWERS

1 lonely, overgrown, pale (sun)
2 two-roomed, dark, dusty, bent (shelves)
3 alone, intense, luminous
4 privately printed, cosmic, astonishing, weighty, limited (production)

5 Ask students to think about the overall impression created by the adjectives individually, then compare their idea with a partner. Elicit responses from the whole class.

SAMPLE ANSWER

You have the impression of an intense, intelligent but eccentric man, living alone in an isolated and slightly wild place, which he loves nevertheless. He lives in a small, dark house where he writes extraordinary poems. Although he writes a limited amount, he seems at peace with this fact.

6 Ask the whole class to suggest answers to this question and illustrate their answers with examples.

ANSWERS

The weather is harsh: *The rain drummed on the tin roof*

He's an eccentric collector: *bent under the weight of books, mineral specimens, Indian artefacts and fossil oysters.*

He has a good sense of humour: *He cackled humorously*

Even though it seems a harsh, lonely existence, you see a glimmer of the beauty that must have attracted him to stay: *Bees hummed around the poet's hives. His apricots were ripening, the colour of a pale sun. Clouds of thistledown drifted across the view and in a field there were some fleecy white sheep.*

Word focus cast

7 Ask the class to find and explain the meaning of the expression with *cast* in the text.

ANSWER

She casts her spell – referring to Patagonia itself. This is an expression used of a witch or a wizard; when they make magic, they 'cast a spell' (on someone). It is also frequently used figuratively, as here, to mean that one is captivated by someone or something.

8 Ask students to work with a partner to complete the expressions with *cast* in the sentences, using the words in the box. Elicit the answers from the whole class as complete sentences.

ANSWERS

1 mind
2 net
3 eye
4 doubt
5 vote
6 shadow

Speaking

9 Ask students to think individually about a person they met when travelling and the effect the meeting had on them. They should then get into groups of four to talk about their experiences and listen to the others. Elicit a few examples from the whole class.

Homework

Ask students to write up their experience of meeting a person whilst travelling into a detailed description 100–125 words long. They can share this with others in a later lesson.

5d I'd like to read

Lead-in

Personal response

Ask students to tell a partner about something (anything, e.g. a novel, a poem, a newspaper article) they have read and found interesting recently. Elicit a few examples from around the class.

Real life reading aloud

1 Ask students to work in pairs and discuss the questions about reading aloud. Elicit some responses from the whole class.

Speaking skill engaging your audience

2 Ask students to complete the sentences in the box about engaging your audience with the words in the word box. They should do this individually, then check with a partner. Elicit answers from the whole class as complete sentences.

ANSWERS

1 background	4 volume
2 enunciate	5 dialogue
3 Pause	6 enthusiasm

3 [1.28] Ask students to read the questions to focus their listening. Play the recording while students answer. They can check with a partner. Play the recording again, if necessary, then elicit the answers from the whole class.

ANSWERS

1 a detective novel or thriller
2 building suspense
3 He thinks he sees a police spy or agent. In fact it is his old friend, Harry Lime.

Audioscript [1.28]

I'd like to read an extract from *The Third Man*, a thriller by Graham Greene. The context for this story is post-Second World War Vienna, around 1948. A writer, Rolly Martins, has come to Vienna to find his old friend Harry Lime, but he discovers that Harry has died in suspicious circumstances. At this point in the story Martins is walking back through the deserted streets of Vienna at night. It's a great example of how to build suspense.

'Passing by the end of the street he happened to turn, and there just around the corner, pressed against a wall to escape notice, was a thick stocky figure. Martins stopped and stared. There was something familiar about that figure: perhaps, he thought, I have grown unconsciously used to him during these last twenty-four hours: perhaps he is one of those who have so assiduously checked my movements. Martins stood there, twenty yards away, staring at the silent motionless figure in the dark side-street who stared back at him. A police spy, perhaps, or an agent of those other men, those men who had corrupted Harry first and then killed him: even possibly the third man? It was not the face that was familiar, for he could not make out so much as the angle of the jaw: nor a movement, for the body was so still that he began to believe that the whole thing was an illusion caused by shadow. He called sharply. "Do you want anything?" and there was no reply. He called again. "Answer, can't you?" and an answer came, for a window curtain was drawn petulantly back by some sleeper he had awakened and the light fell straight across the narrow street and lit up the features … of Harry Lime.'

4 [1.29] Ask students to listen to the recording and follow the notes; ask them to pay particular attention to the notes in red, which show what the reader does to make it more effective. They then practise reading the extract in pairs, following the instructions in red.

Pronunciation enunciation

5a [1.30] Ask students to read the sentence so that they know what they are going to hear; ask them to think about how it should be said. Play the recording and ask which version is clearest. Discuss what the differences are between the two recordings, and what effect this has.

ANSWER

The second version is enunciated more clearly. The speaker also reads with more expression, varying the tone and volume, which makes it more interesting to listen to.

Extra activity

Play the good version of the recording a few times for students to listen to, then again, pausing at suitable points for students to repeat chorally and individually.

5b Ask students to practise reading the sentence out loud with a partner, helping each other with the clarity of the enunciation.

6 Read through the instructions with the class, and ask them to get into pairs and decide who is A and B. They should then find their respective pages and follow the instructions, preparing and then presenting the reading passages to each other for comment and advice. Finally they should read them to another pair and listen to their readings, and discuss the quality of each one.

5e Book of the month

Lead-in

Personal response

Ask students about the last book they bought: What was it? Who was it for? If it was for themselves, have they read it? If so, did they enjoy it? Why / why not? Elicit various responses from around the class.

Writing a book review

1 Ask students to discuss with a partner how they normally choose their books. Elicit some responses from the whole class.

2 Ask students to read the review and answer the questions individually. Elicit responses from the whole class.

ANSWERS

Her opinion is that it's a beautiful reflection on the subject of destiny.

She justifies her opinion with these details: 'elegant prose', 'compelling characters', 'drawn so vividly', 'thought-provoking'.

Background information

Thornton Wilder (1897–1975) was an American novelist and playwright. He published his first novel *The Cabala* in 1926, but it was *The Bridge of San Luis Rey* (1927) which established his reputation as a writer and brought him his first Pultzer prize in 1928. This was followed by Pulitzer Prizes for his plays *Our Town* (1938) and *the Skin of our Teeth* (1942). He continued to write, and also lectured at Harvard and Chicago University.

3 Ask students to read the questions to focus their second reading of the review. They can check their answers with a partner. Elicit answers from the whole class.

ANSWERS

1 a historical novel
2 destiny
3 the present tense
4 (elegant) prose

4 Ask students to read the different ways to begin a review and say which they think are the most effective. They should discuss their ideas with a partner before you elicit answers from the whole class.

ANSWERS

a, c or d might be effective openings; b and e are likely to be less effective.

The reviewer uses d (gives a short summary of the whole story).

Writing skill descriptive words

5a Ask students to underline the adverbs and adjectives and decide what they describe; they should also identify the two compound adjectives. They can then check with a partner before you elicit the answers from the whole class.

ANSWERS

adjectives: short (novel), beautiful (reflection), true (story), real (people), elegant (prose), aristocratic (Marquesa), wise (uncle), lifelong (ambition), compelling, eccentric and human (characters), thought-provoking (book)

adverbs: vividly (drawn), highly (recommended)

The compound adjectives are 'thought-provoking' and 'lifelong'.

5b Ask students to work in pairs to complete the compound adjectives. Elicit answers from the whole class.

ANSWERS

1 provoking
2 fetched
3 going
4 written
5 packed
6 wrenching
7 moving
8 willed

5c Ask students to match the opposite compound adjectives individually, then check with a partner.

ANSWERS

convincing – far-fetched
easy-to-read – heavy-going
happy – heart-wrenching
indecisive – strong-willed
poorly written – well-written
slow-moving – fast-moving
uneventful – action-packed
uninspiring – thought-provoking

6 Ask students to write a review of a novel they have read, following the plan given.

7 Ask students to exchange their reviews with a partner and give feedback on them according to the criteria given.

5f On the road: Andrew McCarthy

Before you watch

1 Students work in pairs. Ask them to look at the photo and discuss the questions.

2 Ask students to discuss ideas with their partner.

While you watch

3 Give students time to read the words in the glossary and the two questions. Play the video for students to answer the questions. Take feedback from the class.

ANSWERS

1 He walked the Camino de Santiago (a pilgrim's route) in northern Spain.
2 He felt taken care of and unafraid in the world for the first time.

4 Give students time to read the words. Then play the first part of the interview (to 02.09) for them to make notes. They then reconstruct the story with a partner.

ANSWERS

a Andrew McCarthy was in a bookstore when he picked up a book about the Camino de Santiago.
b He took the book to read on the plane some months later.
c There was no Internet in those days to do research so he contacted the author directly.
d The author of the book was working for Harper's magazine, so McCarthy contacted him there.
e The author gave McCarthy his home phone number and McCarthy phoned him a number of times.

5 Give students time to read the questions then play the second part of the interview (02.10 to 03.08) for them to answer.

ANSWERS

1 a transformative, terrifying
b lonely, miserable
c religious
d unafraid
2 To see if he could take care of himself

6 Give students time to look at the questions, then play the third part of the video (03.09 to end).

ANSWERS

1 He isn't sure if it's a good idea to go back and do the same things again.
2 a month
3 in refugios (hostels) and in pensione (inns)
4 gold card; he means that he was having the pilgrim experience but with a higher standard of accommodation, etc. than most pilgrims
5 By telling himself he wanted to meet the local people, not just the tourists and pilgrims.

7 Give students time to read and complete the summary. If necessary, play the video again for them to check.

ANSWERS

1 bookstore	5 Internet	9 changed
2 walked	6 author / writer	10 unafraid
3 Spain	7 transformative	11 hostels
4 grabbed	8 lonely	12 locals

After you watch

8 Students work in pairs to roleplay an interview with a traveller, according to the instructions.

9 Students work in small groups to discuss which things make them feel anxious and how they deal with them.

Videoscript

Part 1

00.03–00.23 Unit 5 McCarthy … that every … everybody, but especially every writer, has a trip that changed their life. Do you have a trip that changed your life?

McCarthy Yeah. About twenty years ago now … no, not, less … eighteen, yeah, around eighteen years ago, I was in … I walked the Camino de Santiago in Spain. That changed my life. Yeah. I was in a bookstore waiting for my girlfriend at the time. I just sort of picked up some book, you know, and it was some guy who walked the Camino de Santiago in Spain. I just sort of went … that's kind of weird. I bought it and then it sat on my bookshelf for months, and then I got on a plane, was getting on a plane and I was looking for something to read and I just grabbed it, read it on the plane and when I landed, I said: 'I'm going to do that.'

00.45 So I went, two weeks, I guess … I … but I'd no, then there was no Internet or anything to find out anything and I didn't know, I never heard of the Camino de Santiago, which is this old pilgrim's route across the north of Spain that started in the eighth century, you know, the crusades and reconquests of Spain from the Moors, and … so I … It was written by a guy named Jack Hitt who … I didn't know, I didn't know anyone who wrote books, and so … I … It said he wrote for, I think *Harper's* magazine, or something. Anyway, I called up whatever magazine it was and I said: 'Hi. I'm looking for Jack Hitt.'

'Hold on.' And the guy: 'Yeah, Jack Hitt.' 'Hi, Jack. My name's Andrew McCarthy. I read your book. It was so cool.' And he was like: 'You read my book?'

And so I said: 'Yeah,' you know, so I said: 'I want to go do that. How do I do it?' And so he started to tell me and then he sort of told me, and then I … 'Thanks a lot' and 'Bye', and I had some more questions and the next day, I called him up again.

And he goes: 'I can't talk. Call me at home later.' Well, that was a mistake. So he gave me his home phone number, so I called him that night and I go: 'Listen, how do … so, how do … I need a backpack.' So anyway, I called him pretty much every day for … And finally his wife started answering the phone and: 'Jack's not in. Jack's not in'

02.10 and so I went to Spain and I walked across Spain for a month. And it was … yeah … it was just a transformative experience for me. I found it terrifying and I was lonely and miserable for most of it, and then something happened and I had, sort of, one of those experiences that you have, and it just … I went there to see if I could take care of myself, in a certain way, though I didn't know that at the time. But then I sort of, I just discovered that I was taken care of, in a certain way. I mean, it wasn't a religious experience, but it was some kind of experience that I had where I felt … unafraid in the world for the first time, on a deep level for the first time.

I had the experience of being unafraid and I didn't … I was … carried so much fear with me in the world all the time that I didn't even know that I carried it until it was suddenly absent for a short time. And that changed my life.

And that started me travelling, that experience. Yeah.

03.09 Interviewer That's great.

McCarthy It was great. Yeah, I'd love to do it again someday. With my son if he wants to do it or my daughter, but … But it's one of those things: do you really want to go do those things again? … You know? I don't know. But it was good, yeah, it changed my life.

Interviewer How long did it take?

McCarthy A month.

03.26 Interviewer And you're staying in little inns?

McCarthy You're staying in little … um … uh … little refugios, little sort of pilgrim hostels. Which … you know, truth be told, at a certain point I was a gold card pilgrim. I just said 'I can't take this'. You know? Where's the pensione? You know, I mean … and then I justified this by 'I want to meet the locals; I don't want to meet the Germans walking. I want to meet, you know, the people who live here, you know, and have that experience.' And so … yeah, half the time I slept with the sweaty pilgrims in, you know, with my backpack rolled out on the bunkbeds and half the time I checked into the little inns. You know.

Interviewer It works.

McCarthy It was great, it was great. I much preferred sleeping at the inns. Yeah.

Unit 5 Review

Grammar

1 Ask students to read the description and answer the questions.

ANSWERS

1 There are lots of upmarket hotels for rich tourists, but also less expensive accommodation for backpackers.
2 They are very welcoming and friendly.
3 The main island of Viti Levu is where most of the population lives, where there is real Fijian culture.

2 Ask students to read the description again and find the things in the article that the phrases have been used to substitute.

ANSWERS

a most of the islands
b staying in Fiji
c experience the paradise
d whether it was possible to travel on a limited budget
e the needs of different travellers
f Yasawa
g want to go fishing with them
h the feeling of being a tourist

3 Ask students to find similar sentences in the article.

ANSWERS

1 It's no surprise to find a lot of upmarket hotels.
2 The Fijian's long experience of dealing with the needs of tourists
3 the feeling of being a tourist remains.
4 if your wish is to see a country's true way of life

Vocabulary

4 Ask students to complete the sentences.

ANSWERS

1 trail	3 setting	5 theme
2 no-go	4 wary	

5 Students work in pairs to describe a journey they enjoyed.

Real life

6 Ask students to discuss how to read the extract aloud, and practise reading it in pairs.

7 Students work with a new partner to read aloud and compare their reading.

Speaking

8 Students work in pairs to discuss a place that was not as they expected.

Unit 6 Body matters

Lead-in

Personal response

Ask students to tell a partner about their experience of cycling. Elicit some responses from the whole class.

1 Ask students to work in pairs and try to come up with a snappy title for the cycling photo, one that captures the moment and the feelings the cyclist might have. Elicit some suggestions from the whole class, and discuss which the students like best and why.

SAMPLE ANSWERS

Natural high; Natural thrill; The open road; Adrenaline rush; The need for speed; Wheeeee!; Wild wheels

2 [1.31] Tell students that they are going to listen to two people talking about exercise. Ask students what sort of exercise they do themselves, e.g. do they prefer going to the gym or walking, or doing some other form of outside exercise. Then ask them to read the questions to focus their listening. Play the recording for them to answer. They can check with a partner. Play it again, if necessary, so they can check their answers. Elicit answers from the whole class.

ANSWERS

1 She says intensive exercise is less effective than gentle exercise.
2 She does active things that she enjoys, such as road cycling, rather than going to the gym.

Audioscript [1.31]

W = woman, **R** = Rashmi

W: How do you advise people to stay fit and healthy, Rashmi?

R: You know, there's so much contradictory information out there about how to keep in shape: whether you should watch your weight by controlling what you eat or by exercising; what kind of exercise regime is best, and so on. I was reading a scientific journal just this morning saying that working out at the gym is actually less effective than going for a walk regularly in the park.

W: Really? Why did it say that?

R: I think the idea is that if you do really intensive exercise, then your body demands calorie compensation afterwards – in other words, you're more likely to reward yourself with a bigger snack at the end of the session. Whereas if you just stretch your legs often or take regular gentle exercise, it doesn't have the same effect.

W: So what do you do? You're in pretty good shape.

R: Well, mainly I try not to obsess too much about my weight. I don't go on diets and I don't weigh myself every day. I just do active things that I enjoy. I've never been a fan of the gym, I have to say, and I never go for a run – I find it boring. The kids keep me pretty active anyway. But recently I've got into road cycling. You've got to try it. Every couple of weeks a few of us go out for a ride in the countryside – 40 or 50 kilometres. We often go up in the woods and hills around Springvale. The scenery's beautiful, and it's a great way to enjoy nature and stay fit at the same time.

3 [1.31] Ask students to complete the expressions with a preposition individually, then check with a partner. Elicit answers from the class, but without saying which are correct. Play the recording for them to check, and elicit further responses.

ANSWERS

The four expressions which need a preposition are:

2 keep **in** shape
4 work **out** at the gym
5 go **for** a walk / run / ride
8 go **on** a diet

The other expressions are already complete.

4 Ask students to discuss their personal exercise regimes in groups of four, following the model dialogue and asking follow-up questions. Elicit responses from the whole class.

6a Exercise around the world

Lead-in

Personal response

Ask students to discuss exercise around the world with a partner – which countries do most? Why? Do any countries do very little or none? Elicit ideas from the whole class.

Reading

1 Ask students to read the quotation and discuss its implications with a partner. Check that they understand what a *treadmill* is (an exercising machine where you walk in one position on a moving rubber belt). Elicit ideas from the whole class.

ANSWER

The point he is making is that if you do exercise that you enjoy, the time passes quickly, and it doesn't feel as if you are making an effort.

2 Ask students to read the sentences in the list, then scan the article to match the sentences to the form of exercise they relate to. They should check with a partner before you elicit answers from the whole class.

ANSWERS

1 Yoga
2 Radio Taiso / Yoga
3 Radio Taiso / Yoga
4 Swogging
5 Swogging
6 Radio Taiso

3 Ask students to write a heading for each paragraph individually, then check with a partner. Elicit suggestions from around the class, and discuss which are most suitable.

SAMPLE ANSWERS

1 A positive start to your day
2 No pain, no gain
3 Relax and get fit

4 Ask students to discuss the questions in groups of four. Elicit answers from the whole class, and continue the discussion. Read through the *Wordbuilding* box with the class, and discuss the contents with them. If you think more explanation and practice would be useful at this point, turn to page 51 of the Workbook.

Language focus phrasal verbs

5 Ask students to look at the three expressions in the box, and underline where they are in the first paragraph of the text. They should then answer questions a and b individually, and check their answers with a partner. Elicit answers from the whole class.

ANSWERS

a come out of
b come across, join in with

Extra activity

Ask students to find three more phrasal verbs in the second paragraph and a three-word phrasal verb (verb + two prepositions) in the third paragraph, and discuss the meanings with a partner.

Answers: second paragraph: *put off* (= deter), *dry off* (= dry with a towel or allow to dry) *get to* (= reach) third paragraph: *came up with* (= thought of)

6 Ask students to look at the sentences and answer the questions individually, then check with a partner. Elicit answers from the whole class.

ANSWERS

a *got into* and *taken up* have an object ('it')
b In sentence 2, the object comes after the phrasal verb. In sentence 3, the phrasal verb is separated and the object is between the verb and the preposition.

7 Read through the information about phrasal verbs in the language focus box and discuss the contents with the class. If you feel they need more explanation and practice, turn to page 163. Ask students to read the text and put the objects of the phrasal verbs into the correct positions. They should do this individually, then check with a partner before you elicit answers from the whole class as complete sentences.

ANSWERS

1 get over this
2 setting them up
3 hit on it
4 fell back on some Salsa dance music
5 getting out of dangerous situations
6 carrying them out

8 Ask students to decide on the meanings of the phrasal verbs individually, then discuss their ideas with a partner. Elicit answers from the whole class.

Point out that phrasal verbs often have a very specific, restricted meaning, or they can only be used in particular contexts, e.g. *take off* means 'be successful', but you can only use it of an idea / concept or a product when it becomes popular.

ANSWERS

get over = recover (from)
set up = start (a business or other organisation)
come about = happen
hit on = have (an idea)
fall back on = use as a substitute
take off = become popular
get out of = avoid or leave a difficult situation
carry out = do

Grammar notes

We can classify transitive (i.e. having an object) two-part phrasal verbs into three kinds:

1 always inseparable (i.e. the object must always follow the particle), for example:

to look after sb *She **looks after** her mother at the weekend.*
You cannot say: *She looks ~~her mother after~~ at the weekend.*

(similar verbs: *call for, look through, come after, count on, go into, look for, look through, make of, take after*)

2 separable or inseparable (i.e. the object can either be before or after the particle; however, when it is a pronoun it must come between the verb and the particle), for example:

to put out *He **put out** the cat for the night.*
*He **put** the cat **out** for the night.*
*He **put** it **out** for the night.*
You cannot say: *He put ~~**out** it~~ for the night.*

(similar verbs: *bring out, bring round, call off, drop off, get up, give up, look up, make up, pass round, pick up, put across*)

3 always separable (i.e. the object must always come between the verb and the particle), for example:

to call sb back *Can you **call** Peter **back** this evening?*
You cannot say: *Can you **call** ~~**back** Peter~~ this evening?*

(similar verbs: *call over, invite out, talk round, tell apart*)

Students can find out the word order of a new phrasal verb by checking in a dictionary. Most dictionaries will give the information like this:

look after sb / sth (object must follow the particle, as in 1)

call sb back (object must come before the particle, as in 3)

9 Ask students to order the words into correct sentences and questions individually. Point out that they can use a dictionary to check the correct word order for each verb (see Grammar notes above). They can then check their answers with a partner. Elicit the answers from the whole class and check the meaning of any new phrasal verbs (see Vocabulary notes below).

ANSWERS

1 I'm thinking of taking up Pilates.
2 It took me ages to get over it.
3 He set it up last year.
4 We couldn't get out of it.
5 The doctor is going to carry out some tests on my knee.
6 How did you hit on that idea?
7 What do you put its success down to?
8 It takes me back to my childhood.

Vocabulary notes

take up = to start (usually a hobby)

put sth down to = to think something is because of something else

it takes me back = it reminds me of a previous time

Speaking

10 Ask students to read the questionnaire and check they understand the meaning of the phrasal verbs (using a dictionary if necessary), then interview their partner and note the results.

ANSWERS

1 set aside = reserve
2 go in for = have an interest in doing
3 take up = start (to do)
4 keep up with = stay in touch with / not be left behind by
5 join in = be involved
6 put off = deter from

11 Ask students to work in groups of five or six to discuss their findings, and draw some conclusions.

Extra activity

Ask the groups to appoint a secretary to keep a note of their conclusions in Exercise 11, and then present them to the rest of the class. Were the groups' findings all the same? Were there any discrepancies?

Homework

Ask students to write up the findings about their class's exercise habits in a 150-word report.

6b No pain, no gain

Lead-in

Personal response
Ask students to tell a partner about the most strenuous, exhausting and demanding physical activity they have ever done. It might not have anything to do with sport. Elicit some experiences from the whole class.

Vocabulary injuries

1 Ask students to work in pairs to discuss the picture and what injuries they think the runner risks, then compare ideas with another pair. Elicit answers from the class.

SAMPLE ANSWERS

He might pull a muscle, twist / sprain an ankle, strain his back, suffer from exhaustion / dehydration / nausea (altitude sickness) / sunstroke / hypothermia, damage his knees, break a leg / ankle / arm in a fall, get hit by falling rocks, get blisters and cuts on his feet.

2 Ask students to complete the collocations individually, then check with a partner. Elicit answers from the class.

ANSWERS

1 graze your knee
2 bump your head
3 pull a muscle
4 lose your voice
5 stub your toe
6 sprain your ankle
7 strain your back
8 chip a tooth
9 bruise your ribs
10 break your arm

Vocabulary note

Point out the difference between these two similar verbs:
sprain = an injury in a joint, e.g. ankle or wrist, caused by too much stress
strain = an injury in a muscle caused by overstretching; it can include torn muscle fibres. This is also called *a pulled muscle* in informal English.
strain can also be used as a general word for stress or pressure, either physical stress on the body or mental stress.

Other common injuries:
to graze your knee = to take the top layer of skin off
to bump your head = to knock your head against something (e.g. the door)
to lose your voice = to be unable to speak because of a throat inflammation
to stub your toe = to hit your toe
to chip a tooth = to hit a tooth on something hard so that a corner breaks off
to bruise your ribs = you can actually bruise any part of the body, i.e. hit the body and cause a purple mark
to break your arm = to break the bone in the arm, (or any other part of the body)

3 Ask students to get into groups of four to rank the injuries. Elicit answers from the whole class and discuss their ideas. Encourage students to defend their order.

Listening

4 [1.32] Ask students to read the questions to focus their listening. Play the recording for them to answer, then give them time to check with a partner. Play the recording again if necessary for them to check their answers. Elicit answers from the whole class.

ANSWERS

1 Ultrarunning is where you run further than a normal marathon.
2 The fear of failure.
3 They carry on when they have an injury rather than resting.
4 Listen to your body and do the right kind of preparation.

Audioscript [1.32]

P = presenter, **B** = Ben

P: … thanks for those comments, Sarah. I'd like to turn now to someone who should know more about sports injuries than most and that's ultrarunner Ben Newborn. Ben, before we get into the questions of injuries, can you just explain for our listeners what ultrarunning is?

B: Sure, basically ultrarunning is running distances beyond a usual marathon distance. So, it could mean running 100 kilometres in a single day, or it could involve running several marathons on consecutive days.

P: And how did you get into it?

B: I was a runner anyway and I just wanted to take it to another level – to really test myself physically and mentally. So in 2008, I registered for the Ultra-Trail race in the Alps which requires runners to run 161 kilometres around Mont Blanc.

P: Didn't you worry about doing yourself real damage?

B: Actually, I wasn't so concerned about regular running injuries. I was more worried about failure. And I knew that to succeed in overcoming exhaustion and the things that make you feel nauseous, I had to get my diet and nutrition right. That's ultimately what would let me run in relative comfort.

P: Comfort's not a word I'd automatically associate with a 160-kilometre run, but anyway … What about injuries? This must put intense strain on your body.

B: I think the most important thing in any sport is to recognise when your body's in pain. A lot of sportspeople try to go through the pain. I'm not talking about when they're in a really bad way, but if they have a small muscle strain or a twinge in a joint – an ankle, for example – they tend to take some painkillers or put on some kind of support and just carry on. Because they feel they can't afford to rest. But that, of course, is completely wrong. Pain is your body warning you to be careful – to stop often – because minor problems will inevitably develop into more severe injuries. So that's the first thing: to listen to your body.

P: Yes, but we all get aches and pains. Surely that shouldn't discourage us from doing exercise?

B: Well, my point actually is that if you do the right kind of preparation, you can avoid getting injuries in the first place. I follow a method developed by a sports physiologist which is a series of stretches and gentle exercises that strengthen the key muscles and ligaments. It's definitely prevented me from getting ankle sprains and helped with other things I used to suffer from: lower back pain, runner's knee and so on …

Background notes

The *Ultra-Trail du Mont-Blanc* is a single-stage mountain ultramarathon, and considered the most difficult foot race in Europe. It mostly follows the Tour du Mont-Blanc hiking path, which takes walkers seven to nine days to complete. It starts and ends at 1,035 m height in Chamonix, and the 165 km route crosses the Grand Col Ferret at 2,537 m, its highest point. There are food and drink points every 10–15 km, and four 'life bases' along the course. A maximum of 2,000 participants can take part, and they have to prove their ability before they are allowed to do so.

5 [1.32] Ask students to read the sentences to focus their listening. Play the recording for them to complete the sentences, then give them time to check with a partner. Play the recording again if necessary for them to check their answers. Elicit answers from the whole class.

ANSWERS
1 exhaustion, nauseous
2 strains, twinges
3 severe
4 sprains, back, runner's

Idioms health

6 Ask the class to suggest what the runner meant by the idiom in bold in the quote.

ANSWER
seriously injured or ill

7 [1.33] Ask the students to work in pairs to complete the sentences with the prepositions. Elicit the answers from the whole class, without saying whether they are correct. Play the recording for students to check. Elicit answers and check on revisions to original ideas.

ANSWERS
1 in, up 2 out, on 3 off, under, down

Audioscript [1.33]

1 A: I heard Sarah came off her bicycle. Is she in a bad way?
B: Luckily she didn't break anything; she was pretty shaken up though.

2 A: Is it true that Jack nearly cut his finger off?
B: Yes, he practically passed out when he saw what he'd done. It was quite a deep cut, but he's on the mend now, I think.

3 A: You look a bit off colour. Are you feeling under the weather?
B: No, I'm not ill. I'm just run down from working too much.

8 Ask students to match the words in the box with the expressions in Exercise 7. Elicit answers from the whole class.

ANSWERS
in a bad way = suffering
shaken up = distressed
passed out = fainted
on the mend = getting better
off colour = pale
under the weather = unwell
run down = lacking in energy

Pronunciation linking in idiomatic phrases

9a [1.33] Ask students to reread the conversations in Exercise 7 and think about how the idioms in bold are pronounced. Play the recording for them to listen. Play the recording again two or three times, pausing after the idioms for students to repeat.

9b Ask students to practise the conversations in pairs, helping each other with their pronunciation, and changing roles so that they practise all the idioms.

Language focus verb patterns

10 Ask students to match the verbs with the verb patterns that follow them, then check their answers in the audioscript on pages 177–8. Elicit and discuss the answers with the whole class.

ANSWERS
1 d involve doing (+ *-ing*)
2 b require someone to do (+ object + *to* + infinitive)
3 e worry about doing (+ preposition + *-ing*)
4 c make someone do (+ object + infinitive without *to*)
5 a tend to do (*to* + infinitive)
6 f discourage someone from doing (+ object + preposition + *-ing*)

11 Ask students to find the other examples in the audioscript on pages 177–8. Elicit the answers from the whole class. See also highlighting in the audioscript.

ANSWERS
a wanted to take; try to go; afford to rest
b warning you to be
c let me run
d mean running; avoid getting
e succeed in overcoming
f prevent me from getting

12 Read through the box about verb patterns with the whole class and discuss the contents. If you think it necessary, read the further information and do the exercises on page 164. Ask students to use the patterns from the box to complete the sentences. They should do this individually, then check with a partner. Elicit the answers from the whole class as complete sentences. Note that the preposition after *prevent* is optional.

ANSWERS
1 about suffering, to be
2 damaging, getting
3 on using, to have
4 to warm, (from) occurring
5 on bending, to raise

13 Ask students to discuss which sportspeople are being discussed in pairs. Elicit answers from the whole class.

ANSWERS
1 swimmers
2 runners
3 tennis players
4 footballers
5 cyclists

14 Ask students to choose verbs from the box which could be used instead of the verbs in sentences 1–8. Point out that the verbs in the box are in the infinitive form, and a different form of the verb would have to be used in the sentences. They can check with a partner before you elicit answers from the whole class.

ANSWERS
1 stop
2 blame
3 mean
4 decide
5 appear
6 postpone
7 expect
8 convince

Extra activity

Ask students to write three sentences advising someone how to avoid injuries, choosing a different verb pattern for each sentence. They should then compare their sentences with a partner. Elicit some examples from the whole class.

Speaking

15 Ask students to work in pairs to describe what happened in one of the incidents.

Extra activity

They can write up their description as a more detailed paragraph, and then exchange it with their partner to give feedback.

6c The enigma of beauty

Lead-in

Personal response

Ask students to say which famous person they think is very handsome or beautiful, and why. Discuss the choices as a class.

Reading

1 Ask students to work in groups of three and discuss how beautiful they find the six faces in the photos, and why. Elicit responses from the whole class. You may want to mention that Huli Wigmen (Papua New Guinea, picture 4) paint their faces to make themselves more attractive, as do Geisha girls in Japan (picture 5).

2 Ask students to work in pairs to discuss the statements. Elicit some responses from the class. Then ask them to read the text to find out what the author thinks.

ANSWERS
1 False (*yet it does seem that across different cultures we can agree on certain points*)
2 True (*In almost all cultures a little fat was formerly seen as a positive trait, a sign of wealth and well-being*)
3 True (*We all like to think that beauty is not only skin deep; that personality and charm contribute as much*)
4 False (*perhaps the quest for beauty goes deeper than vanity*)

Extra activity

Ask students to find and discuss the universal characteristics of beauty mentioned in the article with a partner. Did they refer to any of these when they were discussing faces in Exercise 1? Elicit some responses from the whole class.

Universal characteristics mentioned: symmetry, averageness, indications of strength and good health

3 Ask students to read through the phrases, then find them in the article and choose the correct meaning. They can check with a partner before you elicit the answers from the class.

ANSWERS
1 b 2 b 3 a 4 a 5 b 6 a

Vocabulary notes

The following words and expressions from the text may be unfamiliar:
to diminish = to get less
to dissect = to cut up in order to examine
foot-binding = wrapping the foot in tight bandages to keep it from growing
a trait = a characteristic
to preoccupy = to worry
to fuss over = to give something a lot of attention in a caring parental kind of way

Critical thinking identifying aims

4 Ask students to read the statements, discuss them with a partner and decide on the best reason for writing the article.

5 Ask the pairs to compare their ideas with those of another pair. Elicit suggestions from the whole class.

> ANSWER
>
> Number 4 best fits the article (facts about different cultures are presented; historical perspective is presented; *Is it a shallow quest?* invites reflection).

Word focus *face*

6 Ask students to find the two expressions with *face*. Elicit answers from the class.

> ANSWERS
>
> a let's face it (paragraph 6)
> b there are long faces (paragraph 1)

7 Ask students to match the meaning of *face* in each expression to one of the words in the box, then discuss the meaning of the whole expression with a partner. Elicit the answers from the whole class.

> ANSWERS
>
> 1 credibility
> 2 attitude / expression
> 3 surface
> 4 attitude / expression
> 5 confront
> 6 surface
>
> 1 to look silly or foolish, or be taken less seriously
> 2 kept a happy expression, didn't show her disappointment
> 3 for what it seemed to be, without asking questions
> 4 looking serious, not laughing
> 5 accept the consequences, stop hiding from something
> 6 on the surface, superficially, without looking at the details

Speaking

8 Read through the instructions with the whole class. Ask students to work in pairs and read one piece of information each. They should then do the roleplay on the advertising campaign for a face cream. They should keep notes of their decisions. Ask them to discuss their ideas with another pair and find out the similarities and differences in their ideas. Invite the class to have a round-up discussion about the activity.

6d A bold initiative

Lead-in

Personal response

Ask students to discuss the attitude to sport and fitness at the schools they attended. How much PE did they have to do? What did it consist of? Were there sports clubs?

Real life discussing proposals

1 Ask students to read the information about what the six countries do to encourage a healthy society. They should then work with a partner to discuss the questions. Elicit ideas from the whole class.

2 [1.34] Ask students to read the questions to focus their listening. Play the recording for them to answer. Elicit answers from the whole class.

> ANSWERS
>
> 1 The company want to lead the way in encouraging health and fitness. It will improve productivity.
> 2 To encourage health and fitness (e.g. walking to work); to install a gym or fitness centre; to offer fun sports activities; to offer group exercise; to offer personal incentives, e.g. loans for bikes.
> 3 Qatar encouraged companies to install gyms in the workplace.
> 4 B's idea of bikes for employees gets approval from C; A's idea of group exercises is rejected by B.

Audioscript [1.34]

A: So, everyone, this is an initial brainstorming session, to come up with some concrete ideas for promoting health and fitness among employees. As you're probably aware, health is an issue that's very topical at the moment, and our own Chairman and CEO are very keen that we, as a company, take the lead on it. Of course, there's also an obvious benefit to us in terms of productivity and days not lost through sickness. So, I'd like to hear any ideas you have, really. Yes, Michelle …

B: Well, as I see it, there are two routes we could go down: one is just promoting the idea of health and fitness at work by encouraging people to do simple things like walking to work, not spending long periods sitting at their computers, that kind of thing. Or we could spend some serious money on the problem and do something like install a gym or fitness centre on site that people can use in their breaks or after work. But I realise that there may not be a budget for that.

A: Hmm, OK … Yes, Ben …

C: I don't know what others think, but for me the key is getting people to enjoy exercise. If you offer activities that employees think are fun, we'll get much better participation.

A: Such as …?

C: Such as team sports – football, basketball and so on – and we can arrange competitions. Also dance classes. Admittedly, a lot of people may do these things anyway in their free time, but I bet there are a lot more who'd like to and never get round to it.

A: Thanks, Ben. And what about the idea of group exercises in the mornings? The kind of collective warm-up routine you used to see in companies 50 years ago. It's not a particularly original idea, I'll grant you, but it might be fun and also build team spirit.

B: I think you have to be careful there. People may think that you're trying to coerce them into some kind of forced exercise regime. I know that isn't the intention, but it could look that way. I think it'd be much better to give people incentives to do things on their own. So, for example if we had a 'bike to work' scheme where we offered to pay part of the cost of a new bicycle to encourage people to cycle to work – I haven't thought through exactly what proportion of the cost, but I think that that kind of individual incentive probably works much better.

A: Mm, I like that …

B: Of course, it wouldn't be so easy to monitor whether they used the bike to commute to work or for leisure, but you'd probably just have to accept that risk …

C: Yeah, I definitely think that idea could work …

Speaking skill conceding a point

3 [1.34] Read through the instructions and the phrases in the box. Ask them to listen again and complete the phrases.

ANSWERS

1. there may not be a budget for that
2. a lot of people may do these things anyway …
3. original idea … it might be fun
4. that isn't the intention, but it could look that way
5. exactly what proportion of the cost, but I think that that kind of individual incentive probably works much better
6. easy to monitor whether they used the bike to commute to work or for leisure, but you'd probably just have to accept that risk

Pronunciation toning down negative statements

4a [1.35] Ask students to read the two sentences and underline the words which are most strongly stressed. Elicit the answers from the whole class.

ANSWERS

1. It's not a particularly original idea.
2. It wouldn't be so easy to monitor.

4b [1.36] Ask students to practise saying the three sentences in pairs, then play the recording.

5 Ask students to each come up with another idea to promote health, then discuss the ideas in their group.

6e A controversial plan

Lead-in

Personal response

Ask students to say what they think about smoking and the smoking laws and regulations in their countries, towns and work places. Initiate a discussion.

Writing a formal report

1 Ask students to discuss report-writing experiences with a partner. Elicit some experiences from the whole class.

2 Ask students to read the three questions, then read the report and find the answers. They should compare their answers with a partner. Elicit the answers from the whole class.

ANSWERS

1. to decide on the viability of a public health initiative
2. 30 per cent of the interviewees objected on the grounds that the initiative was discriminatory; there were many others – 55 per cent – who took the opposite view: that smokers ought to pay for the consequences of their behaviour; when interviewees were asked if people should be helped to give up smoking, the response was 90 per cent positive
3. we recommend that a pilot scheme be set up where smokers are given free help by their insurance company to stop smoking over a six-month period

Extra activity

Ask students to discuss their personal views of the report and its findings with a partner. Elicit some opinions from the whole class.

3 Ask students to read the description of reports, then find examples of the features in the report in Exercise 2. They should share their ideas with a partner. Elicit answers from the whole class.

ANSWERS

All of these things are found in the report except for bullet points.

Writing skill linking adverbs and adverbial phrases

4a Ask students to read the words in the box, find the equivalents in the text and decide which introduce more subjective comments. They can check with a partner before you elicit answers from the whole class.

ANSWERS
as might be expected = not surprisingly
clearly = evidently
in view of this = accordingly
on the face of it = ostensibly
on the other hand = conversely
whatever the justification = rightly or wrongly
The phrases used to introduce a more subjective comment are:
not surprisingly, rightly or wrongly, ostensibly

4b Ask students to work with a partner to replace the expressions in the sentences with words from the box. Elicit the answers from the whole class as complete sentences. Point out the phrases used in the sentences are less formal than the adverbs that replace them.

ANSWERS
1 Apparently
2 Interestingly
3 Specifically
4 Overall
5 Ultimately
6 Alternatively

5 Ask students to write a 200–250-word report about a company's health initiatives using the ideas from earlier in the unit. They should do this individually, perhaps as homework.

6 Students should exchange reports with a partner, and use the bullet points in the Student's Book to analyse their partner's work and give feedback.

6f Palestinian free running

Before you watch

1 Students work in pairs. Ask them to look at the sports and say whether they are usually done in the street, or only sometimes. Take feedback from the class.

2 Ask students to look at the photo and say what they see, then answer the questions.

While you watch

3 Give students time to read the words in the glossary. Play the video for students to check their answers from Exercise 2. Take feedback from the class.

ANSWERS
1 Moving from one place to another as fast and easily as possible using physical strength and ability.
2 It appeals to young people because it's exciting and good exercise.

4 Give students time to read the sentences. Then play the first part of the video (to 01.44) for them to choose the correct options.

ANSWERS
1 poor urbanised areas
2 Paris
3 any equipment
4 to keep in shape
5 wouldn't know what to do

5 Give students time to read the sentences, then play the second part of the video (1.45 to end) for them to write the missing words.

ANSWERS
1 proud
2 sprains
3 fall *or* land
4 opposing
5 cool

6 Give students time to read and complete the summary. Play the video again for them to check their answers.

ANSWERS
1 spread
2 caught
3 improvise
4 express
5 stay
6 land
7 perform

After you watch

7 Students work in pairs to roleplay planning a campaign, according to the instructions.

8 Students work in groups to discuss the questions about sports.

Videoscript

Narrator The camps of Gaza are rich with the performance arts of the underprivileged. So it's not surprising that a sport that first found expression in the poorer suburbs of Paris before spreading to other urban settings such as London and New York should catch on among the youth of the Gaza strip in Palestine.

00.25 Abed (words translated) My name is Abed Allah Neshi, 22 years old from Khan Younis in Southern Gaza Strip.

Narrator The beauty of parkour is that you don't need any equipment; you just improvise with the environment around you.

00.38 Mohammed (words translated) I am Mohammed Jamal Jakeer, 21, from Khan Younis in Southern Gaza Strip. We practise a sport called parkour, which means the art of moving from one part to another as fast and easy as possible by using physical strength and ability. This is the definition of the parkour that we've been practising for five years.

Narrator With unemployment around 40 per cent, and 35 per cent of the population living below the poverty line, opportunities are limited here. But there is no sense of apathy amongst these youngsters who are highly focused on staying fit and active … and enjoy expressing themselves at the same time.

01.29 Abed (words translated) If I don't practise this sport I feel something away from me, so I can't leave it. I love it. It became part of my life.

01.45 Mother (words translated) I'm very proud of him. I encourage him and I'm happy for him, although he finds some obstacles in this game. His tooth was broken, once he came to me and his mouth was all like this and I was very sad. But now it's fine. Here he is. I'm proud of him, and I encourage him and his friends.

Narrator Injuries – sprains, broken limbs or worse – are an ever-present risk. Landing awkwardly on concrete is a very different matter from landing on a rubber practice mat. So one of the first lessons these parkour artists learn is how to fall.

02.20 Mohammed (words translated) At the beginning, they opposed me a little bit, because it's dangerous and it requires high abilities and skills. But after a period of time, I convinced them and I convinced all people around me about this sport. Thanks for our God because we reached this very good level in this sport.

Narrator As well as giving them a sense of personal achievement, there is always the hope for practitioners of this obviously cool sport that they may one day be asked to perform their art in a competition, a film or even as professional stuntmen.

Unit 6 Review

Grammar

1 Ask students to consider the question. Elicit responses from the class.

2 Ask students to read the blog and answer the questions.

ANSWERS

1 It's very common and affects people all round the world.
2 Exercise classes, painkillers and manipulation

3 Ask students to complete the blog with the correct verb forms.

ANSWERS

1 from working	4 to suffer
2 to become	5 sitting
3 for thinking	6 working

4 Ask students to replace the noun objects with pronouns.

ANSWERS

go in for it
look into them
turn it around
put up with it

Vocabulary

5 Students complete the sentences with prepositions.

ANSWERS

1 down	3 down	5 in
2 On	4 up	6 aside

6 Students work in pairs to discuss the statements in Exercise 5.

Real life

7 Ask students to read and complete the proposal.

ANSWERS

1 particularly	3 through	5 head
2 grant	4 Admittedly	6 out

8 Students work in pairs to prepare and present their proposal.

Speaking

9 Students work in pairs to discuss health and exercise.

Unit 7 Stories from history

Lead-in

Personal response

Ask students to tell a partner a story they know from history. You might encourage them and initiate the process by telling them one you know (e.g. How the geese saved Rome, Paul Revere's ride, Drake playing bowls and the Spanish Armada). Elicit a few of the stories for the whole class to listen to.

1 Ask students to look at the picture and caption, and answer the question in pairs. Elicit ideas from the whole class.

SAMPLE ANSWERS

Students might deduce that Genghis Khan was a Mongolian leader (*his cavalrymen*) who lived in a time when arrows were used as weapons, and that he had a strong cavalry whose soldiers were very skilled at shooting with arrows (*his cavalrymen could fire six arrows a minute*).

Extra activity

Ask students to describe the woman in the picture – what she is wearing, her appearance, her expression.

2 [2.1] Ask students to read the four questions to focus their listening. Play the recording once, and let them discuss their ideas with a partner. Play the recording again for them to complete, correct and check their answers. Elicit responses from the whole class.

ANSWERS

1 He built a great empire across Asia and Europe in the 13th century.
2 People in his native Mongolia have a positive opinion of him. ('His achievements are viewed with great pride')
3 He is seen as a ruthless warlord who crushed his enemies.
4 Opening up trade and cultural links, abolishing the slave trade, giving greater legal rights to his citizens.

Audioscript [2.1]

What do we really know about the Mongolian leader, Genghis Khan? It's a fact that he built a great empire across Asia in the 13th century. But was he a great general that brought peace to these lands, or a cruel warrior? Well of course, there are two sides to every story. In his homeland of Mongolia, his achievements are viewed with great pride, and the stories about him focus on the great Mongolian traditions of archery and skill with horses. Khan's cavalry could shoot with a bow and arrow forwards or backwards while riding at full speed – or so the story goes.

However, in other countries, among the people he conquered, Khan is known as a ruthless warlord, who crushed city after city as his armies swept across Asia. It's often said that it's the victor who writes history, but in the case of Genghis Khan, it's the accounts of those he defeated that seem to have prevailed. These accounts say that the evidence tells its own story, quoting Genghis Khan himself: 'the greatest happiness is to scatter your enemy, to drive him before you; to see his cities reduced to ashes'.

But now some western historians are suggesting that Genghis Khan also had his good points. According to them, he did many positive things: opening up trade and cultural links between east and west, abolishing the slave trade and giving greater legal rights to his citizens, both men and women. So perhaps it's true to say that …

Background notes

Genghis Khan was born with the name Temujin in the Khentii Mountains of Mongolia, possibly in 1162. His father was chieftain of a tribe. At sixteen he married his betrothed, Borte, who bore him four sons. This marriage united her tribe to his, and by 1190 he had united all the nomadic Mongol tribes under his leadership. He invented a civil and military code called the Yassa, which put merit and loyalty above family ties, and used it to control his people. The Mongols were, however, surrounded by enemies, and Temujin set about defeating them one by one. Much of the fighting and strategic planning was done by his loyal generals; they used traditional and modern methods of warfare, and learnt from others. After 1220, his armies went as far as the River Volga, defeating peoples in present-day Azerbaijan, Armenia, Georgia and south Russia. In around 1226 he died in the campaign against the Tanguts to the east, although it is not known how. His body was taken and buried near his birthplace.

3 [2.1] Read the five expressions with the class, and ask if they are familiar with any of them – elicit any suggestions you can, without saying whether they are correct or not. Then play the recording again so that they can hear them in context. Ask them to discuss the meanings with a partner. Elicit ideas from the whole class.

ANSWERS

The expressions the speaker uses are: 'there are two sides to every story'; 'or so the story goes' and 'the evidence tells its own story'

there are two sides to every story = there are usually two views or opinions of an event.

it's always the same old story = it's what usually happens

or so the story goes = or so it is said *or* so people say (but it isn't necessarily the real facts)

the evidence tells its own story = the facts explain the story: no further explanation is necessary

he wanted to get the inside story = get the story from someone inside a group or organisation who had first-hand experience

4 Ask students to discuss famous leaders in the history of their country. In a mixed class, students from the same countries can work together, then share their descriptions with the class.

Homework

Ask students to write 150 words about a great historical leader – perhaps one they admire.

7a The father of history

Lead-in

Personal response

Ask students where history comes from: *How do we get the information we have about what happened in the past? Who writes it down, based on what? How reliable is it?* Elicit some ideas about these issues from the whole class and discuss them.

Reading

1 Ask students to read the quotation and elicit responses from the whole class to the question.

ANSWER

The point that is made is that the way history is reported or recorded can be more important (or influential) than the facts themselves.

2 Ask students to read the rubric and say what they know about Herodotus, the Persians and ancient Greeks.

Ask students to read the four questions, then read the article. Elicit answers to the questions from the whole class.

ANSWERS

1 To conquer it and get revenge because the Greeks had defeated his father.
2 He was a Greek historian, called 'the father of history', and he recorded these events.
3 He believed in *the power of storytelling*: he thought it was important to tell a story as well as give the facts when recording history.
4 That the Greeks, especially the Spartans, will fight even though their armies are smaller.
5 He'll ignore it. He appears confident of his army's superiority.

3 Ask students to read the topics they have to find out about, then read the article again to find the information. Elicit suggestions from the whole class.

ANSWERS

1 Greece was organised into a number of independent 'city' states.
2 He was powerful, determined, arrogant, headstrong.
3 They were afraid of him (Demaratus hesitates to answer his question truthfully).
4 The values that were important to the Spartans were bravery, discipline and honour.

4 Ask students to consider the questions with a partner. Elicit ideas and reasons from the whole class.

Read through the information about noun formation in the *Wordbuilding* box with the class. Elicit some other nouns made from verbs, using *-ment* (e.g. *agreement, government, development*), *-ion* (e.g. *competition, discussion, revolution*) and *-ance* (e.g. *alliance, appearance, insurance*).

If you feel it would be good to work on this more at this stage, ask students to do the exercises on page 59 of the Workbook.

ANSWER

It is an effective story, but is unlikely to be accurate. Herodotus quotes the words the characters use, but he could not have known these details.

Extra activity

Ask students to look for more nouns formed from verbs in the article, and give the verb that is related to each noun.

a defeat (to defeat); *resistance* (to resist); *a surrender* (to surrender); *a commandment* (to command)

Note also *an invasion* (to invade) in Exercise 2.

Language focus linking words

5 Ask students to do this activity individually, then check their answers with a partner. Elicit answers from the class.

ANSWERS

a a contrast: *although, however, in spite of*
a reason: *on account of*
an additional point: *as well as*
time: *after*

b followed by a noun or gerund: *on account of, as well as, in spite of, after*
followed by a clause or a new sentence: *although, however*

6 Read through the language box with the class, and make sure they understand the meaning and use of the linking words. Ask them to complete the sentences in the exercise individually, then check with a partner. If necessary, ask students to read the information and do the exercises on page 165.

ANSWERS

1a Despite only writing one book, Herodotus is one of the world's famous historians.
1b Herodotus is one of the world's most famous historians. However, he only wrote one book.
2a In addition to doubting that Herodotus' facts are reliable, people have even called him 'the father of lies'.
2b Some people doubt that Herodotus' facts are reliable. Moreover, they have called him 'the father of lies'.
3a Some people are suspicious of Herodotus owing to the fact that many of these stories are based on what others told him.
3b Since many of his stories are based on what others told him, some people are suspicious of Herodotus.
4a After completing his *Histories*, Herodotus took them and read them aloud to the audience at the Olympic Games.
4b Following the completion of his *Histories*, Herodotus took them and read them aloud to the audience at the Olympic Games.

7 Ask students to complete the text individually using the linking words, then check with a partner. Elicit the answers from the class as complete sentences.

ANSWERS

1 However	5 since
2 owing to	6 In spite of
3 When	7 as well as
4 and	8 following

Vocabulary and speaking
stories from history

8 Ask students to match the words in the sentences to the words in the box.

ANSWERS

1 explorer	4 a criminal
2 unlucky	5 achievement
3 a bad reputation	6 personal loss

9 Ask students to think of a story they know from history, using the words from Exercise 8. Ask them to make notes about it. They should then get into groups of four and tell each other their story. They should ask and answer questions about their story.

Extra activity

Discuss with the class why these historical stories were so memorable for them. Reasons might include the following: it is a good story; the historical characters stand out in some way, e.g. they achieved something extraordinary; because of the emotional impact the story had on them.

Homework

Ask students to write up their story, or one of the others they heard, in around 150 words.

7b Microhistory

Lead-in

Personal response

Ask students to tell a partner how they used to spend their free time when they were children, between the ages of seven and twelve. Elicit some answers from the class (e.g. watch TV, play computer games, read books, play cards or board games, make models, play with dolls or toy animals).

Listening

1 Ask students to think about the three questions for a couple of minutes, then discuss their responses with a partner. Elicit ideas from the whole class and talk about their replies.

2 [2.2] Ask students to read the definition of microhistory to themselves. They should then read the two questions to focus their listening. Play the recording once. Ask them to discuss their ideas with a partner. Play the recording again for them to check their answers. Elicit suggestions from the whole class.

ANSWERS

1 What were people's attitudes to children?
2 They found out that children in fact did have toys in the Middle Ages and were able to play.

Audioscript [2.2]

P = presenter, J = James

P: A recent archaeological dig on the banks of the River Thames in London has uncovered evidence about the lives of children in the Middle Ages. Archaeologist James Newman is here to tell us a bit more about it. James, correct me if I'm wrong, but compared to children today, I imagine children in medieval times didn't have much of a childhood!

J: Well, as far as historians are concerned, that is – or certainly was – the accepted view of it. In the 1960s, a French social historian, Philippe Ariès, claimed that parents in the Middle Ages didn't really form emotional attachments with their children, but rather sent them off to work as soon as they could to be economic providers for the household. According to Ariès, the idea of a childhood didn't really appear until the 16th or 17th century. Up until then, children were just little adults, expected to do what adults did. If you look at paintings of children in medieval and renaissance times, in fact they do appear as small versions of grown-ups.

P: But considering people had much shorter working lives, you can understand why they'd want to get their children working earlier. Having said that, it does seem a pretty harsh view of human nature: to assume that people in the Middle Ages had no emotional bond with their children. But you think you've found some evidence to show this wasn't actually the case.

J: Yes. I was working on a dig, retrieving objects from mud banks by the River Thames. We found various items dating back to the 13th century: little cannons and guns, metal figurines, and miniature household objects such as chairs, jugs, and even frying pans complete with little fish. And insofar as the objects have great historical value, you could say we've struck gold! Also assuming that these are all medieval toys – and they look just like doll's house furniture – they paint a different picture of childhood in the Middle Ages.

P: You mean that perhaps children were allowed to be children, more than people thought, anyway.

J: Yes, exactly. Someone clearly went to the trouble of making toys for them so they could play. The other interesting thing is that, regardless of what they tell us about children at the time, some of these objects are things we didn't know existed in medieval households, like a birdcage and a three-legged stool.

P: Mmm, sounds fascinating. Now, in case any listeners want to see these items, the collection will be going on tour around the country …

Vocabulary notes

Check some of the key language from the audioscript with the class:

cannon = a large gun that fires metal balls

frying pan = shallow pan used for cooking food in oil (frying)

jug = container for holding and pouring liquids, particularly drinks (e.g. water, milk)

stool = a chair without a back

3 [2.2] Ask students to read the questions carefully. They might circle some of the answers based on what they have already heard. Play the recording, and ask them to check, complete and correct their answers; they can also discuss them with a partner. Elicit the answers from the whole class.

ANSWERS

1 b 2 b 3 b 4 a 5 a 6 b

4 Ask the class to discuss and answer these questions.

ANSWERS

The example given is doll's house furniture.

Other possible answers are: dolls, rocking horses, soldiers

Idioms luck

5 Ask students to look at the phrases and match them to the definitions individually, then check with a partner. Elicit answers from the whole class.

ANSWERS

strike gold = have a big piece of luck (a)

1 d 2 d 3 b 4 c 5 a

Vocabulary notes

Elicit any other phrases students know related to luck, e.g.

to be down on one's luck = to be going through a period when things keep going wrong

Bad luck! = a comment made to sympathise with somebody who loses a competition

to take pot luck = to have to make do with what there is, as there are no other choices

to be in luck = the situation seems favourable to you

6 Ask students to complete the four phrases in a way that is related to their own experience, if possible, or that of someone they know well. They should then get into groups of four and tell each other their sentences. Elicit some examples from the whole class.

Language focus subordinate clauses

7 Learners should already be familiar with the concept of subordinate clauses using words like *when, although, because,* etc. but check the concept of main clause / subordinate clause by writing this example on the board: *Although they are amateurs, the local historians have made some very important historical discoveries.* Ask students to identify the main clause and the subordinate clause in this sentence.

Then, ask them to complete the exercise individually, and check their answers with a partner. Elicit answers from the whole class.

ANSWERS

a yes
b no
c no
d It gives more information through comparison, opinion and additional facts.

8 Read through the language box on subordinate clauses with the class and ensure that they understand the explanation. If you feel that more explanation and practice is necessary, see page 166. Ask students to match the two halves of the sentences in Exercise 8 individually, then check with a partner. Elicit answers from the whole class.

ANSWERS

1 c 2 d 3 b 4 a

Pronunciation intonation in subordinate clauses

9a [2.3] Ask students to listen and say what the intonation does. Ask them why it does this.

ANSWER

The intonation rises; this alerts the listener to the fact that there is more to follow.

9b Play the recording again and have students repeat chorally and individually. Then ask them to practise the sentences in pairs, helping each other with their intonation. Circulate and monitor their speaking.

10 Ask students to complete the passage with the subordinating conjunctions given. They should do this individually, then check with a partner.

ANSWERS

1 insofar as
2 in view of the fact that
3 as far as (some historians) are concerned
4 in spite of
5 Given that
6 Supposing that
7 contrary to

Writing and speaking

11 Ask students to read the four questions, and then discuss the answers in relation to their own families. Elicit answers from the whole class. Open a wider discussion.

12 Ask students to work with their partner, and summarise the ideas that have been discussed in three or four sentences. Encourage them to use subordinate clauses where possible. Elicit sentences from the whole class.

7c Diamond shipwreck

Lead-in

Introducing the topic: shipwrecks

Ask students to talk about any shipwrecks they know about in pairs. Elicit any details they can give you.

These are some of the world's most famous shipwrecks:

The Mary Rose (1545) Henry VIII's English warship, lost 650 crew and equipment in a storm. Salvaged in 1982. Now a museum.

The Vasa (1628) Swedish warship. Salvaged in 1961. A very popular tourist destination.

The Titanic (1912) British liner. Hit an iceberg. 1,517 people lost. Famous film.

The Lusitania (1915) Cunard liner. Hit by a German torpedo off southern Ireland. 1,201 people lost.

The Andrea Doria (1956): Italian liner. Hit a Swedish ship near New York. Few people lost. Popular wreck for scuba divers to visit.

Reading

1 Ask students to look at the map and answer the questions with a partner. Elicit answers from the whole class, and discuss them.

SAMPLE ANSWERS

1 To trade goods, to make money, to discover new lands,
2 Possible dangers they faced were: bad weather / storms, disease, piracy, damage to the ship, lack of food, poor navigational equipment and maps.

2 Read through the three questions with the class before they read the article to focus their reading. They should then discuss their ideas with a partner before you elicit answers from the whole class.

ANSWERS

1 To trade / make money *or* to bring back spices and pepper from India and Africa.
2 The ship was caught in a storm and sank near the Namibian coast.
3 The irony was that the sailors who had set out to seek their fortune were, in fact, shipwrecked off the coast of Namibia where diamonds (and a great fortune) lay beneath the sand.

3 Ask students to read the sentences and the options, then reread the article to find the answers. They should check with a partner. Elicit the answers from the whole class as complete sentences.

ANSWERS

1 a 2 c 3 c 4 b 5 a 6 a

4 Ask students to find the words individually, then check with a partner. Elicit answers from the whole class.

ANSWERS

1 odyssey
2 sturdy
3 sketchy
4 inhospitable
5 inkling

Vocabulary notes

Check students understand these words from the article:

a carat = a measurement of the size of precious stones

chain mail = circles of metal linked together, worn as protection by soldiers

chunk = an irregular piece

coat of arms = the emblem of a king or lord

inhospitable = unwelcoming, difficult to survive in

an odyssey = a long journey of exploration

a port of call = a place where a ship stopped regularly

to shudder = to shake uncontrollably

spices = flavouring, e.g. cinnamon, caraway, nutmeg

sketchy = unclear, limited

sturdy = strong

Critical thinking fact or conjecture

5 Ask students to decide whether the sentences are fact or conjecture and find evidence in the article.

ANSWERS

1 F (*Archaeologists would later find a staggering 22 tons of these ingots beneath the sand as well as … exquisite gold coins bearing the coat of arms of King João III of Portugal*)
2 F (*The ships … were sturdy and capable; two of them were brand-new*)
3 F (*All that remains is a clerk's acknowledgement that the report was received*)
4 F (*a mention that the Bom Jesus disappeared in wild weather*)
5 C (*the theory is that it struck rocks about 150 metres from shore*)
6 C (All we know is that *none of them ever returned home*)

Teaching note

Students should be made aware that the dividing line between conjecture and fact can be very small at times, in the sense that an individual's conjecture can be based on research and factual information. Students need to ascertain that there are clear facts, quoted evidence and references in the text to say with confidence that something is a fact; equally the use of words like *believe, imagine, probably* are more likely to be associated with conjecture.

6 Ask students to compare their answers with a partner, and decide on how believable the 'conjecture' sentences are and why. Check the answers to Exercise 5 and 6 together as a class.

SAMPLE ANSWER

The sentences are believable because the conjectures are based on logical deduction even though there is no hard evidence to prove it.

Word focus *bear*

7 Ask students if they know any meanings of the verb *to bear* and elicit some examples. Then ask the class to explain the meaning of the two phrases from the text.

ANSWERS

a Having the coat of arms on its surface
b carrying

8 Ask students to read the sentences in pairs and decide on the meanings. Elicit answers from the class.

ANSWERS

1 received the main impact or force
2 doesn't look like (*bears a close resemblance* would mean 'looks very much like')
3 felt resentment
4 is the evidence of
5 had a successful result
6 Remember (that)

Speaking

9 Ask students to work in groups of three and read their facts on the appropriate page. They should then take it in turns to read the fact to the other two students who have to try and guess what the irony is. The first student should then tell them the correct answer.

Homework

Ask students to use the details from the various texts and discussions in this section to write a hundred words from a diary of a 16th-century sailor who survived a shipwreck, describing how it happened and what it was like.

7d I blame the weather

Lead-in

Personal response

Ask students to talk in pairs about the weather: their favourite and least favourite kinds of weather, the worst and most extreme weather conditions they have experienced. You might start by describing something you experienced yourself. Elicit some responses from the whole class.

Real life asking for confirmation and clarification

1 Ask students to answer the questions with a partner. Elicit some answers from the whole class.

ANSWERS

Students' own answers.

2 Ask students to read the text for 30 seconds (time them, saying *Start* and *Stop*). Then ask the class for answers to the two questions.

ANSWERS

1 It looks at how weather and climate change affects events in world history.
2 Whether we should pay more attention to the environment when we study the past.

Extra activity

Ask students to look at the photo and ask them what it shows. (Answer: The top part of a statue visible in a flood of the Mississippi; also there is artwork/graffiti on the wall behind the statue which indicates the height the water has risen.)

3 [2.4] Ask students to read the four topics listed, then play the recording for them to order them correctly. Play the recording again for them to check. Elicit the answers from the class in the correct order.

ANSWERS

1 c 2 d 3 a 4 b

Audioscript [2.4]

L = lecturer, **A** = student 1, **B** = student 2, **C** = student 3, **D** = student 4

L: Yes, you in the third row.

A: Yes, hello. Thanks for a very interesting talk. Er, I'd just like to make sure I understood what you said about the plague that affected the Roman Empire so badly. Am I right in thinking that the drought in Africa caused an increase in the number of rats?

L: Well, not exactly … The drought actually caused a lot of animals to die – rats and mice, and also those animals that hunted rats and mice. But when the rains returned, the numbers of mice and rats grew much more quickly than the number of the animals that hunted them, so they quickly spread everywhere and so did the plague. Yes …?

B: I always understood that there were a lot of different reasons for the decline of the Roman Empire, but the logical conclusion of your argument is that it just wouldn't have happened without the drought. No drought, no decline. Is that what you're saying?

L: Well, I don't know – and I don't think anyone knows precisely, but climate change certainly set off a chain of events: the plague was caused by changes in the weather, and in turn a lot of people within the Roman Empire died in the plague and so … the world order was changed … and – girl at the back?

C: Yes, I have a question. You mentioned the 'Little Ice Age'. Can you explain what you meant by that? Was it really that bad?

L: No, the term 'little' really describes both the fact that it was quite short and that it wasn't as intense as a proper Ice Age, but it certainly had an effect – on northern countries in particular. Crops failed and animals died. When people don't have enough food, of course, this has political and social consequences. You can see that throughout history. Yes, you in the blue shirt …

D: Yes, sorry, perhaps I missed something, but how do punishments fit in with the Little Ice Age?

L: Ah, people always look for someone to blame when things go wrong, even if it's something out of our control like cold weather. So they found people that they thought were troublemakers anyway and punished them …

Speaking skill prefacing a question and seeking clarification

4 [2.4] Read through the phrases for prefacing a question in the language box with the class and make sure that they are familiar with the expressions listed, without discussing their purpose. Play the recording while students listen. Play it again and ask them to tick the ones which are used. Ask them to discuss the purpose of the phrases in pairs. Elicit answers from the whole class.

ANSWERS

The phrases which are used to preface each question are:

I'd just like to make sure I understood what you said about …

You mentioned …

Perhaps I missed something, but …

The logical conclusion of your argument is that …

The purpose of these phrases is to be polite and show appreciation for the information that has been given; to specify what you're going to ask about.

5 [2.4] Ask students to work individually to complete the questions for seeking clarification in the language box, then play the recording again for them to check. Elicit the answers from the whole class as complete sentences.

ANSWERS

1 the drought in Africa caused an increase in the number of rats
2 No drought, no decline.
3 that
4 punishments (fit in with), the Little Ice Age

Pronunciation: intonation in questions

6a [2.5] Ask students to read through the questions and think about what the intonation should be in each one. Play the recording and ask students to decide whether the intonation rises or falls. They can check their ideas with a partner. Play it again for them to check. Elicit answers from the whole class, and discuss the rules about intonation in different types of question.

ANSWERS

1 rising
2 rising
3 rising
4 falling
5 falling

The rule they follow is that *wh-* questions fall and *yes / no* questions rise.

6b Ask students to practise reading the questions to each other with the correct intonation. Circulate and monitor their intonation.

7 Read the instructions with the class. Ask them to get into groups of three and decide who will read which text. They should prepare their talks and give them. The other students should then ask suitable questions using the language and intonation practised in Exercises 4–7.

7e Krakatoa

Lead-in

Personal response

Ask students what they know about volcanoes. Elicit the names of a few famous ones (e.g. Etna and Vesuvius in Italy; Mount St Helens in the USA), and the effects they have had (e.g. Vesuvius destroyed Pompei; the Iceland volcano Eyjafjallajökull disrupted world flights in 2010).

Writing describing past events

1 Ask students to look at the photo and caption and answer the questions.

ANSWERS

It is a volcanic island – an island where the whole island is a volcano, rather than an island with a volcano on it.

See Background notes below for further examples.

Background notes

Some well-known volcanic islands are:

Kilauea in Hawaii (where there are several)

Stromboli in Italy

Pico in the Azores

Bora-Bora in Indonesia

McDonald Island in Australian Antarctica

An important example of an island with a volcano on it (i.e. **not** a volcanic island) is Montserrat, where the Soufrière Hills volcano devastated half of the island in 1995, forcing 8,000 people to leave, and making the southern half of the island a forbidden zone.

2 Ask students to read the text and answer the questions individually, then discuss them with a partner. Elicit the answers from the whole class.

ANSWERS

1 That the volcanic eruption on the island of Krakatoa affected global weather patterns *or* caused lasting climatic effects.
2 a 1.2 degree drop in global temperatures the following year; the extraordinary winter in Nebraska in 1888

Writing skill sequencing events

3a Ask students to order the events individually, then check with a partner. Elicit answers from the whole class.

ANSWER

The correct order is: c, b, a

3b Ask students to complete the table individually, then check with a partner. Elicit the answers from the whole class.

ANSWERS
1 until then
2 in the preceding months
3 the following year
4 in those days

3c Ask students to complete the sentences individually, then check with a partner. Elicit the answers as complete sentences from the whole class.

ANSWERS
1 some / a few days earlier
2 the following day
3 at that time
4 the previous day
5 from then on

4 Read the rubric with the class, and encourage students to use as many of the sequencers from Exercise 3 (and other similar ones, e.g. *the following week / month / year*) as appropriate to structure their writing. You may wish to give them this task for homework, depending on the time available in class.

5 Ask students to exchange their writing with a partner and check the four features listed. They should then give each other feedback on those points.

7f Collecting the past

Before you watch

1 Students work in pairs to discuss their favourite museums and answer the questions. Take feedback from the class.

2 Ask students to look at the picture and say what they see, and where they would find it.

ANSWERS
This is a rubbing of China's first emperor, Qin Shi Huang. They would find it in the exhibition of Chinese objects.

While you watch

3 Give students time to read the words in the glossary. Play the video for students to answer the question. Take feedback from the class.

ANSWER
Chinese collectors are collecting these objects; they think it's important that these items are brought back to China.

4 Give students time to look at the table. Then play the first part of the video (to 01.05) for them to choose the correct options.

ANSWERS
1 Qing dynasty
2 private collector
3 foreign auctions
4 a shopping mall
5 $100 million

5 Give students time to read the questions, then play the second part of the video (01.06 to end) for them to answer.

ANSWERS
1 (wealthy) Chinese collectors
2 It's soaring (rising very high).
3 In Japan, in the late 70s and 80s.
4 more affordable decorative pieces
5 They are a good investment; investors / collectors want to bring a piece of their heritage home.

6 Give students time to read and complete the summary. Play the video again for them to check and complete their answers.

ANSWERS
1 collectors / investors / buyers
2 repatriate
3 auctions
4 bidding
5 soared
6 affordable
7 investment
8 heritage

After you watch

7 Students work in pairs to roleplay a meeting to negotiate a solution, according to the instructions.

8 Ask students to work in groups to describe three important objects from their country to the rest of the group.

Videoscript

00.01 Finely embroidered robes once used by an emperor of the Qing dynasty, the last dynasty to rule imperial China. They're part of one man's collection of stately Chinese artefacts, mostly snapped up in auctions abroad, on display in a shopping mall in Hong Kong. It's an unusual setting for such regal finery, but this collector is just happy his treasures are back on home soil.

00.28 Mr Chan (words translated) These antiques originally belonged to China and it would be a real shame for them to be kept overseas. That's why I want to bring back as many pieces as I can.

00.42 Narrator An emperor's own calligraphy and imperial edicts written onto scrolls – a very small part of the total hoard Mr Chan spent 25 years and over 100 million dollars collecting. He's part of a growing breed of wealthy buyers who scan the catalogues of auction houses around the world looking to repatriate pieces from China's imperial past.

01.06 Auctioneer Any kind of Chinese activity, they'll go after it and it will often be Chinese versus Chinese versus Chinese with all the European or American collectors being left behind, sometimes not even being able to raise their hand at the auction.

Narrator Fierce bidding is making prices soar. Last year, Christie's most expensive Chinese lot was this pair of crane statues which sold for 16.7 million dollars. As well as dozens of dollar billionaires, China now counts almost one million millionaires, potential buyers with cash to spend who are emerging as a powerful force in the global art market. Some dealers say they've seen this all before.

01.46 Dealer The late 70s and 80s were the Japanese. Originally they bought very important works of art which they had lost from their country – bought them back from the West, bought them back into Japan. But then soon after that, they still had an interest and a desire to buy, and the wealth, and they bought more affordable decorative pieces.

02.07 Narrator But for now it's the big money that speaks loudest. Each year, record sales keep smashing the old. As auction houses prepare for their spring sales, they'll be looking to meet the demands of clients who have one eye on a good investment and another on bringing a piece of their heritage home.

Unit 7 Review

Grammar

1 Ask students to read the text and answer the questions.

ANSWERS

1a Mount Everest was named after him
b 'the father of geography' (we don't know why)
c helped the army to map enemy positions during the Civil War
d made maps of the US coast
2a not much remembered
b as author of the Iliad and the Odyssey
c for the defeat at the Battle of the Little Bighorn
d as the painter of 'Whistler's Mother'

2 Ask students to choose the correct options.

ANSWERS

1 he had
2 climbers
3 is
4 serving
5 were
6 he was
7 doodling
8 one

Vocabulary

3 Ask students to complete the sentences.

ANSWERS

1 outlaw
2 ill-fated
3 evidence
4 feat
5 sacrifices
6 old

4 Ask students to work in pairs to think of a historical event and describe it.

Real life

5 Ask students to complete the comments.

ANSWERS

1 correctly
2 pick
3 missed
4 in
5 expand
6 fit

6 Students work in groups to ask and answer questions about games they know.

Speaking

7 Students work in pairs to describe an important recent event.

Unit 8 Digital media

Lead-in

Personal response

Ask students to work in pairs and talk about their experience of photography: Were they photographed a lot as children? Did they like having their photo taken? Which photos of themselves do they remember, like and dislike? Are they photographers? Do they own a camera? Do they use a mobile phone or tablet camera? Elicit some responses from the whole class.

1 Ask students to look at the photo and answer the questions as a class.

SAMPLE ANSWERS

They are taking photographs of a work of art on their mobile phones to share with friends and perhaps post online.

2 [2.6] Ask students to read through the three questions, then discuss them with a partner. Play the recording and ask students in their pairs to compare their ideas with those of the speaker. Ask students to comment on the speaker's ideas and have a short class discussion about the issues raised.

ANSWERS

The speaker says:

1 People spend as much time recording and sharing experiences as they do having them.
2 Audiences take photos, send texts and tweet during the event.
3 He thinks we need to be careful not to overuse these tools in case they detract from the experience itself.

Audioscript [2.6]

Do the different types of digital media available today change the way people experience the world? Perhaps. They certainly change the way we record and share those experiences with others. Never before has so much been written for such a large audience; nor have so many photos been taken and distributed so widely. Digital media – that is blogs, social networking sites, internet forums, online photo albums, downloadable music, viral marketing – have increased accessibility to others' experiences enormously.

But do digital media change the experience itself? That's a more difficult question to answer. In a way they do. If you go to a concert or a festival, or even a conference these days, everyone's busy recording and sharing the experience as it happens: taking photos, sending texts or tweeting. In fact, people seem to spend almost as much time recording the experience as they do actually watching or listening to what's going on. Does this detract from the experience itself? Some would argue that it does. I'm inclined to think that it's a question of moderation – as with any tool. It's a good thing as long as you don't let it take over your life.

3 [2.6] Ask students in their pairs to list the digital media mentioned, then play the recording again for them to check. Elicit answers from the whole class and note them on the board.

ANSWER

He mentioned: blogs, social networking sites, internet forums, online photo albums, downloadable music, viral marketing.

4 Ask students to categorise the activities as indicated, and then work in groups of four to discuss their answers. Elicit answers from the whole class. You may wish to make a class table on the board and discuss the differences in use.

Homework

Ask students to write 100–150 words to describe a particular photo and explain why it is important to them. They can bring their writing to class in a subsequent lesson and exchange it with a partner for feedback and comment.

8a Sinkholes

Lead-in

Personal response

Ask students to talk to a partner about when and how they first used a computer, and how and when they first used the Internet. Elicit some responses from the whole class.

Reading

1 Ask students to tell a partner about their use of blogs. Elicit some responses from the whole class.

2 Ask students to discuss the features of blogs listed and their reactions to them. Elicit ideas from the whole class.

3 Ask students to look at the photo and write a list of questions about it. Then ask them to read the blog and see if their questions were answered. Alternatively, when students have made their lists of questions you could ask them to feed back to the class and write all the questions up on the board so that they can check for the answers to all of them while they read the blog.

Background note

The Republic of Guatemala is a Central American country with a population of around fourteen million people. It has a coast on both the Pacific Ocean and the Caribbean. The capital is Guatemala City, which is inland, and is centred on an old Mayan city, some of which is a park museum. In 2002, it had a population of 2.3 million, but it has expanded rapidly in the past ten years. The people are a mixture of indigenous Indian races (descended from the Maya) and (mostly) Spanish-speaking Europeans. The country has very important, rich nature reserves with great biodiversity, and many rare and endangered species.

4 Ask students to choose the options to complete the sentences individually, then check with a partner. Elicit answers from the whole class.

ANSWERS

1 see the holes
2 man-made
3 insecure foundations
4 it was caused by an unexpected weather event
5 not the first of its kind

5 Ask students to work with a partner to find and discuss which of the features listed in Exercise 2 are offered by this particular blog. Elicit suggestions from the whole class. Read the information in the *Wordbuilding* box about compound nouns, and if necessary refer to the information and practice on page 67 of the Workbook.

ANSWERS

a an insider's view (*I decided to head down there to look for myself rather than take anyone else's word for it.*)
b more personal content (*One told me she wasn't waiting to find out. 'My family and I are getting out of here.' ... Whatever you call it, the effect is both amazing and frightening.*)
c a writer's passion for a subject (*I've spent ten years photographing sinkholes ...*)
d a genuine, even if sometimes biased opinion (*So strictly speaking, this isn't a real sinkhole.*)
e the chance of dialogue with the writer (*I'd be very interested to hear from any readers if you've seen anything similar.*)

Language focus passive reporting verbs

6 Ask students to look at the two sentences and answer the questions individually, then check with a partner. Elicit answers from the class and discuss them.

ANSWERS

1 A: + *that* + clause; B: + *to*-infinitive
2 No, but we assume it's some kind of expert.
3 A passive verb is used because either the writer doesn't know who the agent is (or it is a mixture of people that is difficult to specify) or the writer assumes the reader is not interested in who the agent is.
4 Because it is considered more formal, impersonal and objective.

7 Ask students to find the type B passive sentences and what time they refer to individually, then check with a partner. Elicit answers from the whole class.

ANSWERS

1 In 2007, a similar sinkhole ... **was reported to have swallowed** about a dozen homes. (Past)
2 What **is believed to have happened** here is that water leaked from the sewer system ... (Past)
3 **It is not expected to happen** again (Future)
4 Other sinkholes like this **are known to exist** (Present)

8 Read through the information about passive reporting verbs in the language box with the class and check that they understand it. If you feel it useful and necessary at this point, have students read the information and do the extra activities on page 166.

Ask students to use the information to rewrite the sentences in the answers to Exercise 7 as type A. They should do this individually, then check with a partner. Elicit answers from the whole class.

ANSWERS

1 In 2007, it was reported that a similar sinkhole had swallowed about a dozen homes.
2 It is believed that in this case the water leaked from the sewer system.
3 It is not expected that it will happen again
4 It is known that other sinkholes like this exist

Grammar note

Point out to students that a major reason for using passive reporting verbs is for the writer to distance themselves from the people involved, and concentrate on the facts and actions. This style is very often used in academic writing, and also in reports, which need to be impersonal. It is important for students to master this register, particularly if they go on to study in English, or if they use written English in their work.

9 Ask students to rewrite the sentences individually and then check with a partner. Elicit the answers from the class as complete sentences.

ANSWERS

1 are said to be the most beautiful sinkholes in the world.
2 are thought to have been very important to the Mayan people because there were so few rivers in the region.
3 were known to have built important settlements near the cenotes.
4 was believed that the cenotes led to the next world after death.
5 are reported to be increasingly popular with tourists.
6 are expected to be closed to the public.

Speaking and writing

10 Read through the instructions and topics with the class, and give them a set time to think of a specific topic and prepare to talk about it (perhaps ten minutes maximum). You could suggest they make some very brief notes. Then ask them to talk to their partner about their experience.

11 Ask students to produce a 150-word written version of their talk as a personal blog, using passive reporting verbs. You could show them the model below to give them the idea. They could then put their blogs up on the wall, and go round and read each other's. You could ask them which one(s) they like best, and why. Discuss the quality of the writing and invite suggestions for improvements.

MODEL ANSWER

Most people who visit England have heard of Stonehenge, but if you are interested in Stone Age monuments, why not try visiting the Rollright Stones in Oxfordshire, which are believed to have been erected at about the same time? Although they form a much smaller stone circle, the great thing about the Rollright Stones is that they attract far fewer visitors. Situated in a tranquil part of the English countryside, without any visitor centre or coach parks, you can enjoy the Rollright Stones in peace and quiet. In this way you can get a much better feeling of how the original builders experienced them. Like Stonehenge, they are thought to have been used in Neolithic times for rituals and also for burials.

8b Creating a buzz

Lead-in

Personal response

Ask students to say what their favourite sweet snack or drink is. Encourage them to give the name of the producer and the product. They should also say why they like that particular product, e.g. *I like ... Extra Strong Mints because they are really minty and clear my head.* Elicit a variety of responses from around the class.

Speaking and listening

1 Ask students to answer the five questions by themselves first, then get into groups of four to discuss their answers. Elicit responses from the whole class.

2 Ask students to stay in their groups and discuss the questions about the photo.

ANSWER

1 lemonade
2 the chance to use a good wi-fi signal
3 A laptop on display, and home-made posters with the phrase 'hot-spot'.

3 [2.7] Ask students to read through the questions to focus their listening, and elicit what they think the term 'a straight sell' means (selling something immediately, without any customer or brand loyalty). Then play the recording and ask students to listen and answer. They can check their ideas with a partner. Play it again for them to check, complete and correct their answers. Elicit answers from the whole class.

ANSWERS

1 They must become fans of your company and its products.
2 Only occasionally, but they are getting better at it.
3 To interact, for example, sharing stories, doing surveys and entering competitions.
4 By offering an element of fun.

Audioscript [2.7]

P = presenter, S = Sarah Palmer

P: OK, we hear about companies being customer-focused all the time these days, but there's no point being focused on your customer if they aren't focused on you. Sarah Palmer from the e-marketing consultancy firm, Excite, is here to tell us how organisations can generate that kind of interest. Sarah …

S: Thanks, Greg. The key to good marketing is being able to turn your customers into fans, in other words people who want to share a passion for what you do with others. These days, a company has no hope of doing that unless they use social media: not just to sell their products and services, but to really involve people in what they're doing. Basically, customers want to know your story, and they want to learn something. And you, the company, want to get them to buy into your story. There's no doubt that a straight sell can work occasionally, for example, if a customer happens to be looking for a particular thing at a particular time and an ad pops up on their screen. Companies are getting much better at engineering that kind of event, but creating a loyal following is far more effective.

P: So, can you give us some examples of organisations that use social media effectively, in the way that you're describing?

S: Yes, we've been looking at examples of best practice in social media marketing and a good one is *National Geographic*. They actively encourage fan interaction: inviting users to share travel stories, or to do surveys on how ecologically they live, and then compare their scores with their friends. You can enter competitions, and there are also links to different causes you can support – like helping to protect an endangered species.

P: OK. That all sounds great, but is there no mention of selling at all?

S: Yes, there is … there are offers of discounts for magazine subscribers, coupons you can use for *National Geographic* products. It's a business too …

P: And I see how this fan-building works for an organisation with a worthy mission. But what about a company that's just trying to sell a regular product, like bathroom cleaner? They have no alternative but to present the product in an ordinary way.

S: No, it's really no different – the same principles apply. Try to tell a story or engage customers in a way that's fun. No matter what you're selling, if you can involve people, you'll find an audience. I was recently looking at a company that sells tea and their website had this great widget that gave you an interactive tour of the teas of China. It was really fun, and you wouldn't believe the number of varieties and how much some of them cost. It's a whole other world …

4 [2.7] Ask students to read through the sentences and, based on what they can remember, decide if they are true or false. Then play the recording for them to check their answers. Elicit answers from the whole class.

ANSWERS

1 T
2 F ('they want to know your story')
3 T
4 F ('they offer discounts on subscriptions')
5 T
6 T

Idioms business buzz words

5 Read the description of what a 'buzz word' is and elicit examples from students, if possible. Then ask them to discuss the meanings of the buzz words in the sentences in pairs. Elicit suggestions from the whole class.

ANSWERS

1 interested in *or* concentrating on what the customer really wants
2 believe and be interested in (your story)
3 the best ideas and systems used in the industry

6 Ask students to match the words and definitions individually, then check with a partner. Elicit answers from the whole class.

ANSWERS

1 g	4 i	7 c
2 d	5 e	8 b
3 f	6 h	9 a

Vocabulary note

Stress to students that buzz words are useful because they can sum up an idea, or a whole set of ideas, in a succinct and forceful way. This is especially useful when dealing with something very up to date. However, also point out that such expressions can go out of fashion as quickly as they came in, so students need to keep their eye on current use, and not use out-of-date expressions. Also, if buzz words are overused, it can become rather annoying and boring, so they should be used with care.

Language focus expressions with *no*

7 Ask students to match the halves individually and check with a partner before they check in the audioscript at the back. Elicit answers from the whole class.

ANSWERS

1 d 2 a 3 f 4 c 5 e 6 b

Extra activity

Ask students to write a sentence of their own starting with the phrases in 1–6 in Exercise 7. It does not have to be related to business. Ask them to get into pairs to share and discuss their sentences. Elicit examples from around the class.

8 Read through the expressions with *no* in the language focus box with the class and ensure they understand the structures. If you feel it would be useful at this stage, read the further information and do the practice activities on page 167. Ask students to rewrite the eight statements individually, then check with a partner. Elicit the answers from the whole class.

ANSWERS

1 There's no question that it's a well-constructed website.
2 I had no difficulty (in) navigating my way around the site.
3 Also, no matter which page I visited, there was always something interesting to look at.
4 I liked the fact that there was no suggestion of having to buy something / anything.
5 I was surprised that there was no mention of shipping costs.
6 You have no choice but to accept their delivery terms.
7 I think that no matter what the retailer does, they must make the buying process transparent.
8 Personally, I had no intention of buying anything.

9 Ask students to think about a commercial website they have used, and write some sentences about it using the phrases given. They should then discuss their experiences with a partner. Elicit examples from the whole class.

SAMPLE ANSWERS

1 I had no problems finding what I wanted *or* navigating to the relevant page.
2 There's no question that they have done a very professional job.
3 No matter what you do, check the delivery costs before you agree to buy anything.

Speaking

10 Read through the instructions with the class and ensure that they know what to do. Ask them to work in groups of four to discuss ideas. Ask one of each group to be the secretary and keep a record of the suggestions they come up with.

Elicit ideas from the secretaries, and possibly record them on the board. Ask students to vote on the three suggestions they think are best. Discuss their ideas further with the whole class.

SAMPLE ANSWERS

1 A map showing where the van will be on different days and at different times.
2 If they can get twenty friends to suggest a new location where they would like it to be, each of the twenty gets a 15% discount when they visit.
3 A place where you can post pictures or photos of yourself near one of the vans. Winner gets a £20 voucher to spend on snacks.
4 A fun and games area on the site – name the snack, find the van, etc.

Homework

Ask students to write a report to the Mosushi company, suggesting some ways that they can get more of a following on a social networking site. They can bring their reports to class in a subsequent lesson, exchange them with a partner and discuss each other's writing.

8c A hacker's life

Lead-in

Personal response

Ask students to work in groups of four to compare their use of computers, laptops, the Internet, email, social networking sites, mobile devices, tablets, etc. What do they each use most and why? Elicit some details from the whole class.

Reading

1 Check students are familiar with the words in the box. Ask them to discuss the issue in pairs using these words, then compare their ideas with another pair. Elicit ideas from the whole class.

SAMPLE ANSWERS

Change your wi-fi password frequently.

Don't keep details of your identity on your computer.

Don't take part in financial transactions with small unknown companies.

Back up your data regularly on a separate drive.

2 Ask students to read the two definitions and say which one they think is correct for the word *hacker*. Ask them to read the article to see what the author's view is.

ANSWER

The author's view is definition 1.

3 Ask students to read the questions to focus their reading, then answer them individually. They should then check with a partner. Explain to them before they read that DefCon is an annual conference held in Las Vegas each year. Elicit answers from the whole class.

ANSWERS

1 They find gaps in systems where security could be breached (and pass on these findings to the relevant companies).
2 They are not young 'geeks' involved in illegal activities, or criminals.
3 They look at all kinds of security systems (e.g. door locks, mobile phones).
4 They pass on the information to the companies / industries who designed the system.
5 That they are not interested in the usual signs of social status.
6 cyber game
7 They are ignorant about online security issues.
8 They are passionate about online freedom.

4 Ask students to discuss their views on hackers and whether they have changed since reading the article. Elicit some responses from the whole class.

Vocabulary notes

The following words and expressions from the text may be unfamiliar:

an accomplishment = an achievement, a success

to break in = to enter a building without a key, as a criminal does

car marques = the make of a car (e.g. BMW, Mercedes)

to be doomed = to be going to have something bad happen to you

a geek = a boring person who is only interested in technology and has no social skills

gross = (in this context) serious, important (it can also mean *unpleasant*)

to pit someone against = to make a contest between

to plug the holes = to repair the problems

scrutiny = detailed examination

to strew = to throw around randomly

Critical thinking identifying personal opinions

5 Ask students to find and highlight the adjectives and adverbs used to express the writer's personal opinions. They should do this individually, then check with a partner. Elicit suggestions from the whole class.

ANSWERS

(para 1) worrying realisation
(para 2) passionate hackers; a gross misrepresentation
(para 3) an enormous impact; a great service
(para 4) Ironically; Unfortunately,
(para 5) It's kind of refreshing
(para 6) The room is mesmerising
(para 8) There is no greater ignorance; I'm happy to admit; Sadly; passionate about online freedom

Extra activity

Ask students to look at the adverbs and adjectives from the previous activity and discuss their effectiveness: in what ways do they make the article more interesting and the arguments more powerful? Elicit the following points:

- intensifying adjectives, e.g. *enormous, gross,* add strength to the noun or verb they are related to
- exaggeration makes the arguments more powerful, e.g. *no greater ignorance*
- interesting and unusual words make the ideas expressed more striking, e.g. *mesmerising, refreshing*
- several words express personal emotion, e.g. *worrying, happy, sadly*

Point out that all these categories of words indicate that the article expresses personal opinions. They would not be used in an objective or scientific article, or in writing that aims to appear objective and neutral.

6 Ask students to consider these three points individually, then discuss their ideas with a partner. Elicit ideas from the whole class.

SAMPLE ANSWERS

1 It was a refreshing mix of people from different backgrounds.
2 Sadly, our personal data is not really safe.
3 We should respect them because they are dedicated and are trying to help us.

Word focus *break*

7 Ask students to find the expressions with *break* as indicated, and discuss them with a partner. Elicit suggested meanings from the whole class.

ANSWERS

break in = to enter by force

break the habit = to interrupt or stop doing something you often or always do

break the etiquette = to fail to follow the correct procedure

8 Ask students to match the expressions and the definitions individually, then check with a partner. Elicit answers from the whole class.

ANSWERS

1 e 2 c 3 a 4 f 5 b 6 d

9 Ask students to write a sentence using one of the expressions with *break*, then read the sentence to a partner, omitting the expression; the partner has to guess what the missing phrase is.

Extra activity

Once they have done the activity with a partner, they can either go round the class saying their sentences to other people and guessing one another's missing phrases, or give their sentences in a whole-class setting for everyone to guess.

Speaking

10 Ask students to get into pairs and read their information (on pages 154 and 155) to prepare for the roleplay. They should then roleplay the meeting. They could then change role and carry out the roleplay again with a different partner.

Circulate and monitor their roleplays, and feed back to the class on their use of language.

Homework

Ask students to write 100–150 words on their own IT security (without giving away passwords!) and say how they may change after what they have read. They can bring their writing to a subsequent class and exchange it with a partner for comment and criticism.

8d A podcast

Lead-in

Working with words

Write the verb *to cast* on the board, and ask students to say what it means and give some examples of it in use. Meanings include: 1 to throw something as widely or as far away as possible; 2 to mould things in metal; 3 to give somebody a part to play. Then write the verb *to broadcast* on the board and ask for definitions and examples (to spread news or information).

Real life making a podcast

1 Ask students to discuss their views on news with a partner. Elicit responses from the whole class.

2 [2.8] Ask the class to respond to the photo, describing it and suggesting what kind of news story it might relate to. Then play the recording and elicit answers from the class.

ANSWER
A science and environment report

Audioscript [2.8]

P = presenter, **M** = Martin Roddick

P: Hello and welcome to the *Nature Today* podcast. Today we're going to look at some new evidence about what is arguably one of the most spectacular sights in nature: the phenomenon where waves glow at night and mirror the stars with lots of tiny, blue lights. It's been known for some time that the source of this light is organisms called phytoplankton. But how they produce the strange blue light has been a mystery. Until now. Here's Martin Roddick of the Oceanographic Institute.

M: Hello. There are a number of different sea creatures that are bioluminescent, in other words that are able to glow in the dark. The creatures which have this ability tend to spend most of their lives in deep ocean waters, which suggests that being able to light yourself up, as it were, is useful for finding food or scaring away predators, or perhaps just lighting your way as you move around. But the most common bioluminescent organisms – phytoplankton – live near the surface. And it's these that create this strange, blue light that people see on beaches and in waves.

P: And how do they do it?

M: It seems that electrical signals in the phytoplankton cause a chemical reaction to take place, producing a blue light. The light is usually emitted in waves, so it's reasonable to assume that the electrical signal is generated by motion in the water.

P: Thank you, Martin. And if you'd like to know more about this research, you can read details of the study on the OI website at …

3 [2.8] Ask students to read the questions to focus their listening, then play the recording again for them to answer. Elicit answers from the whole class.

ANSWERS
1 That the source of the light is from small sea creatures called phytoplankton.
2 Now they think that motion in the water causes electrical signals to make a chemical reaction in the phytoplankton's body, producing a blue light.

Speaking skill hedging language

4 [2.8] Make sure students understand what *hedging* language is. Ask them to read the six facts. Play the recording, pausing after each expression for students to find the hedging phrase in the language box.

ANSWERS
1 Arguably …
2 tend to
3 which suggests that
4 perhaps
5 It seems that
6 It's reasonable to assume

Vocabulary note

Hedging language is used for a variety of reasons: to sound more objective and scientific, to remain neutral, and to present proven factual information clearly, and separate it from subjective conjecture.

Pronunciation word stress

5a [2.9] Read the question with the class, and ask them to think about where the stress will fall. Then play the recording for them to underline the stressed syllables. Elicit answers.

ANSWER
'**Today** we're going to look at some new **evidence** about what is **arguably** one of the most **spectacular** sights in **nature**: the **phenomenon** where waves glow at night and **mirror** the stars with lots of **tiny**, blue lights.'

In two-syllable words the stress often (but not always) falls on the first syllable. In three-syllable words the stress generally falls on the first syllable (in four syllables the stress is usually on the second).

5b Ask students to practise saying the sentence to themselves, then check their stress with a partner. Allow them further time to practise.

5c Ask students to look at the verbs which are stressed on the second syllable, and work out what they have in common.

ANSWER
All these verbs have a prefix as the first syllable, which is unstressed.

6 Read all the instructions with the class. Ask the groups to prepare their podcast, then deliver the podcast to the other group of three.

8e The invisible man

Lead-in

Personal response
Ask students to discuss the concept of *invisibility*. What things really are invisible to us? (e.g. gases such as oxygen, water vapour, bacteria, electricity) How do we know they are there? (e.g. scientific proof – water vapour condenses on a cold mirror in the bathroom.) Would it be useful if we could be invisible? What would be positive and what negative? (e.g. listening to what others are saying about us could have positive and negative effects.)

Writing an online news report

1 Ask the class to look at the photo and answer the question. Encourage a whole-class discussion, eliciting ideas from everyone. Then ask them to read the report and find out if they were correct.

ANSWER

He has been painted so that he blends into the shelves of cans of drinks behind him (it looks as if he is standing behind the shelves, but he is actually in front).

2 Ask the class to discuss this question together.

SAMPLE ANSWERS

The photos trick you into thinking you see something different, so they are fascinating.

People are interested because the artist goes to extreme lengths (standing perfectly still for several hours) to create an artwork which doesn't last long.

The story appeals to people because the artist is making a statement about issues that affect us all (e.g. plasticisers in drinks) and that he feels strongly about.

3 Ask students to read the advice about what sort of information a news report should give, and then find this information in the news report from Exercise 1.

ANSWERS

Who? Liu Bolin

What? He made a striking photo of himself camouflaged in front of supermarket shelves.

Where? In his studio in Beijing

When? In the summer of 2011

Why? He wanted to protest against the use of plasticiser in foods.

How? He stood there while his assistants 'painted him in'.

Writing skill cautious language

Extra activity

Ask students to explain the meaning of the adjective *cautious* (approaching something with care and respect, exploring the whole situation before getting involved, not jumping in with both feet) and give some examples about times when they were cautious (e.g. *When I was in India I once saw a snake's tail in a pipe I had to walk past every day, so I was always cautious when I approached that particular pipe after that, and whenever I saw any other pipes*).

4a Ask students to read the instructions and descriptions of cautious language, then find examples of the language in the report. They should do this individually, then check with a partner. Elicit answers from the whole class.

ANSWERS

1 he seemed to have disappeared; appear to have struck a chord
2 is supposed to express
3 generally
4 presumably

4b Ask students to rewrite the sentences individually, then compare and discuss their ideas with a partner. Elicit sentences from the whole class.

SAMPLE ANSWERS

1 His pictures generally carry a strong social message.
2 Apparently, he became internationally famous when a New York art dealer bought some of his works.
3 His work might make people think more about their surroundings.
4 He seems to want to draw our attention to what we cannot see in a picture.
5 Bolin is said to have used friends at first to help him paint his pictures. / It is said (that) Bolin used friends at first to help him paint his pictures.

5 Ask students to write the report as in the instructions. They can do this for homework if you prefer.

6 Ask students to exchange their writing and comment on each other's reports, checking that they have followed the criteria in the bullet points.

Extra activity

Based on their partner's comments, students can write an improved second draft.

8f Talking dictionaries

Before you watch

1 Students work in pairs to discuss the questions. Take feedback from the class.

2 Ask students to discuss the questions.

While you watch

3 Give students time to read the words in the glossary. Play the video for students to compare their views in Exercise 2 to what the speaker says.

ANSWER

The speaker says that lesser spoken languages can be saved by spreading the message that these smaller languages and linguistic diversity are important; also by expanding their reach by using technology, for example by putting them on the Internet.

4 Give students time to read the questions. Then play the first part of the video (to 01.02) for them to answer.

ANSWERS

1 half of them
2 There is social pressure which devalues small languages.
3 They are using technology, e.g. social media and text messaging.

5 Give students time to read the summary, then play the second part of the video (01.03 to 02.29) for them to write the missing words.

ANSWERS

1 presence	3 fluent	5 knowledge
2 Internet	4 thousands	6 revitalise

6 Give students time to read the questions. Play the last part of the video (02.30 to end) for them to answer.

ANSWERS

1 to put their language on the Internet
2 Their language is just as good as other languages.
3 It has been launched as an iPhone application.
4 to scientists, journalists and indigenous communities

7 Give students time to read the questions and write the words. Play the video again for them to check.

After you watch

8 Students work in pairs to roleplay creating a talking dictionary, according to the instructions.

9 Students discuss the questions in groups.

Videoscript

It's been estimated that of the 7,000 languages in the world, half of them are endangered and may disappear in this century. And this is happening for a variety of reasons, mostly because of social pressure and attitudes that devalue those small languages and tell people that they're not worthwhile, they're not modern enough to continue using.

00.23 Some people see technology as a threat to the existence of small languages, but the really savvy small language communities are using technology to sustain themselves, to expand their reach, to broadcast themselves out through many different channels, whether it be social media, text messaging, to use technology as a way to survive.

01.03 Under their Enduring Voices programme, which I co-direct, we've been building talking dictionaries. And the goal of the talking dictionaries is to give some very small languages a first-ever presence on the Internet. We've been working with a variety of communities around the world. One of them is the Siletz Dee-ni language, which is spoken in the state of Oregon. Siletz Dee-ni has probably one fluent speaker and a small handful of people who have some knowledge of the language. And we've been working with Bud Lane, who's the … acknowledged as the fluent speaker. He has sat down and patiently recorded thousands and thousands of words in the language. And we bring these recordings back to my lab at Swarthmore College, and my students work on them and create a talking dictionary.

So, you can go to the Siletz Dee-ni talking dictionary, type in the word 'salmon' or the word 'basket' and you begin to see the very rich lexicon of terms that they have, and you can start to appreciate some of the cultural knowledge.

02.06 ***Talking Dictionary*** Basket bottom. Basket design.

02.17 The Siletz nation is using this talking dictionary as a tool to revitalise the language as they are conducting language classes and helping the younger generation acquire some of the language through the talking dictionary.

02.30 We've also built a talking dictionary for a language called Matukar Panau. This is a very small language spoken in Papua New Guinea by six hundred people. They all live in one village. They knew about the Internet before they had ever actually seen the Internet and when our *National Geographic* team visited the village a couple of years ago, they said: 'We would like our language to be on the Internet.' And this was really interesting because they hadn't seen the Internet yet, they had heard about the Internet. And so with collaboration from the community, we built a talking dictionary for the language.

03.06 ***Interviewer*** How about 'a white pig'?

And how about 'a black pig'?

And how about 'my pig'?

03.26 The following year, they got electricity in the village and then eventually they got an Internet connection. And the very first time they went on the Internet, they were able to see and hear their own language spoken. And this sends a very powerful message that their language is just as good as any other, even though it may be very small and no-one has ever heard of it, it's just as good as any other – it can exist in a high-tech medium.

03.50 The very first talking dictionary I built was for the Tuvan language. Tuvan is spoken by nomadic people in Siberia. They're migratory, they raise animals: goats and sheep and camels.

They have a very rich lexicon pertaining to the natural world and the environment that they live in.

I built the Tuvan talking dictionary and I also launched it as an iPhone application, so you can actually hear the Tuvan language, and many other languages in the future, I hope, on a smartphone platform.

04.32 The AAAS is a great venue to talk about language diversity. It's not a topic that you might typically think of in connection with a gathering of scientists, but linguistic diversity is one of the most important parts of our human heritage. It is … It gives us insight into history and to culture, and to how the brain functions. Without linguistic diversity, we really wouldn't be human.

And so scientists as well as indigenous communities are responding to a crisis of language extinction. And that's what this panel is about and that's why we've chosen the AAAS – we want to get the word out to, not only to scientists, but to journalists and to indigenous communities whose languages are struggling to survive, that there's a common goal, that we can work together.

Unit 8 Review

Grammar

1 Ask students to read the blog and complete it using passive reporting phrases.

ANSWERS
1 It is said to be
2 is thought to be
3 it is already known
4 the Mariana Trench was formed
5 is reported to have spent
6 It is hoped that his film will shed

2 Ask students to read the article again and answer the questions.

ANSWERS
1 a great chasm, the deepest part of the ocean
2 to find out more about its biology

3 Ask students to complete the statements.

ANSWERS
1 where, that 2 of, of 3 in, but

4 Ask students to work in pairs to think of the place and write the sentence about it.

Vocabulary

5 Students choose the best options to complete the sentences.

ANSWERS
1 post
2 writes
3 rocket
4 box
5 game
6 win-win

6 Students work in pairs to discuss their favourite websites and answer the questions.

Real life

7 Ask students to rewrite the sentences to make them less certain.

ANSWERS
1 … seems to have an obsession …
2 Arguably the most difficult thing …
3 He is reported to have tweeted …
4 … tend to be scientists, …
5 … are likely to be manned …
6 … is estimated to be 11 km deep.

8 Students work in pairs to prepare and present a podcast.

Speaking

9 Students work in pairs to describe how they use digital media.

Unit 9 The music in us

Lead-in

Personal response

Ask students to tell a partner what the last live music they heard was, answering the questions *who, what, when* and *where*. Elicit some responses from the whole class and encourage other students to express their opinions.

1 Ask the class to look at the picture and describe what they can see, then answer the questions. Elicit ideas, and the meaning of *busker* and *to busk*.

ANSWERS

1 *To busk* means to play music in the street, and a *busker* is the person who does it.
2 Students' own answers
3 Buskers can play all sorts of music, though some kinds of music might be more typical in different countries.

2 [2.10] Ask students to listen and note answers to the questions. Play the recording twice through. Ask them to compare their notes with a partner, and then elicit answers from the whole class.

ANSWERS

1 to get more confidence as a performer
2 She started busking when she was seventeen; then she met and started playing with another musician, and they made a CD together.
3 R&B, (soulful) ballads; soothing and melodic music

Audioscript [2.10]

Like a lot of buskers, I started busking because I wanted to get more confidence as a performer; it wasn't really about the money. I'm a singer-songwriter – I don't have my own band, and it's not as easy to get gigs as a solo artist. Also I'd always been drawn to buskers. I don't think there's anything better than coming across a really good live performance on the street when you're not expecting it.

So, I went out busking when I was seventeen – just me and my acoustic guitar – not in my home town, because I didn't want people to recognise me, but in a nearby town. It was pretty nerve-racking at first, and I think that came across in my performance because I didn't get much attention, nor a lot of money. I think the first time I got about $15 and a cheese sandwich that someone threw into my guitar case.

But I got better at it, no doubt, and it had the desired effect of building my confidence. And then one time around Christmas, another musician approached me, a saxophonist who worked on and off as a session musician, and he asked if I'd like to team up with him. And I did. And I guess that's how my career got started. We play R&B mainly, some soulful ballads, some instrumentals … we prefer music that's soothing and melodic. We've now made our first single together and I'm pretty hopeful it'll get picked up by a record company …

3 Ask students to put the words in the different categories, then elicit answers from the whole class and write them on the board.

ANSWERS

a genres of music: dance, folk
b musicians: busker, solo artist
c compositions: ballad, instrumental
d describing music: melodic, soothing
e describing taste: eclectic, sophisticated

Extra activity

Discuss the meanings of the words in Exercise 3 with the class. Then ask students to work in pairs to add more words to each category. Brainstorm ideas from the whole class and add them to the lists on the board.

4 Ask students to discuss the questions in groups of four, then elicit responses from the whole class.

Homework

Ask students to write around 150 words on *Music in my life*. In a subsequent class, ask them to exchange their writing with a partner for checking and comment.

9a World music

Lead-in

Personal response

Ask the class to say what they understand by the term *world music* and to give examples, if they can. (It means music from outside the mainstream of British / American rock-pop music, particularly traditional, local, ethnic music.)

Reading

1 Ask students to work in groups of four to answer the questions. If it is a class of mixed nationalities, try to organise students into groups of the same culture or nationality as far as possible. Ask them to appoint a secretary to keep notes on their discussion. Elicit answers from the secretaries for the whole class to discuss further.

2 Ask students to read through the statements to focus their reading. Then ask them to read the interview. They can check their ideas with a partner, then discuss the answers as a whole class.

ANSWER

b

3 Ask students to match the sentences individually, then check with a partner. Elicit answers from the whole class.

ANSWERS

1 d 2 c 3 a 4 b

4 Ask students to discuss the influence of western pop music on local music. Elicit ideas from the whole class and discuss the issues further.

Language focus the adverb *just*

Extra activity

Elicit meanings of *just* from the class, and ask for example sentences. Write the ones you are given on the board.

5 Ask students to match the sentences and the meanings individually, and then check with a partner. Elicit answers from the whole class.

ANSWERS

1 e 2 b 3 d 4 f 5 a 6 c

6 Read through the information about *just* in the language focus box with the class, and ensure students understand the examples given. If you feel they need more explanation and practice, refer to page 168. Then ask them to work in pairs to put *just* into the sentences and work out the meaning. Elicit answers from the whole class.

ANSWERS

1 If you **just** took the time to listen to Ry Cooder, / If you took the time **just** to listen to Ry Cooder, you'd definitely like him. (only)
2 I've **just** heard his new single on the radio. (very recently)
3 It's **just** over ten years since they last performed. (a little)
4 You saw her live? Wow! **Just** hearing her sing gives me goosebumps. (simply) / Hearing her sing **just** gives me goosebumps. (no particular meaning)
5 The concert is in an old theatre **just** behind the bank in the High Street. (a little)
6 Thank you for the CD – it's **just** what I wanted. (exactly)
7 I **just** can't understand why so many people like his music! (simply)
8 I'm **just** as interested in the lyrics as the music. (exactly)

Pronunciation word stress: *just*

7a [2.11] Play the recording for students to listen to the stress and pronunciation. Then elicit situations where the phrases might be used.

ANSWERS

1 Someone answering the front door *or* someone getting ready to go out.
2 Someone arriving at a train station / concert / cinema for something scheduled (e.g. a train, film, etc.).
3 A student in a class.
4 Someone being offered a drink.
5 Someone in a shop.
6 Someone on a phone.
7 Someone talking about a friend of the opposite sex.
8 Someone replying to the question, 'Why do you ask that?'

7b Ask students to use the phrases from Exercise 7a in conversations of their own. Circulate and monitor their conversations.

Speaking and vocabulary themes of songs

8 Read through the instructions and the word list with the class, then ask them to think of their five songs individually, and note the incidence of the words in the list. Ask them to get into groups of four to discuss the results and see what the commonest themes were.

Homework

Ask students to write 150 words about their favourite song of all time, including details about the musicians, themes, instruments used, melody, etc. In a subsequent lesson, they can exchange their writing with a partner for comment.

9b Healing music

Lead-in

Personal response
Bring in two completely different pieces of music to class (e.g. a gentle classical piece and a loud rock song) and play a minute of each to students. Ask them to discuss their reaction to each with a partner, then elicit responses from the whole class.

Listening

1 Ask students in pairs to discuss the questions about how music affects their mood. Elicit some responses from the whole class.

SAMPLE ANSWER
Some people might like to play soft, relaxing music after a stressful day at work; lively dance music for a party or when doing exercise or physical activities like cleaning; invigorating, fast or loud music when driving to keep them awake, or more soothing music to calm them down if they are driving in stressful situations.

2 Check students understand the meaning of *therapeutic* (good for physical, mental or social health; curative), and also *therapy* (treatment) and *music therapy* (treatment using music). Then ask them to discuss the effects of music with a partner. Elicit ideas from the whole class.

3 [2.12] Play the recording and ask students to identify the therapeutic properties mentioned.

ANSWERS
She mentions: relieving stress, relieving pain, helping with learning difficulties, helping with speech difficulties, combating memory loss

Audioscript [2.12]

The study of the effects of music on the brain is still a work in progress, but exciting things are coming to light all the time. We know that music activates many different parts of the brain – there's no one music centre. We also know that music has the power to release endorphins. As you're probably aware, endorphins are chemicals that are vital to our well-being, released at times of stress to help us deal with pain, but also used by the body to produce feelings of happiness, elation even. So when we listen to music, we're rewarded with this boost of feel-good chemicals. Hospitals now make use of music to calm people before surgery or for pain relief after an operation.

But what I'm particularly interested in is another recent finding: that of the close relationship between music and language. If you're someone who has to strain so as to hear what people are saying in a noisy room, the chances are that you're not musically trained. That's because we use the same part of the brain to process both music and language. So those people with musical training have improved their brain's ability to distinguish specific sounds, whether musical or simply spoken.

What are the implications of this? Well, I'm not saying you should take up the violin so that you can hear people better at parties, or in order to be a better linguist – though that's not a bad idea. There are some important medical applications here. This relationship between music and language means we could use music to help people overcome conditions like dyslexia, or other learning disorders. At Harvard, a neuroscientist called Dr Gottfried Schlaug has had amazing results using music therapy with people who had suffered strokes. He conducted experiments with people where the stroke had affected the left side of their brain – the side that principally deals with language. Before the music therapy, these patients responded to questions with incoherent sounds and phrases, but when taught to sing phrases or to speak in time to the rhythm of the music, within minutes they were able to recite their addresses, say their names, and even sing extracts of songs. The results were really remarkable.

Similar positive results have been recorded with patients with dementia and memory loss. This news should be music to our ears, if you'll forgive the pun. Degenerative memory function is going to become more of a problem for all of us as we live longer, and we clearly need to find a way to lessen the impact of this on people's lives. Music may just hold the key.

Vocabulary notes

Check students understand the following words from the recording:

dyslexia (n) = a condition that makes it difficult to read and write words correctly

learning disorder (n) = any condition that causes difficulty in an area of learning

stroke (n) = the sudden death of brain cells caused by interrupted blood flow

4 [2.12] Ask students to look at the notes and complete as much as they can in pairs, trying to remember the information from the recording. Elicit responses from the class, without saying whether they are correct or incorrect. Then play the recording again for students to check and complete the notes. Elicit the correct answers.

Read through the information in the *Wordbuilding* box with the class, and refer students to page 75 of the Workbook for further information and practice.

ANSWERS
1 many different parts
2 deal with pain and produce feelings of happiness
3 music and language
4 dyslexia and other learning disorders
5 had suffered from strokes
6 remarkable
7 we are all living longer

Idioms music

5 Ask the class to say what they think the idiom means.

ANSWER

We should be pleased to hear it.

6 Ask students to match the music idioms with their meanings individually, then check with a partner. Elicit suggestions from the whole class.

ANSWERS

1 give a contrary opinion
2 seem very relevant to
3 take things as they come
4 know what's going on
5 shout about one's achievements
6 accept responsibility
7 make a fuss

7 Ask students to think about the phrases in relation to their own experiences, and tell a partner. Elicit some examples from the whole class.

Language focus expressing purpose

8 Ask students to answer the questions about the sentences from the talk with a partner. Elicit answers from the whole class.

ANSWERS

a 1, 3 and 5 (3 and 5 use *to* + infinitive in *so as to* and *in order to*)
b can; *will, could* and *would* could also be used after *so that* in other contexts
c a noun
d more formal

9 Read through the language focus box with the class, and check that they understand the contents. If you feel it necessary at this point, use the explanations and exercises on page 168 before going further. Then ask students to rewrite the three sentences in the exercise individually, then check with a partner. Elicit answers from the whole class.

ANSWERS

1a he could join his brother's band
1b join his brother's band
2a relax
2b relaxation
3a not to confuse the patients
3b confusing the patients

Grammar notes

The negative ways of expressing purpose can be problematic for students, as the simple *to* + infinitive construction cannot be used (at least not in written or formal English). It therefore needs to be replaced by a more complex construction, e.g.

Affirmative: *I left early **to catch** the bus.*

Negative: *I left early **so as not to miss** the bus.*

or by using the more complicated structure *to* + *avoid* + *-ing* verb

*I left early **to avoid missing** the bus.*

10 Ask students to rewrite the phrases in italics individually, then check with a partner. Elicit answers from the whole class, having students read out the text sentence by sentence.

SAMPLE ANSWERS

1 to avoid sounding silly
2 in order to pronounce another set of sounds properly
3 to improve
4 so as to get
5 so that you can lose

Speaking

11 Ask the class to think about public places in which music is used (e.g. supermarkets, shopping centres, lifts) and elicit what the different purposes of playing music might be. Then ask them to suggest further situations in which it could be used. Then read through the exercise instructions with the class. Ask them to get into groups of six, with three in Group A and three in Group B. Each group should consider their situation carefully. They should then present their ideas to the other group.

SAMPLE ANSWERS

Schools: to get children exercising at the beginning of the day, to calm them down before lessons, to teach them languages, to discourage talking in lessons, etc.

Airports: to encourage people to shop, to relax people on the plane, to distract people while they are waiting.

Homework

Ask students to write 100–150 words on their positive and negative feelings about being endlessly surrounded by music in shopping centres, supermarkets, lifts, reception halls, restaurants. In a subsequent lesson they can exchange their writing with a partner for discussion and comment.

9c One love

Lead-in

Personal response

Ask students to tell the rest of the class about a musician (singer, instrumentalist, group) they like very much, saying something about the person / people, the music and why they like them so much.

Reading

1 Ask students to work in pairs and say what they know about the four musicians. Suggest they make notes about each of them. Then elicit information from the whole class; you may want to keep notes of what is said on the board.

Background notes

John Winston Lennon (1940–80) was born in Liverpool, UK. He was a singer and rhythm guitarist with The Beatles (1962–70), and was also the main songwriter with Paul McCartney. He married Cynthia Powell, then Japanese artist Yoko Ono, and had one son with each wife. With Yoko he became a major world peace activist, writing songs about peace (e.g. *Give Peace A Chance*). He was shot dead in New York in 1980, just as he was starting to make a comeback.

Bob Marley (1945–81) was born in Jamaica, and was a singer, songwriter and rhythm guitarist. He played ska, rocksteady and reggae music in the band Bob Marley & The Wailers (1963–81), and helped to spread Jamaican music and Rastafarianism to the world. He died in 1981 of cancer. The 1984 compilation record *Legend* has sold around 25 million copies worldwide.

Elvis Aaron Presley (1935–77) was born in Tupelo, Mississippi, USA, but lived in Memphis, Tennessee from the age of thirteen. He sang and played guitar from an early age, but was shy about performing. In 1954 he made recordings at Sun Records in Memphis, but his first hit was *Heartbreak Hotel* for RCA, which went straight to No 1 in 1956. A string of rockabilly-rock & roll records followed. In the 1960s he lost his way in the film-making and film-album world. He made his comeback in 1968, but he was already taking large numbers of prescription drugs, which gradually destroyed him. He died in 1977.

Michael Jackson (1958–2009) was born in Gary, Indiana, USA, the eighth of ten children, with a strict and physically abusive father. In the 1960s he was in The Jackson Five with four of his brothers, and they had a string of hits. He then started making solo albums, and by the early 80s was the dominant figure in world pop music. His 1982 album *Thriller* is the biggest-selling album of all time. He won many awards for his musical achievements, and has sold more than 750 million records worldwide. He died at home in 2009.

2 Ask students to read the headlines to focus their reading, then read the review and decide if the reviewer would agree with the headlines or not. Students can check their answers with a partner before you elicit answers from the whole class.

ANSWERS

1 Partly agree (he wasn't the first to bring reggae to a wider audience, but he was the first global reggae superstar)
2 Agree (*he is celebrated as some kind of redeeming figure, a symbol of hope*)
3 Agree (*his difficult environment instilled in him a keen sense of social justice, which came to be expressed in his music.*)
4 Partly agree (*there was no sense that he did not have time for them; simply that he was prioritising*)
5 Partly agree (we do learn a lot about him, but *you still feel there are many questions unanswered about this man who became the first Third World superstar*)
6 Agree (*they contain the sentiments of unity and love which run through almost all his work*)

3 Ask students to discuss Bob Marley in pairs, using what they know of him and his music, and ideas from the text. Then elicit some responses from the whole class.

SAMPLE ANSWERS

Ideas from the text include:

… in many developing countries, he is celebrated as some kind of redeeming figure, a symbol of hope.

'People want to listen to a message. I am not a leader, but a messenger.'

Marley experienced genuine hardship and even put his life on the line for justice.

… his songs come from the heart and appeal to others who face hardship …

… but what stays with you … is the magic of his performances. The music still sounds as fresh as it was when it was first recorded …

4 Ask students to find the words individually, then check with a partner. Elicit the answers from the whole class.

ANSWERS

1 footage	4 prevalent
2 a ghetto	5 (warring) factions
3 an outsider	6 ecstatically

Vocabulary notes

The following words and expressions from the text may be unfamiliar:

dislocation = the sense of not belonging (the literal meaning is when part of a joint comes out of it's correct position, e.g. a shoulder dislocation)

to instill sth in someone = to make part of someone

a keen sense of something = a strong feeling about

to prioritise = to put the most important things first

to redeem = to get back a former (better) status; to turn a bad situation into a good one

a shanty town = a poor area made of makeshift huts, often illegally built

Critical thinking identifying text types

5 Ask students to decide in pairs which type of review the text is. Elicit answers from the whole class.

ANSWER
c

6 Ask students to discuss the questions in pairs, then elicit answers from the whole class and widen the discussion.

SAMPLE ANSWERS
a a 'What's on' guide
b a newspaper / magazine review
c a literary review

Word focus *hit*

7 Ask the class to say what *hit* means in this context.

ANSWER
Hit means 'hit record' i.e. a successful music record, one which sells a lot of copies, and may go into the top 50, top twenty, top ten or be a number one hit – the best-selling record that week.

8 Ask students to match the sentences and definitions individually, then check with a partner. Elicit answers from the whole class.

ANSWERS
1 e 2 f 3 b 4 d 5 c 6 a

Speaking

9 Ask students to get into groups of four to discuss the charity concert. All students should keep notes on the group's ideas and decisions, and they should also decide how to present their project to the rest of the class. You might stipulate that each member of the group has to speak. You should also decide if you want students to do a presentation which involves visuals, either simple ones such as flipcharts or the classroom board, or more sophisticated ones using slide presentation software.

When all the groups have given their presentations, the class can vote on which they thought was best, saying why.

Homework

Ask students to research another famous charity concert (e.g. Live Aid, Live 8, Eric Clapton's Crossroads concerts) and write 125–150 words about it, using the five points from Exercise 9 as their framework. In a subsequent lesson, they can exchange their writing with a partner for comment and discussion.

9d Desert Island Discs

Lead-in

Personal response
Ask students to tell a partner about a record (song, piece of music) they really do not like, explaining why. Elicit some answers from the whole class and widen the discussion.

Real life your favourite music

1 Ask students to read about the *Desert Island Discs* radio programme and comment on it to a partner. Elicit some comments from the whole class. Check students understand the concept of a *desert island* (an island in a hot place, where there are no inhabitants) and a *castaway* (a person who has been washed up onto shore after a shipwreck, and is completely alone). Note that this recording is inspired by a real BBC programme, but this castaway is a fictional character.

2 [2.13] Ask students to read through the questions to focus their listening. Play the recording for them to answer and then check with a partner. Play the recording again for them to check and complete their answers. Elicit answers from the whole class.

ANSWERS
1 He's a disc jockey.
2 He has maintained a loyal following of listeners over 35 years, as well as attracting new ones.
3 Blues / Jazz. He associates it with the hot summer of 1976, and with exams.

Audioscript [2.13]

P = presenter, **F** = Frank Steel

P: Today's castaway is a disc jockey who's been hosting his own radio show for over 30 years. Where most disc jockeys come and go with the changing of fashions in music, he has managed to maintain a loyal following of listeners over the last 35 years, and to attract new ones from each new generation. He is Frank Steel. Frank, what's the secret of your continuing success?

F: That's a good question, but it isn't something I've often thought about. I don't think it's a secret, really. I take an interest in what's happening now in the music world, and I look out for new trends. People do that in other fields, like science or art. It's just that with pop music, you're not supposed to stay trendy after you're 30. But I don't agree with that.

P: So you still get excited by new music. What, for you, makes a good record?

F: I honestly don't know. What makes a particular piece of music move you is something that can't really be described or identified. I'd rather not think too much about why I like a particular song or record.

P: And what's your first record?

F: This is a song by John Etheridge, a blues and jazz guitarist. I think it was the first blues record I ever heard and it opened up a whole new world to me. I also associate it with the summer of 1976, which was a really hot summer. I was supposed to be revising for exams, but I spent most of my time lazing around in the park. It was too hot to work.

P: *Crossroad Blues* by John Etheridge. Your taste in music is very wide – eclectic some would say. How did that come about?

F: That's difficult to say. It wasn't planned, if that's what you mean. I just keep my ears open for anything interesting, and I don't confine myself to any particular source for that. It's a question of staying curious, I suppose.

Background note

John Etheridge is a jazz / fusion guitarist who was born in Lambeth, London in 1948. His father was a jazz pianist. His first success was as guitarist with the progressive rock band *Wolf* (1972–1975), and he gained real fame with *Soft Machine* (1976–1978). He also worked with the legendary jazz violinist Stephane Grapelli (1976–81), touring the world as his guitarist. Since the 1980s he has been involved with many bands and artists, not least classical crossover violinist Nigel Kennedy. In 1998, he started his own record label, Dryad, and continues to perform and record widely.

Speaking skill responding to difficult questions

3 [2.13] Ask students to look at the phrases in the language box for responding to difficult questions, then play the recording for them to listen and note the questions and the phrases Frank uses to introduce his answers. Play the recording a couple of times.

ANSWERS

a
What's the secret of your continuing success?
What, for you, makes a good record?
And what's your first record?
How did that come about?

b
That's a good question.
It's not something I've often thought about.
I honestly don't know.
That's difficult to say.

Pronunciation intonation to express uncertainty

4a [2.14] Ask students to listen and follow the pronunciation of the phrases in the box, and note which use a wavering intonation. Explain that 'wavering' intonation often has a lot of small up and down movements rather than strong, confident intonation patterns. Play the recording a couple of times for students to repeat and imitate the intonation.

ANSWER

Expressions 1, 5, 6 and 9 do not use wavering intonation.

4b [2.15] Ask students to work in pairs and listen to each other pronouncing the words with a wavering intonation. They should help each other to improve. Play the recording for them to check. Play the recording again, pausing after each one for students to repeat it chorally and individually.

5 Read through the instructions with the class. Give students time to choose their music and makes notes about themselves, including the details listed, then exchange their notes and prepare questions to ask one another.

Ask them to get into pairs and act out the interview. Then they should change roles and do it again. Encourage them to use the phrases from the language box as they answer the questions.

6 Ask students to tell the class what they found out about their partner.

Homework

Ask students to write up an imaginary *Desert Island Discs* interview with themselves as the castaway. They should write it as a dialogue or a script. In a subsequent lesson, they can exchange their writing with a partner for comment and discussion.

9e Fado

Lead-in

Personal response

Bring in a piece of traditional folk music from anywhere in the world and play it to the class. Ask them where they think it is from, what type of music it is, and what they think of it.

Writing a description

1 Ask students to discuss their traditional music. If you are teaching a monocultural group, ask them to work in pairs to make notes about traditional folk music from their culture. If you are teaching a multicultural group, pair students with people from a different culture and ask them to describe their own traditional folk music. Elicit details from the whole class. With a monocultural class, you can compile a list of features on the board, and have everyone add to it and comment in a whole-class discussion. With a multicultural class, make a chart on the board with a section for each culture, and have students explain their own traditional music to the others.

2 Ask students to read the two questions to focus their reading, then read the article. Elicit answers from the whole class.

ANSWERS

1 Fado is a traditional style of Portuguese music: it's sad, intense, emotional, dramatic, and tells a story, often of the pain of separation.
2 It used to be popular only in Portugal and former Portuguese colonies. Now it has an international following.

3 Ask students to find examples of the elements of description in the article. Before they start, elicit the meaning of *simile* and some examples, or tell students what it is if they do not know (a comparison which uses *as … as* or *like*, e.g. *she is as pretty as a rose; her eyes are like bright stars*). Ask students to do the exercise individually, then check their answers with a partner. Elicit answers from the whole class.

ANSWERS

1 sultry, sheer (drama)
2 sad, pain and hardship
3 one sultry evening, dimly lit café
4 'piercing the listener's body like a knife' (paragraph 1)
5 'you'll either love it or you'll hate it' 'you can't ignore it' (paragraph 1); 'you may hate it, but I suspect you will love it' (paragraph 2)

Background note

Mariza, born Marisa dos Reis Nunes in Mozambique in 1973, has risen to become one of Portugal's top fado singers. Starting out singing gospel, soul and jazz, she moved into fado with her 2001 record *Fado em Mim*, which sold an astonishing 140,000 copies – unheard of for the genre. She has been classified as a member of the 'New Fado' movement, and has on occasions added other musical genres in with her fado singing. She sang a duet with Sting at the Athens 2004 Olympics, and also performed at Live 8. She is now in great demand worldwide, and has sung everywhere from New York's Carnegie Hall to London's Albert Hall and Sydney Opera House, as well as making TV performances around the world.

Writing skill parallel structures

4a Read through the instructions and example with the class, so they can see what is meant by 'balance' and 'parallel structures' in the two parts of the sentence (i.e. using a similar construction or similar order of words). Ask them to find the other structures individually, then check with a partner. Elicit answers from the whole class.

ANSWERS

1 *either* + pronoun + verb, *or* + pronoun + verb
2 *like* + noun + clause, *unlike* + noun + clause
3 *either* + noun phrase, *or* + noun phrase, *or* + noun phrase
4 *by* + *-ing*, *by* + *-ing*

4b Read the instructions and example with the class, and ask them to do the same with the other sentences individually, then check with a partner. Elicit answers from the whole class.

ANSWERS

1 Mariza is young, talented and energetic.
2 She sings both traditional and more modern songs.
3 Either you can book in advance or you can pay on the door.
4 You can spend hours wandering around the old town, visiting cafés and listening to live music.
5 The music fuses both traditional Spanish folk music and elements of North African music.

Grammar note

Explain to students that by using parallel structures, they will help their readers by patterning the language. This can be done by familiar set structures such as *either … or …, neither … nor …, not only … but also …, both … and …*. But it can also be done effectively by repeating the verb form, e.g. *He helped **by working** with them and **by giving** them his free time.*

Point out that such writing has a natural rhythm which makes it more pleasant to read or listen to, and easier to follow. It can also help to highlight contrasts or similarities.

5 Ask students to write about a traditional type of music or dance from their country, giving the information outlined in the bullet points. If they do not have any personal experience of local traditions, ask them to research any traditional music or dance they are interested in on the Internet. It should preferably be from the part of the world that they come from, if not their home country. They can do this for homework.

6 In a subsequent lesson have students exchange their writing with a partner and check that it corresponds to the criteria in the bullet points. They should then discuss the positive and negative aspects of the description, and help their partner improve it, if necessary.

9f A biopic

Before you watch

1 Students work in pairs to read and discuss the quotations. Take feedback from the class.

SAMPLE ANSWERS

optimistic, philosophical, determined, truthful, sincere

2 Ask students to work in pairs to prepare questions to interview the director of a documentary. They then work with another pair to compare their questions.

While you watch

3 Give students time to read the words in the glossary. Play the video for students to compare their questions in Exercise 2 to the ones the interviewer asks. Take feedback from the class.

4 Give students time to read the questions. Then play the first part of the video (to 00.54) for them to answer.

ANSWERS

1 Who Marley really was as a person and what his inspiration was.
2 He says they don't really listen to it properly – it's like background music.
3 He hopes it will make us listen to his music with fresh ears.

5 Give students time to read the words, then play the second part of the video (00.55 to 01.52) for them to underline the words Kevin Macdonald uses.

ANSWERS

fascinating, extraordinary, rags to riches, racial issues, violence, gangsters, amazing

6 Give students time to read the sentences. Play the third part of the video (01.53 to end) for students to write the missing words.

ANSWERS

1 attractive / gorgeous-looking
2 sincere
3 solace
4 believe him
5 universal
6 relate to

After you watch

7 Students work in pairs to roleplay an interview with the director, according to the instructions.

8 Ask students to work in groups to discuss the questions.

Videoscript

00.06 ***Interviewer*** And what was it like to take on a project like this – about someone so popular?

Kevin MacDonald Oh, it was a huge privilege to get to make this film. And obviously things, a lot of things have been made before and written before about Bob, but what I felt was that nobody had ever done anything which was really about the man, which ever really was honest about who he was and where that inspiration to make the music came from, and what the music was really kind of about, what it was really saying.

And also … there's a way in which we hear Marley around us all the time now. You go to a restaurant, it's playing. It's in the toilets, it's on the, in an elevator. It's in a supermarket. You kind of become a bit deaf to it – you don't really listen to it any more because it's just there. So in a way I wanted people to, sort of, listen to the music afresh.

Once you've, once you sort of understand the man, I think then you hear the music in a different way. That's … That's certainly my idea.

00.55 ***Interviewer*** What is there in Marley's life story that recommended itself to you?

Kevin MacDonald Well, it's a, it's a fascinating story. I mean, that's what it is. Most of us go to the movies to see a great story. It's, It's a … His life story to me is in itself extraordinary even if you didn't know his music. I mean, everyone knows his music. I don't think probably there's a person alive who hasn't heard a Bob Marley song.

The story of the rags to riches tale in Jamaica, the dealing with the, with the racial issues that he had to deal with growing up. Dealing with the violence of Jamaica, the gangsters of Jamaica. Touring the world. It's a … It's an amazing, it's an amazing tale.

01.38 But obviously this film is … made for people who have heard Bob Marley and who want to know more about him and understand who the man is. As I say, it's a film about the man.

01.53 ***Interviewer*** Why is Bob Marley so special? What was it about him that touched people?

Kevin MacDonald Well, I think it's … I think what people love about Bob is first and foremost, you know, he's a very attractive, gorgeous-looking guy and that doesn't, doesn't hurt. But, more significantly he has a message which he really means. He's really sincere in what he, in what he says in his lyrics. And he actually is trying to communicate some sort of religious perspective on life, some sort of philosophical perspective on life, which is offering solace to people who are feeling miserable, people who are, who are going through a difficult time, who are politically oppressed or whatever.

And because you know that he's been through a tough time in his life, because he's lived through terrible poverty, because he's had to struggle, you believe him when he says the things that he says in his songs. When he says everything is going to be alright, you know that there's somebody talking who has been through tough times and who has seen that there is light at the end of the tunnel.

02.52 So that, I think, is one of the reasons why he appeals to people who feel like, you know, they're not understood, who feel like they're oppressed. And he is, I think, probably numerically the most listened-to artist in the world, I would think.

Because not only is he listened to in the western world, so to speak, but he's listened to … in Latin America, he's huge. In Indonesia, he's huge. In India and Tibet. Because his message is universal. And the message of freedom and of tolerance and of overcoming the tribulations of your life is something that we can all, at once stage or another in our lives, relate to.

Unit 9 Review

Grammar

1 Ask students to read the article and answer the questions.

ANSWERS

1 to raise money to help the victims of the 1970 cyclone and the Bangladesh Liberation War
2 It raised a lot of money, it made people aware of the problems in Bangladesh, and it started a new movement in benefit concerts.

2 Ask students to read the article again and rewrite the sentences numbered 1–4 in the article using the words given.

ANSWERS

1 so as to help victims of a disaster
2 to relieve the refugee crisis
3 for distribution
4 so that there would be as wide an audience as possible

3 Ask students to add *just* to each of the five sentences in the last paragraph of the article.

ANSWER

But the aim of the *Concert for Bangladesh* wasn't **just** to raise money. The organisers **just** wanted people to be more aware of Bangladesh and its problems. In this sense, according to organiser Ravi Shankar, 'It was **just** fantastic.' It also turned out to be **just** the start of a new movement in benefit concerts. **Just** under fifteen years later *Live Aid*, a response to the Ethiopian famine, was staged in London and Philadelphia and attracted a global TV audience of almost two billion.

Vocabulary

4 Ask students to match words 1–8 with the definitions a–g.

ANSWERS

1 b 2 f 3 e 4 c 5 h 6 a 7 g 8 d

5 Students choose a song or genre and explain to their partner why they like it.

Real life

6 Ask students to read the dialogue and complete the responses.

ANSWERS

1 tell
2 thought
3 interesting
4 say
5 really / 'm afraid I

7 Students work in pairs to ask and answer the questions in Exercise 6.

Speaking

8 Students work in pairs to describe a piece of music and say why they like it or dislike it.

Unit 10 Social living

Lead-in

Personal response

Ask students to discuss what they consider to be the major annual national festival in their country (e.g. National Day, Christmas, New Year). They should list when the festival is, how long it lasts and what people do. If you are teaching a monocultural class, you can do this as a whole-class discussion, listing responses on the board as students give them. With a multicultural class, have students work with a partner from a different culture if possible, to talk about their festivals. Elicit details from the whole class.

1 Ask the class to describe what they can see in the picture. Then ask them to discuss festivals for different communities in their country. Ask: *When and where do they take place, and whose festival is it? What do they do? Is there any special food?* Elicit responses from the whole class.

Background note

Cinco de Mayo celebrates the day (5th May) in 1862 when a group of Mexicans, against the odds, defeated the invading French.

2 [2.16] Ask students to read through the questions to focus their listening. Play the recording for them to answer, then check with a partner. If necessary, play it again for them to complete, correct and check. Elicit answers from the whole class.

ANSWERS

1. Melbourne, Australia (Greek population); London, England (French population); Denver, Colorado, USA (Hispanic population)
2. They are second, third or fourth generation migrants, not first.
3. They have strong family values.

Audioscript [2.16]

P = presenter, **A** = Alejandra Sanchez

P: Did you know that Melbourne, Australia has the third biggest Greek population of any city after Athens and Thessaloniki? Or that London, England is now France's sixth biggest city? In Denver, Colorado, over a third of the population are Hispanic, mostly from Mexico. The majority of these ethnic groups – with the possible exception of the French in London – aren't made up of first-generation migrants, but second, third, fourth, even fifth generation. So what's it like to belong to a long-standing immigrant community? What are the implications for the individual and the community as a whole? I put this question to a resident of Denver, Alejandra Sanchez.

A: My grandparents came here from Mexico 40 years ago as migrant workers, but I'm an American citizen and I participate fully in American life. I'm also Mexican-Hispanic and with that comes certain values, whether you are first or fourth generation. The most important thing for us is not the individual, it's the family. We grow up surrounded by our extended family; our brothers, our sisters, our cousins, our aunts and uncles. They're also our friends, and without them, we're nothing. I think more than anything else, these deep-rooted values make us a very close-knit community. When we Hispanics come together at social gatherings, we celebrate this part of our heritage and treat each other as family. You can see this spirit of harmony at the Cinco de Mayo festivities, which is a wonderful celebration of our rich heritage.

3 [2.16] Ask students to listen for the adjectives used with the words in the box. Play the recording, and elicit answers from the whole class.

ANSWERS

ethnic groups
first-generation migrants
long-standing immigrant community
extended family
deep-rooted values
close-knit community
social gatherings
rich heritage

4 Ask students to discuss these questions in pairs, then elicit some responses from the whole class. If students are all from the same area, town or district, this activity can be a whole-class discussion.

Homework

Ask students to write 150 words on *My Favourite Festival*, in which they describe it in detail and explain why they like it so much. In a subsequent lesson, students can bring in their writing and exchange it with a partner for comment and discussion.

10a Good citizens

Lead-in

Ask the class to discuss what they understand by the section title *Good citizens*. Ask them to define a good citizen and give examples of the type of behaviour which they would expect to find in such a person (e.g. considerate to neighbours over noise, cleanliness, etc. respectful of the environment, responsible in fulfilling civic duties such as voting; helpful to others in the community).

Listening

1 Ask students to complete the collocations with a partner. Elicit answers from the whole class.

ANSWERS
1 b 2 b 3 a 4 c 5 c 6 c

2 Elicit comments on the picture using phrases from Exercise 1.

SAMPLE ANSWER
Rob is doing his bit for the community and taking responsibility for his environment.

Extra activity

Before they listen to the recording in Exercise 3 ask students to discuss the four questions in groups of four and come up with a set of possible answers. Elicit suggestions from around the class.

3 [2.17] Play the recording and ask students to answer, then check with a partner. If necessary, play the recording again for students to check and complete their answers. Elicit answers from the whole class.

ANSWERS
1 They are focusing on laws and political institutions.
2 their duties and responsibilities to society
3 Yes, a huge amount.
4 taking care of the environment; helping poorer people in the community; being open-minded and tolerant of differences

Audioscript [2.17]

P = presenter, **L** = Louis James

P: Citizenship education is a hot topic at the moment and we're seeing more countries introduce it into the curriculum in schools. But many people wonder if the approach of teaching children about the country's laws and political institutions, and so on actually helps them to be better citizens. Here to discuss this is sociologist, Louis James. Louis, surely any training is better than none, isn't it?

L: Well, I'd like to say 'yes' and I know the intentions are good, but I'm afraid this kind of citizenship education is missing the point.

P: And what is the point?

L: Of course, teaching people about the way institutions function is important, but what's far more important is to get people to think about what their duties and responsibilities to society are.

P: And in your view, young people don't know what those are …

L: Well, I don't think there are any clear-cut answers. That's why I said 'get them to think about these things'. It's a question of taking notice of others in your community. There was an interesting survey done, some years ago now, by the ISSP – that's the International Social Survey Programme – which asked people from all around the world what they thought the duties of a good citizen were. People were asked to rate the importance of various duties, for example: 'to be active in social organisations'; or 'always to obey laws and regulations'. But there were some duties on a more human level, like 'to try to help people who are worse off than you'; and 'to try to understand the reasoning of people with other opinions'.

P: And you think that sort of duty is closer to the spirit of good citizenship, do you?

L: Yes, I don't think the starting point should be how we relate to state institutions, but how we relate to each other … at a more basic level.

P: And how did people rate these duties? I imagine there wasn't that much difference in the way different nationalities responded, was there?

L: Actually, there was – huge variation. For example, 60% of Filipinos thought it was very important to be involved in social organisations, whereas only 15% of Japanese did. There were also some unexpected findings. In Switzerland, only half the people surveyed thought always obeying laws and regulations was very important.

P: That is surprising, isn't it?

L: It is. And there were great differences too when it came to feelings of duty to one another. 80% of Mexicans thought it was very important to help people worse off than you. In some other countries, it was as low as 30%.

P: So you'd like to see more discussion in schools about our duties to each other, then?

L: Yes, I think we need to get children thinking about the basic things they can do to help a community function better: taking care of their environment, helping poorer people in the community, being open-minded and tolerant of differences. If you get those things right, the other elements will naturally follow.

4 [2.17] Ask students to read the four phrases, then play the recording for them to decide what they refer to. Ask them to check with a partner, and play it again if necessary. Elicit answers from the whole class.

ANSWERS

1 citizenship education
2 the intentions of people who organise citizenship education
3 'to try to help people who are worse off than you' and 'to try to understand the reasoning of people with other opinions'
4 In Switzerland, only half the people surveyed thought always obeying laws and regulations was very important.

5 Ask students to work in groups to discuss other public-spirited actions; ask one person to be the secretary and keep notes. Ask for responses from the secretaries in a whole-class setting.

Read through the *Wordbuilding* box with the class and discuss compound adjectives with them. Try to elicit other examples that they know, and list them on the board. If you feel it necessary, turn to page 83 of the Workbook, and read the information and have students do the exercises.

Language focus tag questions

6 [2.18] Play the recording and ask students to match the questions and their functions individually, then check with a partner. Elicit answers from the whole class.

ANSWERS

1 b 2 a 3 b 4 a 5 b 6 c

Grammar notes

The usual form of tag question is one where the verb in the tag is the opposite of the verb in the sentence, i.e. a negative main verb is followed by a positive tag, and a positive main verb is followed by a negative tag.

It is also possible to use a positive tag after a positive main verb. This structure can be used to express particular surprise, sympathy or interest, e.g. *So, you won a prize, did you? Well done!*

However, it is **not** possible to use a negative sentence with a negative tag.

7 [2.18] Ask students to read the questions, then play the recording, pausing after each question to let them note the intonation. Allow them time to read through questions 2 and 3 and answer them. They can then check with a partner. Play the sentences again for them to check, complete and correct their answers. Elicit answers from the whole class.

ANSWERS

1 1 rising 3 rising 5 rising
2 falling 4 falling 6 falling
2 1 and 5 would be statements expecting agreement; 6 would become a question rather than a statement
3 It adds more emphasis and offers an opinion.

8 Read through the information about tag questions in the language focus box with the class, and make sure they understand everything. If you feel that students need more explanation and practice, ask them to read page 169 and do the exercises. Then ask students to rewrite the statements in Exercise 8 as indicated, individually. They can then check with a partner. Elicit answers from the whole class, noting that there are several possibilities for question 3 and two for 1 and 4.

ANSWERS

1 You follow the news a lot, don't you?
So you think it's important to keep up with political events, do you?
2 People aren't generally very public-spirited in our city, are they?
3 It's up to each individual how much they participate in public life, isn't it? / Surely it's up to each individual how much they participate in public life?
Yes, but there will always be some people who want to get involved, won't there? / Yes, but surely there will always be some people who want to get involved.
So you think it can just be left to others, do you?
4 It isn't pleasant to live in run-down surroundings, is it?
But surely you care what your environment looks like?
But you care what your environment looks like, don't you?

9 [2.19] Ask students to complete the tags individually, then check with a partner. Elicit answers from the whole class.

ANSWERS

a aren't I? c shall we?
b did it? d will you?

Audioscript [2.19]

a I'm disturbing you, aren't I?
b Nothing bad happened, did it?
c Let's go, shall we?
d Don't be late, will you?

Pronunciation tag questions

10a Ask students to work in pairs to decide what the intonation of each question tag is likely to be, and why they think that. Elicit answers from the whole class, with one student saying the sentence with what they think is the correct intonation, and the rest of the class checking.

ANSWERS

1 rising (checking)
2 falling (agreement)
3 rising (checking)
4 rising (checking)
5 falling (agreement)
6 rising (checking)
7 rising (checking) or falling (agreement)

10b [2.20] Play the recording for students to check their answers. Then play each sentence and pause afterwards for students to repeat chorally and individually. Then ask students to get into pairs and practise saying the sentences while their partner listens and checks their intonation.

Speaking

11 Ask students to get into groups of four to discuss and rank the duties of a citizen in order of importance. Ask one student in each group to act as secretary and note the group's answers. Elicit answers from the secretaries, and open up a class-wide discussion in order to produce a class list on the board.

Homework

Ask students to write 125–150 words on their own attitude to civic duties. In a subsequent lesson they can bring in their writing and exchange it with a partner for discussion and comment.

10b The civilised insect

Lead-in

Personal response

Ask the class to say what they know about insects in general, e.g. they have six legs, most can fly, they have a life cycle involving development from egg to larva (caterpillar / grub) to pupa to adult; in general they are quite small. You might make a list of characteristics on the board as students give them to you.

Reading

1 Ask students to discuss in pairs what they know about ants and make notes of their ideas. Elicit responses from the whole class and make a list of what they tell you, perhaps under different headings, on the board.

Background notes

Ants are insects belonging to the same group as wasps and bees. Around 12,500 different species have been identified, although scientists believe that there could be up to 22,000 different kinds. They live in all continents except Antarctica. They are easy to recognise because of their bent antennae and narrowed 'waist'. Ants mostly live in colonies, ranging from a few individuals to millions. The colony usually consists of sterile female worker ants, a few fertile male drones and one more fertile queen which lays the eggs. Ant colonies are highly organised, with division of labour, communication between individuals (often using pheromones) and an ability to solve complex problems. Ants are typically omnivorous, and range in size from 0.75 to 52 mm.

2 Ask the class to say what the two quotations tell you about ants.

ANSWERS

They exist in large communities.

They have great strength compared to their body weight.

3 Ask students to read the article and explain the success of ants.

ANSWER

The main reason is the highly sophisticated social behaviour they exhibit, achieving a high level of organisation and synchronisation.

4 Ask students to read the statements to focus their reading, then read the text and decide if the statements are true or false individually. They can then check with a partner before you elicit the answers from the whole class.

ANSWERS

1 T (*thriving everywhere except on icy mountain peaks and around the Poles*)
2 T (*the bodies of these sterile females are adapted to the different jobs they have*)
3 F (*are entirely instinctive messages*)
4 T (*attacking in deadly swarms*)
5 F (*they have a collective intelligence greater than the sum of its individual parts*)

Language focus adverbs

5 Ask students to answer the questions individually, then check with a partner. Elicit answers from the whole class.

ANSWERS

1 the verb *know*
2 the adjective *successful*
3 weighs almost nothing
4 adverb (but it has the same form as the adjective *straight*)
5 because some adjectives that end *-ed* and all adjectives ending *-ly* cannot have *-ly* added, or they sound awkward, so instead we use an adjective + *way, manner* or *fashion*

6 Read through the language focus box with the class and check that they understand the information given. If you feel it necessary, have students turn to page 170 to read the information and do the exercises there. Then ask them to find one more example of each type of adverb in paragraphs 4 and 5 of the text. Elicit answers from the whole class.

ANSWERS

+ verb: *readily (take on)*
+ adjective: *completely (fearless)*
same form as the adjective: *long*
almost not: *hardly*
adjective +way / manner: *in this altruistic and dedicated manner*

Grammar note

Elicit the function of adverbs (to say how an action is performed) and what question adverbs answer (*How … ?*), e.g.

How did he walk? He walked ***quickly****.*

Explain to students that whilst many adverbs can be created directly from the related adjective (e.g. *quick – quickly; careful – carefully*) some cannot, in which case they need to use a phrase which contains the adjective, e.g. *in a … way* or *in a … manner*. Hence, *in a lively way, in an organised manner.*

7 Ask students to rewrite the sentences individually, using an adverb form of the word in brackets, then check with a partner. Elicit answers from the whole class.

ANSWERS

1 Ants are **socially** sophisticated creatures.
2 Ants are cooperative, but it would be wrong to say they act **in a friendly manner** towards each other.
3 An ant can lift up to twenty times its body weight, whereas most people can **barely** lift one time their own.
4 You could **hardly** say an ant's brain was big, but in fact it has the biggest brain-to-body size ratio of any insect.
5 A worker ant doesn't live **long** – on average 50 days – but a queen can live for decades.
6 Some ants, when they attack other ant colonies, **cleverly** emit false pheromone signals to confuse the enemy.
7 Not all ants like to work **hard**.
8 The slave-maker ant steals eggs from other colonies. Then it makes the **newly** hatched ants work for it.

Idioms animal verbs

8 Ask students to discuss the animal verbs in the sentences in groups of four, and try to decide what they mean and how they are related to the animal. Elicit suggestions from the class.

ANSWERS

1 working hard (beavers are known for working hard and building dams)
2 behaving in a very self-important way (swans look very grand and imperious)
3 ate very quickly (wolves have very big appetites and tear at their food)
4 avoid doing (ducks put their heads underwater to look for food)
5 chased *or* followed (hounds chase and hunt other animals)
6 repeating *or* copying (parrots can imitate human speech)

9 Ask students to think of similar expressions from their own language, and then see if they work translated into English. This activity can be carried out as a whole-class discussion.

Extra activity

Give students the following examples of animal verbs and ask them to work out the meanings. They could research these for homework:

to hare about
to dog someone's footsteps
to pig out
to ram something hard
to rabbit on about something
to rat on somebody

Speaking

10 Ask students to look at the two photos and the questions. Ask them to work in pairs; A should look at page 154 and B at page 156. Once they have read and memorised their information, they can ask and answer each other's questions. Elicit some comments about starlings and bees from the class when they have finished.

10c Living free?

Lead-in

Personal response
Ask students whether they ever collect any wild food to eat or make drinks from (e.g. blackberries, chestnuts, mushrooms, rose hips, herbs) or whether they ever eat any meat or fish which was wild rather than farmed. Find out what wild foods students have eaten (if any) and what they thought of it.

Reading

1 Ask the whole class to discuss the term *hunter-gatherer* and what the life of a hunter-gatherer is like.

ANSWERS
A 'hunter-gatherer' is a person who survives by hunting animals for meat and collecting (gathering) plants, fruits, etc. to eat. Their life is different to farmers because they don't own animals or land, so they move from place to place to find food and they don't plant crops.

2 Ask students to work in pairs to discuss the meaning of the map. Elicit suggestions from the whole class.

ANSWERS
The map shows that in pre-historic times, most people were hunter-gatherers; by 2000 AD, there were only small areas in the world where people still survived by hunting and gathering.
Reasons include: people wanted to settle down and stop moving from place to place, so they started farming; land became developed and owned, so there was less land to hunt and gather on (and fewer wild animals).

3 Ask students to read the three summaries to focus their reading, then read the article and choose the correct answer.

ANSWER
a

4 Ask students to read the list, then read the article quickly and decide which the Hadza have and which they don't have. Elicit answers from the whole class.

ANSWERS
Things they have: sufficient food, basic tools, a lot of free time, a difficult environment
Things they don't have: working animals, enemies, a government, their own strict routines

5 Ask students to work in pairs and discuss the meanings of the phrases. Elicit answers from the whole class.

ANSWERS
1 There were also disadvantages to the increase in agriculture.
2 They cause no pollution or damage to the land.
3 The fact that a camp is named after a person doesn't mean they have any authority.
4 The Hadza look after the land carefully.
5 In the past, no one else, apart from the Hadza, lived on this land; now that is changing.
6 Their way of life seems very extreme to us, always living in simple, temporary accommodation, like a camping trip that never ends.

Vocabulary notes

The following words and expressions from the text may be unfamiliar:

briny = salty

to confer = to give a position, honour or status to someone

to escalate = to increase

to forage = to search for food

intermittent = happening from time to time

intolerable = impossible to tolerate

a steward = someone who looks after something

a tuber = the root of a plant

Critical thinking reading between the lines

6 Ask students to consider the two questions individually.

7 Ask students to get into groups of four to share and discuss their answers to the two questions in Exercise 6. Elicit answers from the whole class.

SAMPLE ANSWERS
1 Yes. He talks in a positive tone about them, and whilst there are some elements of their existence which appear attractive, he appreciates how hard their life is (*But who of us could live like them?*).
2 Yes, he seems to support being respectful of the land (*the Hadza are gentle stewards of the land*), and he seems opposed to heavy agriculture (*a mistake from which we have never recovered*).

Background notes

The Hadza people are an ethnic group living in north-central Tanzania around Lake Eyasi, the central Rift Valley and the Serengeti Plateau. There are under 1,000 of them, and of these, about 300–400 live as hunter-gatherers. They are genetically unrelated to other groups of people living around them, and the Hadza language is also isolated, although because it contains clicks it has sometimes been incorrectly linked to Khoisan languages. The people are seriously threatened by the encroaching outside world.

Word focus *free*

8 Ask the class to read the phrase and decide what it means.

ANSWER

It means that the Hadza are free from the restrictions and limitations most of us have to live with.

(to be a free spirit = to be free from social conventions and do more or less what you want)

9 Ask students to discuss the meaning of the *free* phrases in each sentence. Elicit suggestions from the whole class.

ANSWERS

1 There's no need to ask if you want to do something.
2 You can't get something for nothing.
3 an uncontrolled discussion with everyone talking at once
4 the freedom to do what we wanted
5 without punishment

10 Ask students to talk to a partner about their experience of two of the situations given. Elicit some examples from the whole class.

Pronunciation notes

Ask students to practise the following words from the article where the stress is on the third syllable:

agriculturist, population, epidemic, intermittent, extraordinary, anniversaries

Homework

Ask students to take one of the situations from Exercise 10 and write around 125–150 words, expanding the details, the lead-up to the event, the event itself, and what happened afterwards. In a subsequent lesson, they can exchange their writing with a partner for comment and discussion.

Speaking

11 Ask students to get into groups of three, and decide who is A, B and C. They should then each turn to their page and read their role card. The three students should then discuss the issue of the future of the Hadza lands, following their role card. Circulate and monitor their roleplays.

10d An interesting subject

Lead-in

Personal response

Ask the class to suggest the characteristics of a good speaker, whether making a public speech, giving a talk, or just talking to several friends in a group. You might note their ideas on the board. (Possible answers: clear voice and pronunciation, variation of voice, enthusiasm for the topic, eye contact with listeners, involving and relating to listeners, use of gesture, clear structure of what is said.)

Real life making conversation

1 Ask students to discuss the characteristics of a good listener in pairs. Elicit responses from the whole class and encourage further discussion.

ANSWER

The characteristics of a good listener are: maintains eye contact, shows appreciation, waits before giving their views, asks questions.

2 Ask students to consider their own listening habits, then have them discuss them with a partner. If you feel it appropriate, discuss the issues with the whole class.

3 [2.21] Read through the instructions with the class, then give them one minute to read the task. Then play the recording once and ask them to answer the questions. Play it again for them to check their answers. Elicit answers from the whole class.

ANSWERS

1 Because she wants a game of tennis.
2 A model society set up in the 1880s in Chicago by George Pullman.
3 Yes, he / she says 'sounds interesting' and 'I'd be very interested to know because it's a really unusual story'.

Audioscript [2.21]

A: Hi Justin! Have you got time for a game of tennis this afternoon?

B: Oh, hi Rebecca. 'Fraid not – I'm too busy.

A: Why? What you are doing?

B: Working. I have to get that sociology essay in by tomorrow afternoon.

A: Oh, yes. I've done mine already. What have you chosen to write about?

B: Er … I've been researching a model society set up in the 1880s in Chicago by George Pullman, the guy who made the restaurant carriages and sleeping cars for trains …

A: Have you? … Sounds interesting …

B: It is actually. What's odd is that he based his society on capitalist principles, thinking that capitalism was the best way for a society to fulfil its material and spiritual needs.

A: Unusual idea.

B: Yes, isn't it? 'Cos usually utopian societies are based on some kind of communal living ideal … principles of sharing and equality, and being unmaterialistic and that kind of thing. As you probably found out yourself.

A: So how did Pullman's society work?

B: Well, I'm still reading about it, but as far as I can see, it was basically a purpose-built town with his factory at the centre. It had a very rigid class structure with everyone knowing their place – manual workers, skilled workers, managers – with Pullman at the top, of course, living in a grand house while his workers lived in small tenements. He owned all the buildings and rented them to the workers.

A: Doesn't sound very utopian.

B: No, it doesn't, does it? And I think the workers weren't very happy. They weren't allowed unions; there was only one bar in the town and that was for visitors …

A: So, it probably failed in the end then, I suppose.

B: I expect so – these things often do. But I haven't got to that bit yet. I'll let you know.

A: Yeah, do. No seriously, I'd be very interested to know because it's a really unusual story. The one I chose was a farming community in Oklahoma … Anyway, good luck and let me know if you want a break from it. I'd love a game of tennis some time.

B: Yeah, me too. See you soon, anyway.

A: Yeah, I hope so.

Speaking skill showing interest

4 [2.21] Ask students to read through the four extracts from the dialogue. Then play the recording again for them to complete the phrases. They can check their answers with a partner. Play the recording once more for them to check and correct their answers. Elicit answers from the whole class.

ANSWERS

1 Have you? Sounds
2 Unusual idea; isn't it
3 Doesn't sound very utopian; it doesn't, does it?
4 I suppose; I expect so

Extra activity

Read through the phrases for showing interest in the language box with the class, and ensure that they understand the meaning and use of the examples. Point out the elliptical use of *Waiting* (instead of *I'm waiting*) in the first example of 'Responding naturally', and explain that the present participle on its own is frequently used in response to this particular present continuous question.

Pronunciation intonation and elision

5a [2.22] Ask students to look at the responses in the 'Showing interest' part of the Speaking skills box, and think about the intonation. Play the recording and ask them to note whether it rises or falls, and what this indicates about the response. They can discuss their ideas with a partner. Play the recording once or twice more, as necessary. Elicit responses from the whole class. Play the recording again, pausing after each response for students to repeat it chorally and individually.

ANSWERS

Really? (rising: shows interest and invites further comment)
Are you? (rising: shows interest and invites further comment)
Yes, wasn't it? (falling: shows agreement)
No, it doesn't, does it? (falling: shows agreement)
He didn't, did he? (rising: shows surprise)
Yes, do. (falling: shows agreement)

5b Ask students to work in pairs to help each other practise their intonation. One student should make the statement in the 'Showing interest' section of the box, and the other should respond, then they should change roles. Circulate and monitor their intonation.

5c [2.23] Read through the full versions of the phrases (e.g. *I'm afraid not*) with the class, then play the recording of the elided versions. Ask students to note how they are elided by striking through words or letters that are not pronounced. You could write the full phrases on the board and ask students to come up and mark the elided sounds (unstressed vowels are suppressed or omitted completely, including the personal pronoun 'I').

ANSWERS

1 'Fraid not
2 S'pose so
3 Spect so
4 Hope so
5 Doubt it

6 Read through the instructions with the class. If necessary, play the recording from Exercise 3 again for them to listen to as a model. Then ask them to get into pairs to make up their own similar conversation. Circulate and monitor their speaking.

10e A good start in life

Lead-in

Personal response
Ask students to think of people who have been successful despite having a poor start in life; how have they achieved success? In what ways might a poor start have contributed to their success?

Writing a discursive essay

1 Ask students to tick four of the items listed individually.

2 Ask students to get into groups of four to discuss their answers to Exercise 1, and the relationship between social background and a child's prospects in life. Elicit ideas from the whole class.

3 Ask students to read the questions to focus their reading, then read the essay to find the answers. Elicit answers from the whole class.

ANSWERS
1 That your prospects are determined by your own opinion of what you can achieve.
2 Students' own answers.

Vocabulary notes

Point out the use of *provided that, as long as* and *on condition that* in this essay. Ask students to explain the meaning of each one, and identify the construction used. Elicit that the meanings are the same (that something will happen only if a condition is met, e.g. *the school offered cash prizes on condition that their grades improved*), and all three are used with a clause.

Writing skill critical thinking in writing

4 Ask students to decide what steps in an argument the ideas correspond to, and to discuss their ideas with a partner. Elicit answers from the whole class.

ANSWERS
hypothesis: c
thesis: a
analysis: b

5 Ask students to write the essay as detailed. They might do this for homework.

6 Ask students to exchange their essay with a partner and read their partner's essay with the four points in mind, then give and receive feedback on the essays.

10f Initiation with ants

Before you watch

1 Students work in pairs to think of ceremonies for the different occasions. Take feedback from the class.

2 Ask students to predict what part ants might play in the ceremony in the video.

While you watch

3 Give students time to read the words in the glossary. Play the video for students to check their predictions from Exercise 2. Take feedback from the class.

ANSWER
Boys as young as twelve must put their hands into gloves full of stinging ants, as initiation into adulthood.

4 Give students time to look at the table. Then play the first part of the video (to 00.50) for them to complete it.

ANSWERS
1 sound of the horns
2 11 hours
3 12 years and upwards
4 giant tropical bullet ants
5 initiation into adulthood
6 20 times

5 Give students time to read the questions, then play the second part of the video (00.51 to end) for them to answer.

ANSWERS
1 It's 30 times worse than a bee sting.
2 They drug the ants / put them into a stupor.
3 The ants are trapped.
4 to help distract the initiates
5 The stinging gets worse and the hands are paralysed.
6 He says he'll wear the gloves 19 more times.

6 Ask students to discuss the chief's comments.

ANSWER
It marks the entrance into adulthood; it makes them better men; you need to suffer to become a true adult.

7 Give students time to complete the paragraph. Play the video again for them to check.

SAMPLE ANSWER
The Sateré-Mawé tribe of the Amazon hold an extreme ritual for boys that acts as initiation into manhood. Bullet ants are thrust into gloves, which are worn by the initiates for more than ten minutes while they dance around a pole. These ants have a sting 30 times worse than the sting of a bee and the initiates must wear the gloves not just once, but twenty times. After the gloves are taken off, the toxins dissipate over 24 hours. The chief of the tribe says that if you live your life without suffering, it won't be worth anything to you.

After you watch

8 Students work in pairs to roleplay an interview about a ceremony, according to the instructions.

9 Ask students to work in groups to discuss the question.

Videoscript

00.05 In the remote Amazonian village of Inhube, the moan of the horns means a gruelling initiation is about to begin. Several times a year, the Sateré-Mawé Indians hold a painful eleven-hour ritual in which boys as young as 12 must stick their hands into a pair of specially-made gloves, each one infested with a swarm of angry, stinging jungle carnivores – giant tropical bullet ants.

No initiate can be considered a true Indian, a warrior, until he has worn the gloves not just once, but 20 times.

00.46 ***Ted*** People say that I don't have the courage to do it. I have and I will do it.

00.51 The men face the prospect of getting stung even before the ritual starts, when they head off to capture the ants. A stab from this predator's abdominal spear is 30 times worse than a bee sting.

01.08 The tribe's medicine man drugs the ants by soaking them in an herbal solution. But their stupor will only last long enough for them to be thrust, one by one, stinger first, into the gloves. According to the Sateré-Mawé legend, these menaces provide the perfect test of one's worthiness to take on adult roles.

01.34 In less than an hour, the ants are awake. Trapped in the woven mitt, they writhe in angry desperation. They're ready to be inserted into the ceremonial gloves. One by one, each young man steps up to the sacred pole and submits his hands to the swarm. Their agony is unmistakeable. To help distract them, the medicine man leads them in a dance around the pole.

02.10 To be seen as a true tribal warrior, each must endure the ants' punishment for more than ten minutes. With each sting, the bullet ants' neurotoxic venom attacks the nerves, causing paralysis and terrible pain, and this is only the beginning. Once the gloves are off, the stinging and burning will only grow more excruciating.

02.39 Now, after watching the others suffer, Ted's moment of truth has arrived. Unfazed, he keeps dancing while all around him the others succumb to the poison. Slowly, the neurotoxic venom is turning their hands into swollen, simmering, paralysed stumps.

Finally, the gloves come off and Ted remains standing.

03.08 ***Ted*** My body feels like a motor that's heating up. If you throw water here, a lot of smoke will come out.

03.15 It takes 24 hours for the toxins to dissipate completely. As the chief sees it, the ritual not only marks the initiate's entrance into adulthood, it makes them better men.

Chief If you live your life without suffering anything, or without any kind of effort, it won't be worth anything to you.

03.38 Despite his long hours of agony, Ted has promised the chief he will wear the gloves 19 more times, until he becomes a true adult.

Unit 10 Review

Grammar

1 Ask students to read the interview and complete it by making the transformations.

ANSWERS

1 in a concerted way
2 fast
3 hard
4 hardly
5 incredibly
6 in a friendly way
  a Your main purpose was to protect the coral reef, wasn't it?
  b You got the help of the government, didn't you?
  c That has changed, hasn't it?
  d You can relax now that you have won this particular battle, can't you?

2 Ask students to read the article again and answer the questions.

ANSWERS

1 getting fishing banned / stopping the intensive fishing
2 The impact on the environment will be considerable.

Vocabulary

3 Ask students to complete the collocations.

ANSWERS

1 knit	4 bit
2 generation	5 hand
3 extended	6 heritage

4 Ask students to discuss in pairs which statements are true for them.

Real life

5 Ask students to match the statements with the short responses.

ANSWERS

1 e 2 b 3 f 4 d 5 a 6 c

6 Ask students to have a conversation to exchange news, show interest and ask questions.

Speaking

7 Students work in pairs to discuss social living.

Unit 11 Reason and emotion

Lead-in

Personal response

Give students one minute to write down all the words describing emotions that they can think of on a piece of paper. They should then get into a group of four to share their words and add to their lists. Elicit words from the class, and write them on the board; try to organise them in groups with similar meanings (e.g. happy, sad, angry emotions). Elicit where each word should go from the class, and also elicit the differences between words with similar meanings.

1 [2.24] Elicit from the class what the boys in the photo are doing, then ask them what the boy's feelings are. Play the recording, and ask students to listen and see if what the photographer says corresponds to what they suggested.

ANSWER

He's having fun and feeling quite proud and pleased with himself. He's smiling in a rather mischievous way.

Audioscript [2.24]

I've spent the last ten years documenting – through photos – how people express their emotions. The thing is that wherever you go in the world, emotions are expressed in more or less the same way. People used to think facial expressions were something culturally specific, like language or certain gestures, but that isn't actually the case. Expressions are universal; everyone can identify with a picture showing a look of surprise on a person's face, like someone who's taken aback when you take their photo; or showing someone looking despondent because things aren't going well. There are endless shades of emotion too: a look of contentment or sheer unadulterated happiness; someone who's absolutely livid or just feeling mildly irritated.

Children are great to photograph, because they tend not to hide their emotions as much as adults do. I love this one. These two are obviously having a great time, but the boy looking at the camera is also feeling quite proud and pleased with himself. He's smiling in a rather mischievous way as if to say 'Look at me. I know it looks a bit risky and I oughtn't to be doing this, but I'm having fun and you can't stop me now.'

2 [2.24] Ask students to read the three topics to focus their listening. Play the recording and ask them to confer with a partner. Play it again for them to check their ideas, then elicit answers from the whole class.

ANSWERS

1 People used to think facial expressions were culturally-specific, but they are actually universal.
2 There are many emotions and also different degrees of emotion – a look of contentment; sheer, unadulterated happiness; livid to mildly irritated.
3 Children are great to photograph because they tend not to hide their emotions as much as adults.

3 Ask students to categorise the adjectives individually, then check with a partner. Elicit answers from the whole class and check they understand the meaning of the words. Discuss how these words tie in with the words students thought of in the lead-in activity. Encourage students to create word banks by topic, and add to them on a regular basis as they meet new words.

ANSWERS

* = stronger meaning
Anger: cross, livid*
Fear: petrified*, scared
Surprise: astonished*, taken aback
Happiness: content, ecstatic*
Sadness: despondent, miserable*

Vocabulary notes

petrified = very frightened (literal meaning = turned to stone)

livid = very angry (from the original meaning of a purple-blue colour, suggesting that a person who is livid has gone purple in the face)

ecstatic = very happy (from *ecstasy*, meaning a trance-like state: a person who is ecstatic may behave as if they are in a trance)

Pronunciation notes

Note that these adjectives have the stress on the second syllable:

astonished
content
despondent
ecstatic
(taken) aback

All the others have the stress on the first syllable.

4 Read the instructions and the example with the class, then ask them to think of a similar incident when they have felt a strong emotion, and tell their partner about it, using adjectives from the list in Exercise 3.

Homework

Ask students to write 100 words about a real or imaginary event where people displayed different emotions about it (e.g. someone happily giving a tarantula as a present to a child who is terrified of spiders, and parents getting angry). In a subsequent lesson, they can exchange their writing with a partner for discussion and comment.

11a Emotional intelligence

Lead-in

Personal response

Ask students if they have heard anything about multiple intelligences, and if so, elicit anything they can tell you about the concept. (It is the idea, first put forward by Howard Gardner in *Frames of Mind* (1983), that we do not simply have one cerebral intelligence, but that each individual has the potential to use many intelligences and tends to be better in some areas than others. Emotional intelligence is one of these.)

Listening

1 Ask students to look at the definition and answer the questions. They can tell a partner about themselves and other people. Elicit some responses from students and ask them to give reasons.

2 [2.25] Ask students to read the two questions to focus their listening. Play the recording and invite them to check their answers with a partner. Play it again, if necessary. Elicit answers from the whole class.

ANSWERS

a She offers emotional intelligence training to help people understand their own emotions and those of people around them. She can help people overcome their fears and build better rapport with others.

b Modern life is stressful and confusing, and an increasing number of people are suffering from anxiety disorders. Training people to understand other people's emotions can help them to do their jobs better.

Audioscript [2.25]

I = interviewer, N = Naomi Myers

I: Now, does modern life stress you out? Do you wish that you felt more in control of things? If so, perhaps it's time you looked into 'emotional intelligence training', a fast-growing area in the field of practical psychology. Our guest today is Naomi Myers, from the EIQ institute: EIQ being Emotional Intelligence Quotient. Naomi, can you tell us a little more about how this works?

N: Sure. Simply put, emotional intelligence is about two things. One is understanding your own feelings so that you can recognise which are constructive and which are harmful emotions; when to follow your gut feeling and when to follow your head. The other's about understanding how others around you are feeling, and that can be particularly useful in work relationships.

I: And why do people need this training? We've got along without it up to now.

N: Well, as you said, modern life is stressful and confusing. And it's led to an increase in anxiety disorders across the world. In Japan right now there are nearly one million hikikomori: young people who have withdrawn totally from society and stay shut up in their bedrooms at home. We're able to help people understand their fears and overcome them. Suppose you were someone who felt very on edge when speaking in public – we have techniques for helping you deal with that.

I: Such as?

N: Well, I'd rather your listeners took one of our courses than got advice free over the radio! But, for example, we help people to eliminate negative predictions about how they're going to perform.

I: Mmm … And what about reading other people's emotions? How do you help people do that?

N: OK, well one thing we do is train people to read micro-expressions.

I: And what are they?

N: Well, most facial expressions remain on the face for several seconds, but micro-expressions – and we all make them – appear for only a fraction of a second. They're so short because they're a glimpse of a concealed emotion or an emotion that's been very rapidly processed. What if I were to tell you that you'd already made one of these during our discussion?

I: I'd be a bit alarmed.

N: No need to be – it was just a momentary look of shock when I said I wasn't going to tell you about our training techniques. The point is that an ability to read these micro-expressions is very useful – in a business negotiation, for example, or when deciding whether to trust someone. A doctor came to me recently and said, 'If only I was better at building rapport with my patients, I'd be so much better at my job' and we were able to help by training him to read people's emotions better.

Vocabulary notes

Students may be unfamiliar with these words:

gut feelings = very important instinctive feelings

anxiety disorders = illnesses caused by worrying

a glimpse of = to see something for a very short time

concealed = hidden

rapport = relationship, understanding (generally positive)

3 [2.25] Ask students to read through the sentences. Then play the recording again for them to answer. They can check with a partner. If necessary, play the recording again, then elicit answers from the whole class.

ANSWERS

1 emotions
2 nervous and worried
3 other people
4 speaking
5 parts of a second
6 hidden
7 surprise
8 closer to

4 Ask the class to consider their own views on these questions in pairs, then discuss them as a class.

Idioms feelings

5 Ask students to match the idioms and their meanings individually, then check with a partner. Do not elicit answers from the class at this point.

6 Ask students in pairs to check their answers to Exercise 5 against the phrases in context in sentences 1–8. Elicit answers from the whole class.

ANSWERS

a bit down = sad
all over the place = confused and disorganised
done in = very tired
on edge = tense and nervous
hot under the collar = angry
speechless = very surprised
thrilled to bits = very happy
upbeat = optimistic

Extra activity

Ask students to look at the three pictures of the woman and decide what emotion she displays in each. They should then check with a partner before you elicit the answers.

Answers: 1 annoyed or worried 2 surprised or excited 3 happy

Language focus unreal past

7 Ask students to match the extracts from the interview with the descriptions individually, then check with a partner. Elicit answers from the whole class.

ANSWERS

a 1, 6 b 3, 5 c 4 d 2

8 Read through the language focus box with students and check they understand the models. If you feel extra explanation and practice would help at this stage, refer to page 171. Then ask students to rewrite the eight sentences using the prompts. They should check with a partner before you elicit answers from the whole class.

ANSWERS

1 Supposing we offered him more money.
Supposing we were to offer him more money.
2 It's high time he sorted his life out.
3 I wish I didn't have to drive an hour to work each day.
4 If only I was / were able to take a proper holiday.
5 I'd rather you showed me the letter before you send it.
6 I wish people would slow down.
7 What if he said no? What would you do then?
What if he was / were to say no? What would you do then?
8 What would you do if you were me?

Grammar notes

Remind students that we use *were to* + infinitive after *what if* or *supposing* to ask about possible future situations, e.g.

What if it were to rain while we were in the mountains?

Supposing you were to fall over on that steep path?

A simple past form could also be used with the same meaning, but this sentence would be slightly less formal and less hypothetical or 'unreal', e.g.

What if it rained while we were in the mountains?

9 Ask students to complete the conversation individually, then check with a partner. Elicit answers from the class.

ANSWERS

1 were	5 could
2 would	6 would
3 would / might	7 Suppose / Supposing
4 rather	8 soon

Pronunciation word stress: wishes

10a [2.26] Ask students to discuss in pairs where they think the stress falls. Elicit suggestions from the class, then play the recording for them to check. Play it two or three times if they are unsure.

ANSWERS

1 I wish he would listen to me.
2 I wish you were coming with me.
3 If only it were true.
4 If only you would relax a bit.

10b Ask students to say the sentences in pairs and help each other with their stress.

Extra activity

If students have problems imitating the stress patterns, try backchaining and asking students to repeat the sentence in stages, e.g.

***listen** to me / he would **listen** to me / I **wish** he would **listen** to me.*

***coming with** me / you were **coming with** me / I **wish** you were **coming with** me.*

Speaking

11 Read through the list with the class. Ask students to share their ideas in groups and explain why these things irritate them. Ask each group to decide which three things are most irritating.

Homework

Ask students to write 150 words about what they find most irritating in modern life.

11b Thinking fast and slow

Lead-in

Personal response

Ask the class to look at the spread heading, *Thinking fast and slow,* and discuss what they think it might mean. Ask if there are times when they think faster or slower, and if so, why do they do that. Encourage the class to discuss these questions.

Reading

1 Ask students to discuss the questions in pairs, then elicit some responses. Ask if students feel they are generally more intuitive or more careful in their decision-making, and try to elicit examples of the two kinds of thinking.

2 Ask students to read the three statements to focus their listening, then read the article and answer. Elicit answers from the class.

ANSWER

a

3 Ask students to read the three statements and match them to the questions in the article individually. They can then check with a partner before you elicit answers from the class.

ANSWERS

a 1 b 3 c 2

4 Ask students to find adjectives which match the meanings given. They should do this individually, then check with a partner. Elicit answers from the whole class.

ANSWERS

1 intriguing
2 overwhelming
3 plausible
4 deliberate
5 imperfect

Pronunciation note

Ask students to be aware of the syllable stress in these words.

Second syllable: *irrational, intriguing, preferring, intuitive, financial*

Third syllable: *overwhelming, psychological, unreliable*

5 Ask students to respond to these questions in a whole-class setting. Do not push it if nobody answers, as the issues involved could be personal.

Read through the *Wordbuilding* box with the class and ensure that they understand the difference in pronunciation. If you feel it necessary at this stage, ask students to turn to page 91 of the Workbook and read the information and do the exercises there.

Pronunciation heteronyms

6 [2.27] Ask students to read the sentences, and tell a partner what they think the difference is between the pronunciation of the two words. Play the recording for them to check their ideas. Elicit answers from the whole class.

ANSWERS

1 a /ət/ b /eɪt/
2 a /eɪt/ b /ət/
3 a /ət/ b /eɪt/
4 a /eɪt/ b /ət/

Language focus inversion in conditionals

7 Ask students to rewrite the sentences individually using *if*. They should then check with a partner. Elicit the answers from the whole class.

ANSWERS

1 If you should get them wrong, don't worry *or* If you get them wrong, don't worry.
2 If someone had already mentioned that the temperature today was 82° Fahrenheit, your answer would have been a higher number.
3 If the same question were / was presented as a logical formula, few would make this mistake.
4 Some even say that if it hadn't been for this irrational thinking, the banking crisis of 2008 may not have occurred.

8 Read through the information about inversion in conditionals in the language box with the class and check that they understand it. If necessary, have them read the information and do the exercises on page 171. Ask them to rewrite the sentences using inversion individually, then check with a partner. Elicit answers from the whole class.

ANSWERS

1 Should someone ask who told you, don't give them my name.
2 Had I thought about it for longer, I would have got the answer right.
3 They wouldn't be in this situation now had they taken my advice.
4 Were we to take the risk, I am sure that we wouldn't regret it.
5 Would the world be a better place were everyone to think more carefully before acting?
6 Should something be unclear, you can always call me on this number and ask.

Grammar notes

Point out to students that when we invert conditionals, *should* is not used with its usual meaning of giving advice or making recommendations, but to replace *if*, e.g. *Should you want more details, give me a call.* = *If you want more details, give me a call.*

Should can also be used to express an uncertain and more tentative future possibility after *if*, e.g. *If you should want more details, please call me*. This use is also more formal.

9 Ask students to use the sentence stems given to write sentences using the inversion techniques in Exercise 8. They should do this individually, then share and compare their sentences with a partner. Elicit some examples from the whole class.

Speaking

10 Read through the instructions carefully with the class and make sure that they know exactly what to do. Ask them to get into pairs to do the puzzles as indicated, then discuss the point of each case. Elicit answers and ideas from the whole class.

ANSWERS

1 The bat costs $1.05. If you got the puzzle wrong (most people say $1.00), don't be discouraged – so did more than 50 per cent of students at Harvard, MIT and Princeton.
2 Most answer yes, but according to probability it should be an equal number of yes and no.

Extra activity

Ask if students know any other mind puzzles like these. If so, have them ask the class.

Homework

Ask students to write around 150 words about intuitive and considered thinking. In a subsequent lesson, they can exchange their writing with a partner for comment and discussion of the content.

11c Us. And them.

Lead-in

Personal response

Ask students to discuss their use of *us / we / our* and *them / they / their* in English, but also when they use their mother tongue. In what situations and about what do they use these words? (It often has to do with identity and belonging, inclusion and exclusion: *we do this, they don't*, etc.)

Reading

1 Ask students to look at the photos and read the questions. Elicit ideas from the whole class. There will be more information about question 2 in the article; at this point students should discuss their own preconceptions about robots.

ANSWERS

1 The photo on the left is real; it shows an industrial robot. The other photos are science fiction (the photo in the middle is an android from the film *Blade Runner*, the photo on the right is R2D2 from the film *Star Wars*).
2 Students' own answers

2 Ask students to read the three statements, then read the article to decide which one is correct. Elicit answers from the whole class.

ANSWER

b

3 Ask students to work with a partner and produce a list of what the three robots can and can't do. They should then share and compare their answers with another pair. Elicit answers from the whole class.

ANSWERS

Actroid-DER (Yume)

Can raise her arms, smile, blink, turn to face someone, speak

Can't think (*Unlike Yume, HERB does have something like a mental life.*)

HERB

Can take in information and process it intelligently, i.e. he can 'think' for himself; move around without bumping into things, including moving people; recognise specific objects, e.g. a juice box

Can't talk, so he communicates with a bicycle horn; can't deal with crowded places very efficiently

Vanderbilt prototype

Can play simple ball games, recognise human emotions and adjust behaviour accordingly

Can't listen or talk (*There is no linguistic interaction*)

4 Ask students to find the words individually, then check with a partner. Elicit answers from the whole class.

ANSWERS

1 jerk
2 nod off
3 cascade
4 catapulting
5 uninitiated
6 replicating

Vocabulary notes

Check students understand these words from the article:

corporate events = social occasions organised by big businesses

inelastic = not moving or stretching

folding the laundry = folding washed sheets, etc. to put away

creepy = something or someone that makes you feel uneasy or frightened

a structured environment = a place or action which never changes

to boil down to = when reduced to basics

to probe = to investigate

Critical thinking understanding style

5 Read through the instructions with the class and check that they understand what the purpose of the techniques is. Ask students to match the style techniques a–c to the extracts 1–6 individually.

6 Ask students to check their answers to Exercise 5 with a partner and discuss the effect the techniques had on the article. Ask them to think in particular about whether they made the article more entertaining, interesting or easier to understand. Elicit answers from the whole class.

ANSWERS

1 b 2 c 3 b 4 a 5 b 6 a

Word focus *move*

Extra activity

Ask students what the usual meaning of *move* is (to go from one place to another), then to think of any phrasal verbs they know with *move*. Elicit answers from the whole class. List the verbs they suggest on the board, with their meaning.

Sample answers:

move on (progress to the next thing)

move out (leave where you live to go and live somewhere else)

move in (to start living in a place or with somebody else)

move over (make space for someone else)

move up (to improve your position, e.g. at work)

7 Ask students to work in pairs to discuss the meaning of *on the move* in the example, then complete the other expressions. Elicit answers from the whole class and check students understand the meanings.

ANSWERS

1 to tears (made everyone cry)
2 up in the world (becoming richer or more successful)
3 a muscle (stay still)
4 the goalposts (change the terms of an agreement)
5 up a gear (raise one's performance to a higher level)

Speaking

8 Ask students to discuss the issues about robots in pairs. Elicit answers from the whole class.

SAMPLE ANSWERS

Robots could work in public transport as some jobs here are mainly mechanical.

There might be issues with robots working in healthcare and childcare as emotional support is likely to be needed in both these areas.

Robots might be useful in police work as they would not be influenced by emotional responses.

9 Ask the class to discuss the three issues in depth, taking them one by one.

Homework

Ask students to write 150–200 words about the issues surrounding one of the three areas they have discussed in Exercise 9, discussing the pros and cons of their chosen topic. In a subsequent lesson, they can exchange their writing with a partner for comment and discussion of the content and the language.

11d A sensitive subject

Lead-in

Personal response

Ask students to tell a partner about a time when they saw someone who was very sad, and another time when they saw someone who was very happy. How did they recognise the people's emotional states? What was the situation? You might elicit one or two examples from the whole class.

Real life recognising feelings

1 Ask students to read the extract and discuss a situation when they didn't follow the advice given. Elicit some examples from the whole class if it seems appropriate.

2 [2.28] Ask students to read the two questions to focus their listening. Play the recording and ask them to answer the questions for each conversation. They can check with a partner. Play the recording again, if necessary.

ANSWERS

1 Conversation 1 work colleagues
Conversation 2 work colleagues – one is senior to the other and may be her boss
Conversation 3 old friends

2 Conversation 1 being on time for a meeting
Conversation 2 the design of an advertisement
Conversation 3 a new job

Audioscript [2.28]

Conversation 1

A: Hi there, Phil, good to see you. How are you? Do we have time for a coffee before we go into the meeting?

B: Actually, we're late already – we really need to go in straightaway. Do you have the report and other papers with you?

A: Yes, I have all that. You look a little troubled, though. Is everything OK?

B: Do you know, Fernando, it's just that perhaps you had a different attitude to time-keeping in your previous company. Punctuality is very important here, particularly for people like Jeff Kravitz, who we're about to see, and I'm very anxious to start this meeting on the right note.

B: Oh, sorry, Phil. Honestly, I didn't realise. You're right, it wasn't such a big deal in my last company – the attitude to time was much more laid-back. I'll definitely try to be more punctual in future. And don't worry – I'm very well prepared for this meeting. It's going to be good.

Conversation 2

C: Becky, have you got a minute to talk about your design for the new advertisement? I don't think it's quite there yet and we need to send it over to the web designer tomorrow.

D: Oh, I'm surprised. I included all your suggestions from our last meeting. I thought it was looking OK. Mmm, perhaps you should get another person in to look at it …

C: Sorry, I didn't mean to offend you. These things are always subjective, but please don't take it personally …

D: No … I'm sorry, Alicia, that came out wrong. I'm not offended. I genuinely meant it would be a good idea to get a third opinion. But whatever you want. I'm very happy to work with you to get it looking right.

C: Thanks. I appreciate that. I'll call Stacey and see if we can arrange a meeting with all three of us to look at it this afternoon.

Conversation 3

F: Hi Megumi. I haven't seen you for ages. How are you? Jen said you'd got a new job with an American company in Tokyo.

E: That's right. With Disney. I'm going to be in charge of all the merchandise for classic storybook characters, like Winnie the Pooh, Alice in Wonderland, Pinocchio. I'm very excited. Why are you smiling? Did I say something funny?

F: Oh, sorry, please don't think me rude – I wasn't laughing at you. It was just the idea of being in charge of all those characters, like a playgroup leader or something. It conjured up a funny mental picture. But it sounds great fun. When do you start?

3 [2.28] Ask students if they picked up what the point of misunderstanding was in each conversation, and play the recording for them to check. Elicit answers from the whole class.

ANSWERS

1 whether it was important to be on time or not
2 whether the boss thought the other's design work was sub-standard
3 whether the man was laughing at Megumi's new job

Speaking skill recognising others' feelings

4 [2.28] Read through the phrases for recognising others' feelings in the language box with the class, and ensure that they are familiar with the language and how it is used. Then have students read the five situations from the dialogues. Play the recording again and ask them to identify which expressions were used in which situation.

ANSWERS

The underlined phrases are the key expressions from the box.

1 You look a little troubled, though. Is everything OK?
2 Sorry, I didn't mean to offend you.
3 I'm sorry Alicia, that came out wrong.
4 Why are you smiling? Did I say something funny?
5 Oh, sorry, please don't think me rude – I wasn't laughing at *you*.

Pronunciation adjectives ending in *-ed*

5a [2.29] Ask students to work in pairs and decide on the pronunciation of the nine adjectives. Point out that they should focus in particular on the pronunciation of the *-ed* ending. Elicit ideas from the whole class, and encourage discussion, but do not say if they are correct or not. Play the recording for them to check.

ANSWERS

-ed = /t/: distressed; embarrassed; shocked

-ed = /d/: alarmed; concerned; surprised

-ed = /id/: insulted; offended; worried

5b Ask the class to say what the rules are for *-ed* pronunciation, and check they can pronounce the endings of the words in Exercise 5a correctly. They should then suggest other adjectives describing feelings ending in *-ed*. Play the recording again, pausing after each adjective for students to repeat them chorally and individually.

ANSWERS

if the root verb ends in /s/ or /k/, *-ed* is pronounced /t/

if the root verb ends in /m/ or /n/ or /z/ , *-ed* is pronounced /d/

if the root verb ends in /t/ or /d/ or /y/, *-ed* is pronounced /id/

5c Ask students to work in pairs and help each other with the pronunciation of the adjectives. Circulate and monitor their pronunciation.

6 Read through the instructions and options with the class so that they are clear about what they have to do. Ask them to work out a dialogue using the expressions from the box. They can write it down in note form if they need to. They should then practise it a couple of times to themselves. Circulate and monitor their conversations. You might ask some pairs to perform their dialogue for the whole class if they are willing to do this, or you could ask students to act out their conversation for another pair.

11e Don't get me wrong

Lead-in

Personal response

Ask the class to say what they think the expression *Don't get me wrong* means (i.e. 'I don't want you to misunderstand what I'm saying'), and to give some examples of how it is used (e.g. Peter: *I was talking to John yesterday – now, don't get me wrong – I think John's a great guy, but he said something that surprised me.* Peter wants the colleague to understand he isn't trying to criticise John.)

Writing an email message

1 Ask students to discuss these questions in pairs. Elicit some examples from the whole class.

2 Ask students to read the extract, then discuss it as a whole class in the light of their own ideas.

Vocabulary notes

Ensure students are familiar with these expressions from the text:

to treat something like something else (*people treat email like face-to-face conversation*) = to use something or deal with something in the same way as something different

to take offence at something (*she might take offence at something that the writer intended to be a joke*) = be upset or annoyed by something someone says

to interpret something as something else (*the reader might interpret this as impatience*) = to understand something in a certain way

3 Ask students to match the emails to the interpretations individually, then check with a partner. Elicit answers from the whole class.

ANSWERS

1 B 2 D 3 E 4 A 5 C 6 F

Writing skill avoiding misunderstandings

4 Read through the instructions and phrases with the whole class, and ensure that they understand what to do. They should work individually, but then check with a partner. Elicit the answers from the whole class, having some students read the whole email and others comment on their version.

SAMPLE ANSWERS

A I got your report. **Many thanks for getting back to me so quickly. I do appreciate all your work on this.**

B Thanks for letting me know about Jessica's farewell party next Saturday. I had hoped that you would change the day of the party to one that I could manage, **but, of course, I understand and I am not offended in any way**.

C I read your suggestions and I think we will stick to the original plan. **Don't take this the wrong way. I do appreciate all your work on this**.

D As you know, five of us have been offered the chance to visit the new Williams factory next week. There are two other people who I want to invite, not **including** you / besides you / as well as you – Fergus and Marcin. What do you think?

E Thanks for the email. I don't know about the 'optinos' because I don't know what the word means! **I'm joking, of course**. If you want my opinion, I think the Berkeley chairs are the best option.

F You haven't replied to the email I sent you two days ago. **I don't want to pressure you, but could you** reply today or we'll miss the deadline?

5 Read through the situation with the class and ensure they understand what they have to do. They should write the email individually. They might do this for homework.

SAMPLE ANSWER

I understand from a colleague that the foreign dictionary department is going to be closed down. This took me rather by surprise as nobody in the department has been informed of this. Do you know why this decision has been taken and what will happen to those of us who work in this department? Don't take this the wrong way, but were you involved in discussions about this? I don't want to pressure you, but I would really appreciate any further information.

6 Ask students to exchange their email with a partner for comment and discussion, using the three questions given.

11f Self-teaching robots

Before you watch

1 Students work in pairs to discuss the 'intelligent' machines and programmes and how useful they are. Take feedback from the class.

2 Ask students to discuss how a robot might 'learn' new things.

While you watch

3 Give students time to read the words in the glossary and the questions. Play the video for students to answer. Take feedback from the class.

ANSWERS

1 It uses the Internet to search for information.
2 to work with the elderly

4 Give students time to look at the notes. Then play the first part of the video (to 01.22) for them to complete the information.

ANSWERS

1 General Problem Solver
2 Institute of Technology
3 Head
4 build a bridge between
5 a cold drink
6 what an item looks like
7 images

5 Give students time to read the sentences, then play the second part of the video (01.23 to end) for them to decide if the sentences are true or false.

ANSWERS

1 F 2 T 3 T 4 F

After you watch

6 Students work in pairs to roleplay presenting an idea for a household robot, according to the instructions.

7 Ask students to work in groups to discuss the question.

Videoscript

00.03 Everybody knows robots are built to do what they're told. Only science fiction has robots that can think and learn like a human. Until now. Step forward the real-world general problem solver.

Researchers at the Japan's Tokyo Institute of Technology have developed the RW-GPS to teach itself how to perform a new task by scouring the Internet and finding the information that it needs. Heading the project is Dr Osamu Hasegawa.

00.35 Dr Osamu Hasegawa Most of the existing robots are good at processing and programming – the tasks they're pre-programmed to do. But they know little about the real world where we humans live. So our project is an attempt to build a bridge between robots and the real world.

00.50 On this occasion, the robot was given the task of serving a cold drink. Just like a human baby, the robot does not have prior knowledge of what a cup looks like or what it's used for. So the RW-GPS analyses images of cups and drinks collected from the Internet, applies filters for better accuracy, and successfully pours liquid and puts an ice cube, made of plastic in this experiment, into what it recognises as a cup.

01.23 Researcher We did not teach this robot what a cup or a bottle looks like, or how to fetch those items. That kind of information was not programmed into him.

01.32 At the core of this robot's self-learning mechanism is a new computer system called the SOINN. The system allows the robot to gather information on the Internet, and helps it filter out irrelevant or less accurate information so it can make the best educated guess and act accordingly.

01.53 Dr Osamu Hasegawa This robot can learn by itself. There's a huge amount of information available on the Internet, but at present only humans are making use of it. This robot can connect its brain directly to the Internet.

02.09 For example, even if the robot had no prior knowledge of human items like a wristwatch or a keyboard, it can Google their images and find out what they are in a matter of seconds. Hasegawa and his team hope that the robot could eventually be used to help care for the elderly, a situation where the ability to learn could be invaluable.

The engineers say the next challenge for this robot is to learn moral values, which would help it to decide what is right or wrong.

Unit 11 Review

Grammar

1 Ask students to complete the article with the correct verb forms.

ANSWERS

1 give
2 told
3 could
4 had
5 someone praises
6 Were I asked
7 Had you been instructed

2 Students read the article again and answer the questions.

ANSWERS

1 It relies on the participants being truthful and knowing themselves well.
2 No, it's natural human behaviour.

3 Ask students to work in pairs to do the test and discuss the statements 1–6.

Vocabulary

4 Ask students to choose the correct option to complete the sentences.

ANSWERS

1 on edge
2 livid
3 speechlesss
4 thrilled to bits
5 a bit down
6 petrified

5 Ask students to talk in pairs to describe their first day in a job or on a course. Circulate and monitor their speaking.

Real life

6 Ask students to complete the phrases.

ANSWERS

1 You seem
2 sounded a bit abrupt
3 think me ungrateful
4 I didn't offend you
5 out wrong

7 Ask students to improvise this conversation in pairs. Circulate and monitor their speaking.

Speaking

8 Ask students to discuss what type of person they are.

Unit 12 Landscapes

Lead-in

Personal response

Either take in some smaller pictures of different landscapes or one big one that all the class can see. Ask students to talk about the landscape(s) to a partner, saying what they can see, what they feel about it, where they think it is, what it reminds them of and so on, and then elicit some comments from the whole class. If you are using several smaller pictures, have students hold them up for the others to see while they talk about them.

1 [2.30] Ask students to read the questions to focus their listening. Play the recording and ask students to discuss the answers with a partner. Play the recording again for them to check their answers. Elicit answers from the whole class.

ANSWERS

1 Speaker 1: desert
Speaker 2: urban landscape *or* city skyline
Speaker 3: green countryside
2 Speaker 3

Audioscript [2.30]

Speaker 1

People think of the desert as a bleak environment – sparse vegetation and a monotonous, flat landscape. But actually, it's those things that make it so beautiful for me. A vast expanse of sand and rock under a cloudless sky … it just feels very pure. I think what appeals to me is a place which is completely untouched by people. You don't find that so often these days. I'm not saying I'd want to live there, mind you, but as a place to be alone with nature, you can't beat it.

Speaker 2

I prefer an urban landscape myself. I don't really go in for the chocolate-box vista, I have to say – snow-capped mountains or a pretty rustic scene with a farmer ploughing the fields. That's most people's idea of a landscape; they don't seem to count urban features like buildings and factories because they think of those as blots on the landscape. But my favourite views are those you see from rooftops looking out over a big city, particularly a night-time skyline, because I love to imagine what all the people there are doing.

Speaker 3

I love this landscape with its old farmhouses, rolling hills and lush meadows because it feels as if nothing's changed for hundreds of years. I guess that's because it's very rich farmland – they grow olives and grapes and cereal crops, and raise animals, so its use hasn't had to change. It hasn't been artificially preserved, like some scenery can be. We used to come here on holiday when I was young. We'd drive through some dramatic changes of scenery to get here: across the open plains of northern Italy, through medieval towns in the mountains and then we'd arrive here, in this idyllic, gentle countryside.

2 [2.30] Ask students to read through the gapped sentences and think about what adjectives are missing. Play the recording again and ask them to complete the phrases individually, then check with a partner. If necessary, play the recording again for them to check, correct and complete their answers. Elicit the answers from the whole class as complete phrases.

ANSWERS

Speaker 1: a **bleak** environment, **sparse** vegetation, **monotonous** flat landscape, a **cloudless** sky
Speaker 2: **snow-capped** mountains, a pretty **rustic** scene, the **night-time** skyline
Speaker 3: **rolling** hills, **lush** meadows, **rich** farmland, **open** plains, **idyllic**, gentle countryside

Vocabulary note

Students may not be familiar with these adjectives:

bleak = exposed, bare, empty
sparse = thin, not dense
lush = rich, full growth
idyllic = attractive, calm, charming
vast = huge, wide
chocolate-box = a pretty picture (but this has negative implications, suggesting it is clichéd or unoriginal like those traditionally used on boxes of chocolates)
rustic = traditional, rural

3 [2.30] Elicit the answers to this question from the whole class. Play the recording again for them to check.

ANSWERS

Speaker 1: likes the purity of a place untouched by people.
Speaker 2: loves to imagine what people are doing in the city.
Speaker 3: loves the fact it has been like this for hundreds of years.

4 Ask students to think of three landscapes they know that correspond to the criteria given. Then ask them to get into groups of four to talk about them. You might elicit some responses from the whole class after they have talked in groups.

Homework

Ask students to write 150 words about *A landscape that is important to me*. In a subsequent class, they can exchange writing with a partner to comment on and discuss the content and the language.

12a Under the big sky

Lead-in

Personal response

Ask students to look at the photo and the article heading, and discuss what the meaning and connotations of 'big sky' might be. (It often refers to wide, open, flat spaces where nothing limits the edge of the sky. It is used in particular in the USA of counties like Montana that have this sort of landscape.)

Reading

1 Ask students to read the two quotations and say what they think 'the West' represents and what they associate with the word.

SAMPLE ANSWER

For Americans 'the West' represents the pioneering spirit and the bravery of those that kept moving west to colonise new land. People might also associate it with cowboy films, and conflicts between white settlers and native American Indians. In modern-day terms it can also represent big open spaces, sparsely inhabited countryside, wilderness, small remote farming communities, the warmer pacific climate (particularly in California) and more exotic surroundings.

Background notes

Horace Greeley (1811–1872) was a newspaper editor with the New York Tribune. He was also a founder of the Liberal Republican Party, stood for President and lost, but on the way espoused many good, radical causes such as the abolition of slavery. The quotation is supposed to come from an editorial of 1865, though there is some dispute over it.

Robert Penn Warren (1905–1989) was a distinguished literary figure, winning the Pulitzer Prize for his novel *All The King's Men* (1947), and twice more for his poetry in 1958 and 1979. He was an important literary critic and was closely associated with the black civil rights movement.

The quotation comes from his prize-winning novel.

2 Ask students in pairs to discuss the picture and adjectival phrases that could be used to describe it. Elicit ideas from the whole class. Remind students that they can use some of the adjectives from the previous page, if appropriate.

SAMPLE ANSWERS

flat plains, cloudless sky, distant mountains, remote places, broad vistas, endless fields, wide open space, lonely lands

3 Ask students to read the questions to focus their reading, then read the article and answer the questions individually. They can check with a partner before you elicit answers from the whole class.

ANSWERS

1 All over the world; he takes photos of people and places.
2 He loves the grand expanse; it's special to him and he keeps coming back to it.

4 Ask students to work individually to find the phrases which match the sentences. They can then check with a partner. Elicit the answers from the whole class.

ANSWERS

1 William Albert Allard has shown us people and places as he sees them.
2 the stuff in the magazine was travel-postcard photography
3 you can tell it's really dry when a single rider can kick up a dust trail
4 It kept drawing me back.
5 high mountain meadows, the wisps of clouds within my reach

Language focus approximation

5 Ask students to look at the pairs of sentences and discuss the differences with a partner. Elicit answers from the whole class.

ANSWER

They make the details seem more vague or less precise. They also give the writing overall a laid-back, relaxed feel.

6 Ask students to look through the text for the examples indicated. Elicit answers from the whole class.

ANSWERS

1 (well) over 40, dozens of
2 around 1965
3 some place (paragraph 6)

7 [2.31] Read through the phrases for approximation in the language focus box with the class, and ensure that they understand the examples and their use. If you feel it necessary, ask them to read the additional information on page 172 and do the exercises there.

Ask students to decide which expressions of approximation could accompany or replace the underlined words and phrases in the text in Exercise 7. They should do this individually, then check with a partner. Then play the recording and ask them to note which expressions were used. Elicit answers from the whole class.

ANSWERS

1 Around five years ago
2 some party
3 two months or so
4 shortish
5 stuff
6 some 2,000
7 kind of varied
8 well over 200,000

Audioscript [2.31]

Around five years ago, I took a trip to Madagascar to photograph the landscape. An amateur photographer I had met at some party told me it had the most wonderful scenery. Normally I spend two months or so researching a place before I go there. But in this case, I had only a shortish amount of time before I had to be back. So, I packed my stuff and left the next day. During the course of the assignment, I took some 2,000 pictures. The photographer that recommended Madagascar said the landscape was kind of varied. That was a huge understatement. There's desert, marshes, rainforest, sandy beaches and rocky coves; and all of this is home to well over 200,000 different species of plants and animal.

8 Ask students to describe the things listed using the words in brackets. They should tell a partner. Elicit answers from the whole class.

Speaking

9 Ask students to think about a special place and follow the guidelines to prepare a description of it. They can make brief notes to help them talk, but shouldn't write it out completely. They should then tell a partner about their place and listen to their description.

Homework

Ask students to write 150–200 words comparing their special place and their partner's. In what ways are they similar and different. In a subsequent lesson, they should exchange writing with the same partner and comment on and discuss the content and language used.

12b Nature close up

Lead-in

Personal response

Ask the class to describe the last wild place where they were, what was there – plants, birds, animals – what they saw, heard and felt about it. Ask if they enjoy going out into the countryside and looking at wildlife and why / why not.

Listening

1 Ask students to read the haiku and work out the form and tell the class.

ANSWER

17 syllables, arranged 5–7–5

Background note

Haiku is a form of short poetry that emerged in Japan in the 16th century, and was very popular from the 17th to the 19th century. It is still written today, and has become popular around the world. Originally each haiku had to state or imply a season, and was restricted to natural world subjects. This was connected to the symbolism central to Buddhism, Taoism and animism. Nowadays people use the form to make any kind of observation.

2 [2.32] Ask students to read the questions to focus their listening. Play the recording, and ask students to check their answers with a partner. Play the recording again, if necessary, for them to check their answers. Elicit answers from the whole class.

ANSWERS

1 He liked to observe nature's details and she wanted to do this too.
2 He wanted to escape his celebrity and get closer to nature again.
3 Because they capture its beauty and simplicity in just a few words

Audioscript [2.32]

I = interviewer, **B** = biographer

I: Sophie Huxter, you're best known for writing travel guides, but recently you've been writing about the Japanese poet Matsuo Basho. Can you tell us what attracted you to him?

B: Yes, it was the subject of observing nature, especially its little details – the brilliant colour of a particular flower or the way light catches the spray from a waterfall and makes a rainbow. When I started to look into it, it really struck me how much I took the natural world for granted. And I think that's probably true for most of us: that observing nature is either a bit of a luxury, or just something that gets forgotten, because we all get rather caught up in our own busy lives.

I: And how does that relate to Basho?

B: Yeah, well, that's quite interesting, because as a poet one of his preoccupations was observing nature and writing down his thoughts. But fairly late in life, he decided he needed to get away from it all and get closer to nature. You see, Basho was already quite a well-known poet in his lifetime, and he wanted to escape his celebrity and live a more simple life. So at the age of 46, he set off on a journey across the island of Honshu. That journey was the background to his masterpiece in poetry, *Narrow Road to a Far Province*.

I: Ah, yes, I know it … at least parts of it.

B: So, he travelled on foot through Japan's backcountry – a distance of slightly less than 1,200 miles – and he kept a kind of diary of the things he saw in poem form as he went. So he would stop along the way to observe nature's modest dramas: a leaf floating through reflections in a crystal clear stream, the splash of a frog as it hopped from a leaf into the water, the sunlight on an avenue of trees on an autumn evening.

I: That's a lovely way of putting it – nature's modest dramas.

B: Well, what I love about the poems is that the language he uses is rather plain and simple, but the overall effect is very profound. Each haiku is like a polished stone; it captures the beauty and simplicity of nature in just a few words. I'll read you an example of one which pretty much sums this up. At one point he came across an old ruined military fort, overgrown with grass and it upset him rather. He wrote: 'Mound of summer grass / Are soldiers' heroic deeds / Only dreams that pass?'

3 [2.32] Ask students to discuss with their partner what they remember about the poet's description of the five things listed. Play the recording and ask them to check their ideas. Elicit answers from the whole class. Read through the *Wordbuilding* box and refer to Workbook page 99 for further information and practice if necessary.

ANSWERS
1 its brilliant colour
2 the way it makes light into a rainbow
3 the way it floats through reflections in a clear stream
4 the splashing sound as it hops into the water
5 the evening sunlight on them

Idioms adjective collocations

4 Ask the class to say what *crystal clear* means. Explain that it can also have a figurative meaning of 'easy to understand' (e.g. *Her instructions were crystal clear*).

ANSWER
extremely clear

5 Ask the class to read through the phrases and say which two are different.

ANSWERS
worried sick
scared stiff

Vocabulary notes

It might be helpful to explain the meanings of the less obvious intensifiers:

lightning quick (lightning moves extremely fast)

freezing cold (cold enough to freeze water)

worried sick (so worried you feel ill)

scared stiff (we tend to become rigid if we are frightened)

Less obvious or familiar are these:

sopping wet (*sopping* means 'completely soaked'; the word can also be used alone)

pitch black (pitch is a dense black substance made from tar, which is used for making boats and other things waterproof)

brand new (*brand* has to do with fire, so this means *just produced* – hot off the production-line)

fast asleep (this comes from a less common meaning of *fast* – constant, firm; so here completely asleep)

6 Ask students to make three sentences using a different phrase in each, based on real experiences. They should then tell a partner. Read the example with them first. Elicit answers from the whole class.

Homework

Ask students to write about their experiences using the expressions which they didn't use in Exercise 6. Ask them to write in more detail, with several sentences about each event. In a subsequent lesson, they can exchange their writing with a partner for comment and discussion of the content and the language.

Language focus qualifiers

7 Ask students to answer the questions about the sentences individually, then check with a partner. Elicit the answers from the whole class.

ANSWERS
1a noun (luxury)
b adjective (interesting)
c adjective (late)
d adjective (well-known)
e comparative adjective (less)
f verb (upset)
2 It tones it down a little in sentences: a, c, e, f
It intensifies it a little in sentences: b, d

8 Read through the examples in the language focus box with the class, making sure they understand the expressions and their use. If you feel they need more help, read the information on page 173 and have them do the exercises there.

Ask students to cross out the qualifiers which do not fit in the sentences in Exercise 8. They should do this individually, then check with a partner. Elicit answers from the whole class, having students explain why the word doesn't fit.

ANSWERS

1 fairly	5 quite
2 quite	6 fairly
3 a bit of	7 pretty
4 pretty	8 a little

Pronunciation *quite, fairly* and *pretty*

9a [2.33] Ask students to read through the phrases and think about how they might be said to intensify the meaning or tone it down. Play the recording and ask them to tick which meaning they think it has. They can check with a partner, then play the recording again. Elicit answers from the whole class.

ANSWER

Slightly intensifying: 2, 3, 5
Toning down: 1, 4, 6

9b Ask students to work in pairs and say the phrases in each way for the partner to guess what meaning is intended. Circulate and monitor students' speaking.

10 Ask students to talk to their partner about their feelings on the topics given, using qualifiers. Circulate and monitor their speaking.

Speaking and writing

11 There are various ways of doing this activity. You can ask students to imagine a natural event – something they have seen in the past, maybe many times (e.g. crocus flowers appearing from the earth in spring, horse chestnuts falling in autumn) – that they find beautiful, and describe that to their partner. Alternatively you can provide them with a set of suitable photos cut from newspapers and magazines, or printed from the Internet, and they can choose one of those to work from. Or you can ask them to select a photo they particularly like from the Student's Book. Or finally, you could ask them to photograph something digitally themselves and use that picture to talk about.

12 Ask students to put some ideas about their chosen picture (from whichever of the sources mentioned above) into haiku form. They might do this for homework. They can then put up the picture and the haiku on the wall, and walk round and read other people's writing.

12c Room with a view

Lead-in

Personal response

Ask students to tell a partner how their ideal bedroom would be furnished and decorated. Elicit some responses from the whole class.

Reading

1 Ask students to tell their partner what paintings, pictures or posters they have on their own walls at home.

2 Read the instructions with the class to ensure they understand what to do. Ask them to look at the pictures and note the information from the article, then discuss their answers with a partner. Elicit answers from the whole class.

ANSWERS

1 cover the windows (with plastic) to make the room dark
2 cut a small hole in the plastic
3 the image is then projected (upside down) on the wall

Vocabulary notes

to go haywire = to go wrong
inverted = turned the other way round (top to bottom)
to right something = to put something the correct way up
enthralling = catching and keeping the attention

3 Ask students to read through the statements to focus their reading, then read and decide if the statements are true, false, or if there is not enough information to say. Ask them to check with a partner before you elicit the answers from the whole class.

ANSWERS

1 F (*covered with a fuzzy image*)
2 T (*Aristotle described the phenomenon in the fourth century BC*)
3 T (*and the ancestor of the photographic camera*)
4 T
5 T (*was used by painters like Vermeer as a drawing aid*)
6 N (*to his knowledge he was the first*)
7 F (*He chose a room in his own house*)
8 N

Critical thinking identifying aims

4 Ask students to look for the information in the text to carry out the three activities. Elicit answers from the class.

ANSWER

There is enough information to do 1, but there isn't a full explanation of how to do 2 and 3.

5 Ask the class to discuss which of the three options is the author's aim.

ANSWER
b

Word focus *space and room*

6 Ask students to read the sentences and discuss the meaning of *space* and *room* with a partner. Elicit answers from the whole class.

ANSWERS

Space and *room* are not interchangeable in a and b. *Space* has a more general meaning than *room*, which is used here to mean a section of a house.

1 yes
2 no
3 no

Generally, if the meaning is uncountable, meaning an area available for use, *room* and *space* are interchangeable.

7 Ask students to choose the correct word to complete each sentence, then decide what the expressions mean. They should then check with a partner. Elicit answers from the whole class.

ANSWERS

1 give her some space = let someone be alone for a while; not interfere
2 watch this space = wait and see how things develop
3 the elephant in the room = the thing everyone is aware of but no-one wishes to talk about
4 breathing space = time to prepare or collect your thoughts
5 room for improvement = areas that could be better

Speaking

8 Ask students to discuss in pairs how they think the photo might have been taken, then check on page 153. Discuss the question with the whole class.

9 Ask students to choose one of the four subject areas and think of a technique to explain to their partner. Circulate and monitor their explanations. Have some students explain their technique to the whole class.

Homework

Ask students to write a 100-word explanation of a technique from one of the other areas listed. In a subsequent lesson, they should exchange their writing with a partner for comment and discussion of content and language use.

12d A blot on the urban landscape

Lead-in

Personal response

Elicit the meaning of *a blot on the landscape* (something that spoils the countryside or the view) from the class. Ask for examples of blots on the landscape.

Real life a debate

1 Ask students to complete the text and check the answers individually. Elicit the answers from the whole class.

ANSWERS

1 air
2 light

2 Ask students to guess the cities individually, then check with a partner. Elicit suggestions from the whole class, then tell them the correct answers.

ANSWERS

1 São Paulo
2 Beijing
3 Brussels
4 Paris
5 Warsaw
6 Mexico City

3 Ask students to discuss the problem of congestion in pairs and note some ideas to combat it. They should then discuss their thoughts with another pair. Elicit suggestions from the whole class. Note them on the board and discuss them further.

SAMPLE ANSWERS

Congestion charging (i.e. charging for cars to come into the city centre)
Road tolls
High parking charges
Better public transport systems
Cheaper public transport systems
Incentives to share cars / use public transport

Speaking skill interrupting

4a [2.34] Ask students to read the questions to focus their listening. Play the recording for them to answer. They can then check with a partner. Replay the recording if necessary, then elicit answers from the whole class.

ANSWERS

1 a congestion charging scheme, and a park and ride bus service
2 cost and exemptions

Audioscript [2.34]

A: OK, so we'd like to hear your views about two possible ways of relieving traffic congestion in the city centre. Craig is just going to summarise the two main proposals before we open up the discussion. Craig …

B: Thank you. The first proposal is a congestion charging scheme, that's to say creating a zone in the centre of the city which vehicles have to pay a fixed charge to enter. The exact limits of the zone haven't been defined yet, nor has the exact amount of the charge. The second proposal involves simply banning all private cars from the centre, and providing a park and ride bus service from various points on the outskirts of the city into the centre.

A: Thanks, Craig. So now we'll open the discussion to the floor. Please try and keep your comments reasonably short so that everyone gets a chance to have their say …

C: Well, I don't see how we can really comment on the first proposal without knowing what the scope of the zone is and how much it's going to cost: those really are key issues. I mean, if it's going to mean that local residents have to pay to get into the centre, then that's not really fair is it? I live in Charles Street which is …

D: Sorry, can I just say something in answer to that? We had a similar scheme where I used to live and people who lived within the zone were exempted from paying the charge.

B: Yes, I think that's absolutely right and you can also give a discount to people who need to come into the centre for their work so that it doesn't discriminate against them either. Otherwise you find that a lot of people who really need their cars …

D: No, hang on a minute. If you keep making exceptions for different groups of people, you're going to end up with a system that costs a lot of money and doesn't bring much benefit. I think you have to be strict about this …

C: Yes, but how much is the charge going to be? No one's given us any …

D: Sorry, can I just finish what I was saying? The point is that unless you're strict about it, the scheme won't bring in enough revenue to pay for itself, and so those who do pay will question the whole scheme.

4b [2.34] Read through the phrases for interrupting in the language box with students, then play the recording while students underline the phrases which are used in the discussion. Elicit answers from the whole class.

> ANSWERS
> Can I just say something in answer to that?
> No, hang on a minute …
> Sorry, can I just finish what I was saying?

Pronunciation intonation in interruptions

5a [2.35] Read the rubric with the class, emphasising the *polite* and *firm but gentle* tone used for the phrases. Then play the recording of the phrases for interrupting from the box, for students to hear the intonation. Play the recording again, pausing after each phrase for students to repeat it chorally and individually.

5b Ask students to practise the phrases in pairs and help each other with their intonation. Circulate and monitor their speaking.

6 Ask students to work in groups of four. One should be the chairperson, the others are speakers in the debate. Give them time to prepare what they want to say. Make sure the chairperson knows the phrases to use (*hear your views / open the discussion to the floor / so that everyone gets their chance to have their say / these are the key issues*). You may wish to put the chairpeople together to prepare, with the speakers from the floor preparing in small groups that are different to the groups carrying out the debate. Then they can return to their own original groups of four to have the debate. Circulate and monitor their speaking.

Homework

Ask students to write 150 words about congestion problems in the place where they live or another town they know well. Say what the main problems are and how they think they could be solved, using ideas discussed in this section. In a subsequent lesson, they should exchange their writing with a partner for comment on the content and language used.

12e A unique service

Lead-in

Personal response
Ask students to think of a business (a company, a shop, a service provider) which they know well. What is good and bad about the way it is run? How could it be improved? Ask them to tell a partner. Elicit some ideas from the whole class.

Writing a speculative letter

1 Ask students to work with a partner and make a list of suggestions about how to attract customers to their new business. Elicit ideas from the whole class and list them on the board.

SAMPLE ANSWERS

Advertising in local newspapers, on TV
Posters around town
People giving out fliers around town
People with sandwich boards around town
Mail shot to local homes
Website on the Internet
Some special opening event, with gifts, reduced price bargains, famous person attending

2 Ask students to discuss in pairs the tips for approaching clients cold and decide which are the most important. Elicit responses and reasons from the whole class.

Vocabulary note

Elicit / explain the meaning of *bait* and the expression *to bait the hook* – meaning to put a worm or some other attractive thing for fish to eat on the hook in order to catch them. By analogy, to provide something to attract and then 'catch' the client.

3 Ask students to read the letter and check which of the tips it follows. Elicit answers from the whole class.

ANSWERS

a *local businesses like yours*
b letter
c *medium-sized businesses*
d *you don't want to spend a lot of money on this*
e *unique service* and *specialise in transforming the outer appearance of buildings and grounds*
f *Currently we are offering an initial 30-minute consultation free of charge*

Vocabulary notes

to landscape = to change the appearance of an area of land to make it more attractive

to expire = to end, to run out

Writing skill persuasive language

4a Read through the list of persuasive techniques, then ask students to find examples of them in the letter. They can then compare their answers with a partner. Elicit answers from the whole class.

ANSWERS

1 the unique service we offer; it's amazing what effects can be achieved
2 *Exoscape* is a young team of landscape gardeners and exterior designers. We specialise in transforming the outer appearance of buildings and grounds.
3 Clearly, you don't want to spend a lot of money on this.
4 We all look at our surroundings from time to time and think they need freshening up.
5 You might like to take advantage of this offer before it expires at the end of the month.

4b Ask students to match the phrases with the techniques listed in Exercise 4a. They should do this individually, then check with a partner. Elicit answers from the whole class.

ANSWERS

1 d 2 b 3 a 4 e 5 c

5 Read the instructions with the class and ensure that they know what to do. They should use the ideas discussed in the previous exercises to plan and write their letters, and use the Exoscape letter as a model. They can do this for homework.

6 Students should exchange their letters with a partner and check them against the three criteria. Then they should comment on and discuss their letters.

12f Canada oil sands

Before you watch

1 Students work in pairs to discuss where oil is found and how it is extracted, using the words in the box. Take feedback from the class.

SAMPLE ANSWER

Oil is normally found underground. Once an oil deposit has been located, extraction takes place. This is a complicated process: an oil rig drills an oil well through rock until the oil deposits are reached. Then the oil is pumped out of the ground to the surface.

2 Ask students to look at the photo and video title, and answer the questions.

While you watch

3 Give students time to read the words in the glossary. Play the video for students to check their answers to Exercise 2. Take feedback from the class.

ANSWERS

1 It's found on the surface, in the sand.
2 It has a dramatic effect – the forests have to be cut down in order for extraction to take place.
3 Because of the high demand for oil.

4 Give students time to look at the questions. Then play the first part of the video (to 02.13) for them to answer.

ANSWERS

1 trees
2 billions (and billions) of birds
3 It has levels comparable to those in Saudi Arabia.
4 To capture the changing landscapes / to photograph the connection between the forest and the mining.

5 Give students time to read the description, then play the second part of the video (02.14 to 02.37) for them to write the missing words.

ANSWERS

1 forest 2 soil 3 collected 4 trucks 5 pipeline

6 Give students time to read the question, then play the third part of the video (02.38 to end) for them to say what the effects are on each aspect of the area.

ANSWERS

a N b P c P and N d N e N f N

After you watch

7 Students work in pairs to roleplay an interview about the Canada oil sands, according to the instructions.

8 Ask students to work in groups to discuss the questions about exploiting natural resources.

Videoscript

In Alberta, Canada, a new method for extracting petroleum is having a big effect on an environment that's been unchanged for thousands of years. We're on assignment with *National Geographic* magazine to document this changing landscape. This mining operation continues 24 hours a day, 365 days a year, extracting oil from just beneath the surface of what was once Canadian wilderness.

00.28 Celina Harper I could just cry when I see what they've done to our land. There was just sea, that's all you could see, just sand as far as you could see. Nothing, just nothing. Not even one, one stick. Not even one tree standing.

00.46 This is Canada's boreal – one of the largest intact forests on Earth. It's northern America's nesting spot for billions upon billions of birds that migrate across North America and even as far as South America. It's also the site of something called oil sands – a naturally occurring mix of sand and a viscous form of petroleum known as bitumen.

Bitumen must be heavily processed before it is becomes crude oil, then refined into gasoline and diesel fuels. This section of northern Alberta has the largest oil sand deposits in the world and some estimates suggest Alberta's oil reserves are comparable to those of Saudi Arabia. But to get to this oil, Canada has been strip mining large sections of former wilderness.

National Geographic magazine photographer Peter Essick journeyed to Fort McMurray to capture the changing landscape.

01.52 Peter Essick You can take pictures sort of of the wilderness part, which is sort of the trees and the muskeg that hasn't been developed. And then you can take a picture of some of the mining, the big trucks, but I was trying to show some ways that you could see, sort of, the connection between, sort of, the wildlife, or the nature, and the mining.

02.14 First the forest is cut down. The top soil is removed and the sand is collected by massive shovels. It's then carried by dump trucks to a processing facility. Each truck can carry almost 400 tons of oil-rich sand. After processing, the synthetic crude is shipped via pipeline to refineries in the United States.

02.38 Canada has been extracting oil here for almost a century, but higher fuel prices in recent years and new processing technologies have led to a major oil boom. This part of Alberta has been completely transformed.

02.53 Mike Noseworthy You're looking at high rent costs, high food costs and high fuel costs.

Brenda Hampson It's just money and it's all over the place. And the jobs are all over the place. In Alberta, there's ten jobs for one person.

03.09 People's lives have been changed. Some for the worse, but many, arguably, for the better. But conservationists say the landscape is also being changed – for the worse. They worry that stripping the boreal of thousands of square miles of forest is hurting a major ecosystem.

Some argue that destruction in the boreal forest is a major contributor to global warming. The forest is so enormous that it helps control the Earth's thermostat. Its wetlands and bogs absorb carbon, helping cleanse the atmosphere of the greenhouse gases that contribute to higher temperatures throughout the world.

03.53* *Steve Kallick This is the peat. It's spongy, there's no strength to it. This is accumulated carbon from millennia. It's been exposed now to the surface, the protective cover's been removed and all the carbon that's been stored in this is starting to come back out into the atmosphere. Development across the boreal is going to continue to do this. We don't know how much. We don't know what the ultimate result is going to be.

04.15 Already temperatures here are climbing, while there's been a corresponding drop in rain and snow. But the country is not planning to stop oil sand processing any time soon. Dozens of companies are planning nearly a hundred more projects worth 100 billion dollars.

Canada is working to reduce the amount of greenhouse emissions and to reclaim land that's been stripped in the mining process, but some conservationists hope vast sections of the boreal forest will be set aside and protected from future strip mining.

04.52* *Steve Kallick By having a large undeveloped area for wildlife can move and adapt to change, we may be able to protect them from some of the worse impacts of global warming. As climate change is affecting their habitat they'll be able to migrate into other areas if we set aside millions and tens of millions of acres in large, intact natural landscapes.

05.18 It would seem the needs of the land, its wildlife and the planet's thermostat are in conflict with our demand for oil.

Unit 12 Review

Grammar

1 Ask students to look at the photo and answer the questions, then read the article to check.

ANSWER

It's an island near Iceland. The man is catching puffins in a net to eat.

2 Ask students to use the words 1–8 to qualify or approximate the words in italics in the article.

ANSWERS

1 quite a dynamic landscape
2 some ten kilometres
3 fifty years or so
4 smallish
5 a bit like
6 dozens of puffins
7 rather taken aback
8 kind of tasty

3 Ask students to work in pairs to describe a sight they can see in the countryside. Elicit ideas from the class for open discussion.

Vocabulary

4 Ask students to complete the descriptions using the words in the box.

ANSWERS

1 rolling, lush, rustic
2 wide, bone, monotonous
3 brand, skyline

5 Ask students to talk in pairs to describe a landscape they know. Circulate and monitor their speaking.

Real life

6 Ask students to rewrite the phrases so they are less direct.

ANSWERS

1 Sorry, can I just interrupt you there?
2 Can I just say something in answer to that?
3 No, I'm sorry I have to stop you there …
4 Sorry, can I just finish what I was saying?
5 OK, you can make your point in a moment.
6 Just a moment, please.

7 Ask students to have this conversation in pairs. Circulate and monitor their speaking.

Speaking

8 Ask students to choose a photo they liked from the unit and explain why they like it. Circulate and monitor their speaking.

Grammar summary: answer key

Unit 1

1

2 Prior to that time
3 Nowadays
4 Over the last few decades
5 currently
6 in the coming days

2

2 had been running
3 were living
4 will be
5 has been saving
6 will realise

3

2 will have doubled
3 hasn't been doing
4 will have been
5 have missed out
6 had forgotten
7 will have been studying
8 had been working

UNIT 2

1

2 is always singing
3 was shaving
4 had been trying
5 've put
6 'll still be working
7 'll finish
8 've been having / 've had

2

2 Having spent
3 twisting
4 Not having flown
5 Having considered
6 Being
7 not wanting
8 not having spoken

UNIT 3

1

2 foolish
3 entirely
4 extremely
5 quite
6 exhausting
7 dirty *or* filthy
8 quite
9 really
10 absolutely

2

2 Never had I witnessed such a violent thunderstorm.
3 What we could really do with is more storage space.
4 It's the lack of facilities in the area that I'm particularly concerned about.
5 Rarely do houses come up for sale in this village.
6 Not once did he complain about the poor living conditions.
7 Never again will I believe a word he says.
8 I didn't buy any trousers but I did buy a belt.
9 It's this wonderful view that / which I'll really miss.
10 No sooner had she arrived home than the doorbell rang.

UNIT 4

1

2 Andy may / might / could have fixed it.
3 He can't have liked it.
4 There may / might / could have been a power cut.
5 That must have been frustrating.
6 You should have used your sat nav.
7 So we needn't have pre-booked our tickets.
8 He may / might not have realised it was happening.

2

2 unlikely that the company will upgrade its computers
3 chances are (that) we'll be living abroad
4 might well be re-elected.
5 it's bound to break
6 Is the DVD player definitely not
7 may not need to buy
8 should receive a call
9 likelihood is that she'll find an excuse

UNIT 5

1

2 This queue is for e-passport holders only. You haven't got **one** so you need to join the longer queue.
3 If I can take time off work next month, I will **do**.
4 The rooms were very expensive, but ours was one of the cheaper **ones**.
5 You could hire a car when you go abroad, but to **do so** you need to have held a licence for a year.
6 'Did you book the flights?' 'I meant to but I didn't get a moment.'
7 Hindi and English are both spoken in New Delhi. **The former** is the principal spoken language and **the latter** is the principal written language.
8 This train goes to the airport, but that one doesn't.
9 'Did you remember to bring the map?' 'I'm afraid I didn't.' *or* '**I'm afraid not**.'

2

2 the exact location of the hotel.
3 a preference for an earlier start date.
4 by my knowledge of the region.
5 several attempts to contact you …
6 been an improvement in the weather conditions.
7 by our quick recovery from jetlag.
8 on receipt of your deposit.
9 your assistance in this matter.
10 his early arrival.

UNIT 6

1

2 'll be looking after them
3 run through them again.
4 that he'd made it up.
5 take it back.
6 put them off

2

2 talk her out of
3 do away with the monarchy
4 put up with racial abuse
5 take you up on your offer
6 live up to our expectations

3

2 from bringing
3 not to approach
4 for violating
5 being
6 from becoming

UNIT 7

1

Possible answers:

2 In addition to being an enjoyable subject to study, history can help us understand the present.
3 The event was cancelled owing to the lack of funding.
4 Since we hadn't heard from you, we assumed you weren't coming.
5 The Pharaohs of ancient Egypt were seen as gods as well as kings.
6 Although Herodotus was a very famous historian, little is known about the man himself.
7 I've lived in this flat since moving / since I moved to Madrid in 2002.
8 The new law was passed despite the objections.

2

2 Contrary to
3 Given that
4 regardless of
5 provided that
6 since
7 in case
8 in view of
9 insofar as

UNIT 8

1

2 was reported to have occurred off the coast of Mexico.
3 is known to have taken place in the early hours …
4 is said not to have been selected for the Olympic team.
5 are thought to have been wiped out …
6 fell 100 metres down a steep ridge is said to be recovering well.
7 is expected that the finance minister will announce …
8 are believed to have been present.

2

1 no harm (in) applying for the job.
2 no doubt that the advertising campaign has been effective.
3 no point in paying for an expensive laptop …
4 no matter how many possessions we have, we always want more.
5 no use calling him as he never answers his phone.
6 they will have no alternative but to go on strike …
7 no way of accessing the data without a password.
8 I have no intention of leaving before …

UNIT 9

1

2 We stood just in front of the stage.
3 The reviews were just raving about the new single.
4 I bought the CD just after it came out.
5 Tickets for the music festival often sell out in just one day.
6 We've been waiting for just over an hour.
7 I was just wondering where you were.
8 I've just about finished my essay.
9 She's just as talented as her sister.
10 It was just an unfortunate misunderstanding.

2

2 in order to block out the surrounding noise.
3 to get rid of my headache.
4 to avoid causing a scene.
5 so that I would feel fresh on the day of my exam.
6 so as not to leave fingerprints.
7 in order that he could work on the train.
8 so that he will get / he gets them by Friday.

UNIT 10

1

1 hasn't it
2 has there
3 did they
4 does he
5 aren't I
6 won't you
7 shouldn't she
8 didn't we
9 shall we
10 will you

2

2 I was completely speechless when I heard the news.
3 It was so airless in the room that I could barely breathe.
4 The best way to get rid of ants is to go straight to the source: the nest.
5 He hungrily devoured everything that was on his plate.
6 She pushed him aside in an unfriendly way / manner.
7 It solved the problem instantly.
8 He reluctantly agreed to let me pay for the taxi.

UNIT 11

1

2 I'd rather you broke the news to her.
3 What if she left him? Then he'd be devastated.
4 I wish he wouldn't be / wasn't so critical.
5 It's high time the government changed the laws.
6 Supposing we employed someone to clean the flat?
7 If only I / we had more free time.
8 I'd just as soon you drove as James (did).

2

2 Were it not so cold, we could walk into town.
3 Should our plans change, I'll let you know.
4 Should you experience any technical problems, please call the helpline.
5 Were I to be offered a promotion, I would stay at the company.
6 Had the weather been better, we would have stayed longer.
7 Were it not for your help, I wouldn't have known what to do.
8 Had my alarm not gone off, I would still be asleep.

UNIT 12

1

2 kind of
3 ish
4 stuff
5 or so
6 things
7 well
8 around

2

2 quite / bit
3 quite
4 fairly
5 a bit
6 quite
7 bit of / bit of a
8 a bit of / pretty

Photocopiable tests

Unit 1 Test

Grammar

1 Complete the sentences with the correct time phrase.

since Friday	next month	every week	at the moment
how long	last year	already	while

1 Paul has a piano lesson ________________ .
2 ________________ I was walking to work, I met my brother.
3 We will introduce new rates ________________ .
4 I haven't heard from Mike ________________ .
5 They had ________________ lived there for five years when I arrived.
6 He's working in the garden ________________ .
7 They visited the Maldives ________________ .
8 ________________ has she been working there?

(8 points)

2 Match each time phrase to one of the sentences in Exercise 1. You do not need to use all the sentences.

a in June 2008 ______
b for how many years ______
c when ______
d each Tuesday ______
e for several weeks ______
f recently ______
g in six weeks ______
h two months ago ______
i in the future ______
j at present ______

(10 points)

3 Match the beginnings (a–f) with the endings (1–6).

a They haven't studied so hard ______
b In five years' time ______
c Joan and Paul have often done ______
d They had worked in Africa ______
e Paul had been hoping ______
f She has been living with her mother, ______

1 before they came to India.
2 looking for a flat of her own.
3 for many years.
4 for this kind of chance for five years.
5 she will have moved away from here.
6 this kind of work before.

(12 points)

Vocabulary

4 Underline the correct word pairs.

1 There are a few *odds and ends / ends and odds* to complete at work before Friday.
2 They did a good job, *large and by / by and large*.
3 You must be home by 11. No *buts and ifs / ifs and buts*.
4 He's rather *rough and ready / ready and rough*, but he's a good person at heart.
5 He put his *heart and soul / soul and heart* into the game.
6 You can't do that *in this age and day / in this day and age*.
7 I need a bit of *quiet and peace / peace and quiet*.
8 It's important to keep *law and order / order and law*.

(8 points)

5 Put the words in the box into the correct sentences.

chatterbox	drifter	joker	free spirit
control freak	go-getter	outgoing type	doer

1 The boss won't let us do anything without asking him first. He's a real ________________ .
2 Julie's such a ________________ , but she has nothing interesting to say.
3 She's a ________________ . She likes to do her own thing.
4 Jim's very hard-working. He's a ________________ who gets things done.
5 She's fun at parties because she's such an ________________ .
6 Don't believe everything he says. He's a bit of a ________________ .
7 He knows what he wants and makes sure he gets it. He's a true ________________ .
8 Unfortunately Paul never settled anywhere long. He's just a ________________ .

(8 points)

6 Match the expressions with the correct definitions.

1 a life-saver
2 the time of your life
3 all walks of life
4 the story of my life
5 a fact of life
6 larger than life
7 bring to life

a a noisy outgoing personality
b something that helped a lot
c to make something interesting
d a very good time, lots of fun
e something unlucky which always happens
f different jobs and lifestyles
g something you can't change

(14 points)

Functions

7 Complete the conversation with these expressions.

I lost the thread	as I was saying	I'll begin again
just look at my notes	I'll just have a sip of water	

So, [1] ______ in the first part of my talk, the situation is very serious – if I can [2] ______ – we can see a 12% loss this quarter. Now, this is due to … this is because … sorry [3] ______ … this is due to various factors: the recession and (*cough, cough, cough*) …excuse me, [4] ______ . That's better … er, ummm … oh, [5] ______ … oh, yes, and due to other things which are beyond our control …

(10 points)

Writing

8a Read this letter and decide in which paragraphs the candidate does these things.

a shows his enthusiasm for the company
b describes his education
c talks about his personal current situation
d talks about his past work experience
e talks about contact

> Dear Mrs Roberts
>
> I am writing in response to the advertisement in yesterday's *Swindon Advertiser* for a shop assistant. I am interested in the position because your shop is looking for someone with experience, who is prepared to stay in the job for a number of years. I have recently moved to Swindon and got married last month; I am now looking for a job which will allow me to settle here permanently.
>
> As you will see from the enclosed CV, I have a relatively long experience of shop work, having started helping out in my father's newsagent's as a teenager on Saturdays. Since then I have completed my A-levels and a College Diploma in Commerce and Shopkeeping. I have also worked as an assistant in a shoe shop and a bookshop.
>
> I know Roberts Department Store and it is certainly the kind of environment in which I would like to be employed. I am available for interview at any time. Please do not hesitate to call me either on the home phone number or the mobile number, or email me.
>
> I look forward to hearing from you.
>
> Yours sincerely
>
> Clarence Posslethwaite

8b Write a letter of application to Mr Bagley at Belford's Furniture Store in Milton Keynes. They are looking for a Warehouse Manager.

____
____
____
____
____
____
____
____

(15 points)

Speaking

9 Give a full description of a person you know well. Talk about his / her most important qualities and weaknesses, as well as giving information on his / her education, interests, work / study and future plans.

(10 points)

Unit 2 Test

Grammar

1 Complete the sentences with a continuous form of the verbs in brackets.

1 I think Paul ____________ still ____________ (work) with them next Christmas.
2 The boys ____________ (live) in a flat in the city now.
3 She ____________ (study) whales for two years before the accident happened.
4 While we worked, the others ____________ (eat) lunch.
5 Doctors ____________ (try) to find a cure for years.

(10 points)

2 Complete the sentences with the present or perfect participle of the verbs in the box. Use a negative (–) or a positive (+) form.

live	watch	work	want	meet	pay	hope	play

1 ____________ attention to the instructions leads to problems. (–)
2 ____________ there for a long time, he knew the local people. (+)
3 ____________ on a building site can be dangerous. (+)
4 ____________ him before, I didn't recognise him. (–)
5 ____________ the first part of the film, I went home. (+)
6 They left early, ____________ to avoid the traffic. (+)
7 He went to the party, ____________ to miss the chance of seeing Jane. (–)

(14 points)

3 Complete each sentence with the correct form of an expression with *foot* from the box.

to shoot oneself in the foot	to get one's foot in the door
to foot the bill	to put one's foot in it
to put one's foot down	to follow in someone's footsteps

1 The dinner was expensive, but my boss ____________ .
2 Jane had hoped for promotion, but she ____________ when she refused to work late.
3 Mike's dad is a lawyer and Mike started studying law last month, ____________ .
4 If you do a good job on this article, you ____________ .
5 I won't take any poor work, I am ____________ now.
6 I asked about his wife, but he isn't married. I really ____________ .

(6 points)

Vocabulary

4 Circle the correct option.

1 I hope we have enough money to get *by / through / on* on for the next month.

2 If he wants to pass his exam, he needs to get *down to / up to / over to* some serious study.

3 I have to finish by Friday, so I need to get *up with / through to / on with* this project.

4 If you want to get *ahead / past / down* you will need to pass some exams.

5 I really can't understand what Bill is getting *to / at / on* when he says that.

6 She is so lonely that she watches a lot of TV just to get *with / on / through* the day.

(12 points)

5 Match the idioms a–h with 1–8.

a to be second nature	**1** to follow the rules
b to be on the safe side	**2** to not do a good job
c to do something by the book	**3** to take no risks at all
d to cut corners	**4** to do something automatically
e to wrap someone in cotton wool	**5** to be careful
f to take every precaution	**6** to have a lot of risks
g to be fraught with danger	**7** to have protection
h to have a safety net	**8** to overprotect someone

(8 points)

6 Write the meaning of these abbreviations.

1 Mon ____________	6 1st ____________
2 docs ____________	7 + ____________
3 Uni ____________	8 sts ____________
4 p.w. ____________	9 incl. ____________
5 sthg ____________	10 e.g. ____________

(10 points)

Functions

7 Complete the speech with the phrases for keeping people's attention.

that's the key thing	so what does this tell us
I remember when I first	I'd just like to say one thing
how many of you actually	

Before I continue, [1] ______ about office relationships. I wonder [2] ______ are on good terms with all your colleagues. [3] ______ started working for Johnsons, we were all terrified of the office manager. There was a negative feeling throughout the office. [4] ______ about office relationships? Well, we do not have to be best friends with everyone – but it is important to maintain polite relationships with everyone. [5] ______ .

(10 points)

Writing

8a Complete the story with the adjectives in the box.

sheer	bright	confident	slick	daring

It was a [1] ____________ August morning when Martin started off up the [2] ____________ face of the Big Pear Mountain. He was a [3] ____________ young man, attempting something which no other climber had done before – free climbing up the Big Pear! It had been cold the night before, and the surface of the rock was [4] ____________ , so he had to be careful where he put his hands and feet. It all went well at first. Then just 200m below the summit, Martin's normal [5] ____________ movement stopped. He was paralysed. He didn't know what to do next.

(5 points)

8b Now continue the story, describing what Martin did, what happened to him and how the story ended. Use as many descriptive adjectives as you can.

____
____
____
____
____
____
____
____
____
____

(15 points)

Speaking

9 Talk about an adventure that you or someone you know had. It can be real, or something from a book or film. Describe what happened in detail, using adjectives to make it interesting.

(10 points)

Unit 3 Test

Grammar

1 Circle the correct intensifying adverb.

1 Paul is *completely / absolutely / really* strong.
2 They live in *a so / an absolutely / an entirely* beautiful village.
3 She would *really / completely / very* like to see the film.
4 We're *entirely / totally / extremely* sorry that it happened.
5 It was *so / completely / utterly* kind of them to offer.
6 The answer he gave was *so / very / totally* wrong!
7 It was *entirely / extremely / very* my fault.
8 It wasn't their best performance, but it was *so / incredibly / quite* good.

(8 points)

2 Rewrite the sentences, using the word or words in brackets to give emphasis.

1 The colour of the flowers attracts you. (what)
____
2 You notice the height of the trees first. (it's)
____
3 You don't see so many different plants together. (rarely)
____
4 Nobody has created a garden like this before. (never)
____
5 He really likes exotic plants. (does)
____
6 The care he has taken is noticeable. (the thing)
____

(12 points)

3 Complete the text with the words in the box.

although	but	however	so	indeed

Designing beautiful buildings is a wonderful profession, [1] __________ it is not always easy. [2] __________ some people might like your ideas, others will not. [3] __________ , they may hate them so much that they ask you to start again, or invite another architect to present a design. [4] __________ you always feel very relieved when they do accept your plans. [5] __________ , this may just be the start of another long discussion about the inside of the building!

(10 points)

Vocabulary

4 Match the words (1–8) to the definitions (a–h).

1 brick — **a** a small country house
2 concrete — **b** a strong alloy of iron
3 cottage — **c** wood
4 shack — **d** a tall building, often part of a castle
5 steel — **e** small building blocks made of clay and sand
6 tower — **f** a large building used for storing goods
7 warehouse — **g** a strong building material made cement, sand and stones
8 timber — **h** a small wooden building

(8 points)

5 Put the words in the box into the correct gap in the text.

conservatory	courtyard	gym	veranda	sauna

This house has a lovely [1] __________ all along the side of it, where you can sit in the shade in the summer and look out at the garden. In winter, you can sit inside the glass [2] __________ , which is full of lovely plants. The property is built as a square, around a lovely [3] __________ , with a garden and a fountain in the centre. Under the house, there is a fully equipped [4] __________ where you can work out and get fit, and next to it is a Swedish-style [5] __________ to relax in. I think it would make an excellent home.

(10 points)

6 Complete the sentences with the correct form of these expression with *wall*.

bang your head against a brick wall	be off the wall
drive someone up the wall	go to the wall
the writing is on the wall	be a fly on the wall

1 With all the problems they've had, I'm afraid his company will soon __________ .
2 Robert keeps asking me such silly questions! It's __________ .
3 I just cannot solve this problem. I feel as if I'm __________ .
4 I'd love to know what happened in that meeting. I wish I could have been __________ .
5 Julie has such strange ideas. Sometimes they __________ !
6 The company profits were even worse than expected. I think __________ .

(12 points)

Functions

7 Complete the speech with these expressions.

what I mean is	also, the fact that	I have to say
it seems	I think this is important, given	

First of all, [1] ______ that I think this new office block is great. [2] ______ to have all of the features that our company wanted and much more besides. [3] ______ it is so centrally located is a real bonus. As you may have heard, the design has been entered for the annual Stirling prize for architecture, and [4] ______ the prestigious international nature of that prize. [5] ______ that the publicity from this will give a very positive view of our company worldwide.

(10 points)

Writing

8a Read this short article and look at the four key elements (a–d). Find each element in the essay and write the correct order (1–4)

a a description of the building ______

b information about what the building is ______

c an explanation of why it is a good development ______

d details about how it has changed the area around it ______

The Wilson-Morgan Tower was officially opened last Tuesday, although Wilson-Morgan Insurance already established their working headquarters in the building a month ago.

The Tower is set to become one of the new landmarks in London, along with the London Eye and the Shard. This is largely due to its unusual design, but also its location next to the River Thames. The 200-metre tall triangular steel building with its blue glass windows is very striking.

The landscaped gardens around the base of the tower have opened up a previously closed part of the waterfront which was dirty and run down, creating a pleasant park for workers and passers-by to use. It seems to be the ideal combination of a purpose-built and functional office block for Wilson-Morgan and an attractive piece of public property for everyone else.

(4 points)

8b Write a similar piece about the following new building.

- a new warehouse for Jones & Sons furniture company
- located between the park and the local church
- built of green brick with green glass
- large car park and children's playground included

____

____

____

____

____

____

____

____

(16 points)

Speaking

9 Make a case for why a 200-year-old disused church should not be knocked down in your city centre in order to build a new office block. Explain the importance and attractiveness of the church for the town, and suggest uses that it could be put to.

(10 points)

Unit 4 Test

Grammar

1 Use the modals and verbs in brackets to make sentences about the past.

1 They ______________ more sandwiches for the party yesterday. (ought to / make)

2 She ______________ visiting the waterfalls if she hadn't felt ill. (might / enjoy)

3 I ______________ here sooner because the traffic was so bad. (not / could / get)

4 We ______________ in order to catch the last train. (have to / run)

5 He ______________ them everything about it. (not / should / tell)

6 She ______________ that there was something wrong. (must / notice)

(12 points)

2 Rewrite these sentences so that they express a degree of probability, using the words in brackets.

1 This will revolutionise work in the kitchen. (may well)

____

2 They will win the match on Saturday. (likelihood)

____

3 It will snow tomorrow. (chances)

____

4 Travel to the Moon will be open to everyone by 2050. (almost certainly)

____

5 Solar power will save the planet. (good chance)

____

6 I don't think that people will live on Mars. (unlikely)

____

7 Everyone will have robots in their homes in 50 years' time. (perhaps)

____

8 We will soon stop using petrol cars. (likely)

____

9 These cells are the answer to the problem. (might)

____

(18 points)

Vocabulary

3 Circle the correct option in each sentence.

1 While she was exploring the forest, she came *up with / up against / across* a new species of flower.

2 We know that he discovered it, but we don't know how it came *about / off / across*.

3 The professor was always ready to help when his students came *down to / up against / about* a problem.

4 They tried many times, and in the end it finally came *off / about / across*. They had done it!

5 You must admit that in the end good results usually come *up against / up with / down to* hard work.

6 Do you think you can come *up with / about / down to* some new areas for us to research?

(12 points)

4 Complete the sentences with the phrases in the box.

have a bright idea	make a breakthrough	spot a trend
take it one stage further	fill a need	reinvent the wheel

1 The basis of this project is good, but you really need to ______________________ .

2 It is important to ______________________ in society and then think of a product that relates to this.

3 We seem to be a bit stuck with this project. Let me know if you ______________________ .

4 We already know how to do that. There's no need to ______________________ .

5 This product will really ______________________ – there's a big gap in the market there.

6 If rival companies ______________________ in this area, it will be very difficult for us.

(6 points)

5 Complete the sentences with a word from the box.

scrap	stroke	shred	drop	flash	hint

1 He had a ____________ of inspiration for his new project.

2 There wasn't a ____________ of food in the house.

3 There wasn't a ____________ of sadness in his face after the murder.

4 It was a real ____________ of luck that I found my keys.

5 By the end of August there wasn't a ____________ of water in the riverbed.

6 There wasn't a ____________ of evidence to support his accusations.

(12 points)

Functions

6 Complete the speech with the rhetorical questions in the box.

So what, I hear you say?	What is it?
So, how do we achieve this?	How does it work?
Isn't it going to be expensive?	

I would like to present you with our latest product. [1] ______________________ Well, it's a pen. And here it is. [2] ______________________ There are thousands of pens in the world, you say. But our new pen is completely different. It's a laser pen. [3] ______________________ Well, all I can say is that it involves state-of-the-art technology. [4] ______________________ No it isn't, it's going to be so cheap that everyone can afford one. [5] ______________________ By carefully planned advertising which targets teenagers. …

(10 points)

Writing

7a Choose the correct type of punctuation in this text.

There is always a market for new ideas [1], / : especially ones which address a real public need. But where do such ideas come from [2]! / ? There are basically three sources [3]; / : examining other similar inventions, reading books and articles, and flashes of brilliance. This last one is very rare – [4] / ! However, new ideas certainly do keep coming all the time and [5] : / – I can say this from personal experience – it is essential to note down all of your thoughts for the future.

(5 points)

7b Write about a piece of equipment which you use regularly, and say why it's important to you and what you like and/or dislike about it. Do you have any ideas about how it could be improved? Use the following punctuation: comma, semi-colon, colon, question mark, exclamation mark, dash.

____

____

____

____

____

(15 points)

Speaking

8 Talk about an idea which you want to sell to the listener. Say what it is, how it will work and why it's important or necessary for the listener.

(10 points)

Unit 5 Test

Grammar

1 Choose a word or phrase from the box that could replace the phrase in bold in the sentences.

a lot	don't	others	one	it

1 Some people like to visit wild, lonely places, but I **don't like to visit them**. ____________
2 Mike likes to go cross country cycling, and he also likes to write about **cross country cycling**. ____________
3 He used his old jeep for that trip; it is an old **jeep** which he has had for 30 years. ____________
4 While some people don't do work for charity, Steve has done **much work** to raise money. ____________
5 Some tourists go there for the sun, while **other tourists** visit the place for its history. ____________

(10 points)

2 Rewrite these sentences using nominalisation. Note that sometimes you have to find a noun which isn't from the same root as the verb or adjective.

1 Maria's work was influenced by Henry Moore's sculptures.
One of Maria's ____________________ .
2 French impressionism interested her especially.
She had ____________________ .
3 She enjoyed being in the hills because it was so silent.
She enjoyed ____________________ .
4 Although she paints in very bright colours, most of her works are small and delicate.
Despite ____________________ .
5 Maria has been recognised for succeeding as a painter with a special exhibition in London.
A special exhibition in London recognises ____________________ .

(10 points)

3 Change the words in bold into a noun.

1 I've just read a novel **about** people trafficking.
The ____________ of the novel is people trafficking.
2 It **describes** the narrator's life in the desert.
It is a ____________ of the narrator's life in the desert.
3 The story is **set** in Mexico.
The story's ____________ is Mexico.
4 What **attracted** me most was the characters.
The main ____________ for me was the character.
5 The author **is commenting** on the situation of the poor.
It's a ____________ on the situation of the poor.

(10 points)

Vocabulary

4 Complete the sentences with a word from the box.

ascent	path	track	trail
street	motorway	route	way

1 We walked along the ____________ through the trees.
2 We asked an old man the ____________ to the farm.
3 We followed an old Native Indian ____________ .
4 We drove 200 miles on the ____________ .
5 The ____________ was busy with pedestrians.
6 The guidebook described the ____________ to follow to get to the castle.
7 The tractor drove along the muddy ____________ and into the field.
8 The ____________ was steep and difficult.

(8 points)

5 Circle the correct rhyming expression.

1 Now we've talked about your general ideas, let's get down to the *nitty-gritty / wishy-washy.*
2 Paul was just joking. There's no *fine line / ill will* between us at all.
3 We wanted to visit the south of the city, but since the riots it's been a *hot spot / no-go* area.
4 She's looking prettier and happier – those are *tell-tale / real-deal* signs that she is in love.
5 Andy's success in this prestigious competition shows that he is the *fair share / real deal.*
6 There's a very *fine line / hot spot* between what is acceptable and what isn't.
7 Let's go down to the harbour – that's the *nitty-gritty / hot spot* for nightlife.
8 I don't like this deal. The contracts are too *no-go / wishy-washy* and vague.

(16 points)

6 Match the expressions 1–6 with the definitions a–f.

1 cast the net wide
2 cast one's mind back
3 cast doubt on something
4 cast a shadow on
5 cast one's vote
6 cast one's eye over

a make a choice
b spoil something
c include a wide range
d have a quick look
e suggest something may not be true
f remember something

(6 points)

Functions

7 Complete the text with the words from the box.

technique	character	enunciate	stress	extract

When you are reading aloud to an audience, it is very important to choose the [1] ____________ which you are going to read very carefully, so that it gives a good picture of the author's writing [2] ____________ . As you practise reading it, make sure that you [3] ____________ everything very clearly – hold your head up and not in the book! [4] ____________ the key words to help the audience follow, and if there is a dialogue, give each [5] ____________ who speaks a different voice.

(10 points)

Writing

8a Complete the text with the compound adjectives from the box.

thought-provoking	strong-willed	heart-wrenching
fast-moving	well-written	

Brian Smith's new novel is another [1] ________________ action story, starring his well-known and [2] ________________ female detective Janice Clay. Smith is an accomplished and respected writer, and, as usual, this is a [3] ________________ novel – the writing is so much better than most novels of this genre. And it is not just an all-action story. As we have come to expect from Smith, there are some [4] ________________ passages on urban life, the isolation of the individual and the nature of pain. From its dramatic opening, to the [5] ________________ tragedy of the last chapter, this is a book which you will not want to put down.

(5 points)

8b Write a review of a film you have seen. Use adjectives (single and compound) to make your writing more interesting. Refer to the story, the setting, the characters and the themes, and say why you like the film.

____

____

____

____

____

____

____

____

(15 points)

Speaking

9 Describe a journey you have made or that you make regularly. Include details about the things that can be seen and heard, the people involved and any particular events you recall. Make your description as colourful and vivid as possible.

(10 points)

Unit 6 Test

Grammar

1 Complete the second sentences in each pair with the correct form of the phrasal verb in brackets.

1 Birdwatching is interesting. (take up / it)
I'm thinking of ________________ .

2 Look at this old book. (come across / it)
I ________________ in a second-hand bookshop.

3 They expect me to help. (get out of / it)
I want to ________________ .

4 I didn't enjoy the film. (put off / you)
But I don't want to ________________ .

5 He doesn't enjoy singing now. (put down to / it)
He ________________ a horrible teacher at school.

6 It's a very good idea. (come up with / it)
Julie ________________ yesterday.

7 He used to teach some years ago. (fall back on/it)
Since he lost his job he ________________ again.

8 My sister started her own company last year. (set up / it)
She ________________ in an old paper factory.

(16 points)

2 Match the verbs (1–6) with the patterns that follow them (a–g).

1 prevent	**a** to do
2 invite	**b** someone do
3 tend	**c** about doing
4 suggest	**d** someone from doing
5 worry	**e** doing
6 make	**f** someone of doing
7 accuse	**g** someone to do

(14 points)

Vocabulary

3 Choose the correct word to complete the sentences.

1 When Liz fell over, she ______ *chipped / stubbed / grazed* both her knees.

2 I always ______ *bump / bruise / break* my head when I walk through that door!

3 When I slipped on the ice, I ______ *lost / grazed / sprained* my left ankle.

4 She ______ *pulled / stubbed / lost* her toe on the bed leg when she got up in the dark.

5 I hit my mouth on the car door and ______ *chipped / sprained / bruised* my front tooth.

6 When I reached for the book of the top shelf, I ______ *stubbed / pulled / grazed* a muscle in my back.

(6 points)

4 Complete the sentences with the correct form of the expressions in the box.

to lose face	at face value	to have a long face
to keep a straight face	to put on a brave face	
to face the music	on the face of it	let's face it

1 You have got away with your mistake for now, but you will have ________________ at some point.
2 She ________________ at the funeral, but inside she was very upset.
3 You're a good guitarist Mike, but ________________, you're not Eric Clapton or B B King!
4 He kept his personal problems secret because he didn't want ________________ with his colleagues.
5 Why ________________ ? I know the news is bad, but smile in the face of adversity!!
6 ________________ their offer seemed to be genuine, but I have my doubts.
7 Richard looked so ridiculous when he walked in that I couldn't ________________ .
8 I don't really know him yet, so I have to take everything he says ________________ .

(16 points)

5 Match the two parts of these expressions to do with health and fitness.

1 keep in	**a** a run
2 take	**b** active
3 go for	**c** a diet
4 watch	**d** shape
5 go on	**e** your weight
6 work out	**f** your legs
7 stretch	**g** at the gym
8 keep	**h** exercise

(8 points)

Functions

6 Complete the speech with phrases from the box.

admittedly	It's not a particularly
I haven't thought through	I know that
I'm just thinking off the top of my head	

Good morning, everyone. I asked you here because I need to talk to you about the company's financial position. [1] ________________ pleasant task because, as you know, the situation we are in at present is difficult. [2] ________________ many of you had hoped to hear good news, but I'm afraid I do not have anything very positive to say. To start with, [3] ________________ exactly what I wanted to say to you. I hope that if you ask any questions you have, we can have a worthwhile discussion.
[4] ________________, this is a fairly open approach, but it could prove useful. [5] ________________, but I suggest we start with the HR department.

(10 points)

Writing

7a Read the brief report and match the words in bold to the phrases in the box with a similar meaning.

on the whole	at first	to be exact
therefore	it seems that	

The aim of the study was to try to determine whether children and parents are satisfied with the playgrounds in the town, or whether we could improve them in some way.

[1]**Accordingly**, throughout the month of June, two researchers were sent to each playground on a daily basis. One was an observer who noted the total number of children in the playground and the use of the different structures available. The other researcher had a two-page questionnaire which she completed with parents. [2]**Overall**, at the end of the month, from the three parks we had 540 hours of observed play by the children and 274 completed questionnaires.

The results of observing children's play showed us that the sandpits and the slides were the top two attractions, closely followed by the climbing frame and the swings. Interestingly, there was an age-group difference, which we had not [3]**initially** considered, and younger children preferred the sandpit, while older ones preferred the climbing frame. [4]**Apparently**, parents were quite critical of what was available. [5]**Specifically**, they questioned the lack of rubber matting under the swings, the climbing frames and the slide.

(5 points)

7b Write a similar report about car-parking in your town, or area. Consider

- what the study aims to find out
- what information the study will collect, and how
- what the results show (you can invent these based on your experience)

____
____
____
____
____
____
____
____

(15 points)

Speaking

8 Talk about your health, and your approach to exercise and sport, in the past and at present. How could you improve your health and well-being?

(10 points)

Unit 7 test

Grammar

1 Complete the sentences with phrases from the box.

as well as	in spite of	on account of	following
after	however	although	

1 __________ she likes fish, Paula didn't order the salmon.

2 __________ the bad weather, the match was played.

3 We didn't go away last year __________ the economic situation.

4 Tom visited France and Spain, __________ Italy last summer.

5 Jane doesn't get on with Sue. __________, they still manage to work together well.

6 __________ meeting the new boss, I feel happier.

7 __________ his interview, Ian waited three days to hear about the job.

(14 points)

2 Complete the subordinate clauses using the words in brackets. Use the correct form of the verb.

1 ______________ new to the job, he's very good at it. (considering / he / be)

2 ______________ about our plan to leave before we tell her? (supposing / the boss / find out)

3 Office work is easy ______________ economics at university! (compared / study)

4 ______________, the relationship was over. (as far as / Liz / be concerned)

5 I don't know if it's a good idea, ______________. (think / about / it)

6 They checked with the porter ______________. (in case / door / be locked)

7 We'll go ahead with the project, ______________. (assuming / they / like / it)

8 People will buy them, ______________. (regardless / their quality)

(16 points)

Vocabulary

3 Complete the sentences with the correct form of the verbal expressions.

to miss the boat	to strike gold	to blow one's chance
to get a break	to hit the jackpot	to not go one's way

1 Mike really ______________ when he bought those prize-winning tickets!

2 You need some help if you are going ______________ in the business world.

3 You're too late! I'm afraid you have ______________ by not buying when I told you.

4 I'm in financial trouble. Things have ______________ recently.

5 Janet said Paul could work with her, but he really ______________ when he was rude to her.

6 If you invest in this new company, you might just ______________.

(12 points)

4 Choose the correct option to complete the sentences.

1 Mike and I bore ______ of the boss's anger.
a in mind **b** the brunt **c** a grudge

2 That statue bears a close ______ to your brother!
a witness **b** fruit **c** resemblance

3 The designers he worked with bore ______ to his wonderful new creations.
a witness **b** fruit **c** resemblance

4 She worked very hard, and eventually her efforts bore ______.
a witness **b** fruit **c** resemblance

5 Bear ______ that he always wants the presentation to be in English.
a the brunt **b** a grudge **c** in mind

6 I'm afraid I will always bear ______ against her for what she did.
a a grudge **b** resemblance **c** witness

(12 points)

5 Match the verbs (1–6) with the definitions (a–f).

1 to defeat
2 to invade
3 to resist
4 to surrender
5 to command
6 to get revenge

a to give in and stop fighting
b to fight someone who attacks you
c to be in control of an army
d to beat in battle
e to do something to someone who hurt you
f to go into another country with an army

(6 points)

Functions

6 Match the phrases for clarification in bold (1–5) with the speakers intention (a–e).

1 **Am I right in thinking that** you basically want an increase in salary?

2 **Can you expand a bit more on** those ideas?

3 You think it's a mistake. **Is that what you're saying**?

4 **Can you explain what you mean by** outside help?

5 **How do** your plans **fit in with** what the report says?

a Asking for clarification of a specific detail.
b Asking the speaker to relate what they were saying to a wider context.
c Asking the person to go deeper into what they were talking about.
d Clarifying that the speaker has understood what the person wants.
e Checking understanding of the other person's opinion.

(10 points)

Writing

7a Match the sequencing phrase in bold to the time it refers to.

1 **Up to now**, the weather has been perfect. ______
2 **Nowadays**, people don't do things like that. ______
3 **From now on** we will always use them. ______
4 They informed us about it **some weeks ago**. ______
5 **In those days** people often worked in that way. ______

a at the current time
b at a time in the distant past
c at a time in the recent past
d until the present time
e in the future

(5 points)

7b Write about the development of an invention from the past 100 years (e.g. the motor car or the personal computer) using time sequencers to structure the past, present and future details. You can invent details such as dates if you need to.

____
____
____
____
____
____
____

(15 points)

Speaking

8 Work in pairs. Student A: talk about your topic from 7b. Student B: listen to your partner and when he/she has finished, ask questions for clarification or further information. Change roles.

(10 points)

Unit 8 Test

Grammar

1 Complete the second sentence so that it means the same as the first.

1 It is believed that some jaguars still live there.
Some jaguars ______________________________.
2 It is known that a big cat is killing animals in the area.
A big cat ______________________________.
3 It wasn't reported that footprints were seen.
Footprints ______________________________.
4 It is said that the locals feared going out at night.
The locals ______________________________.
5 It isn't expected that the mystery will be solved soon.
The mystery ______________________________.
6 It wasn't thought that anyone had been attacked.
No one ______________________________.
7 It is estimated that the damage is around £ 2,000.
The damage ______________________________.

(14 points)

2 Complete the sentences with the words in the box.

point	question	difficulty	matter
suggestion	mention	choice	intention

1 I'm afraid you will have to do it, James. You have no ______.
2 There is absolutely no ______ that what she did was right.
3 He really had no ______ of upsetting her, I can assure you.
4 It will not make the slightest difference, no ______ what you both say!
5 There was no ______ of what Jane did or said in the paper, thank goodness!
6 The boy had no ______ climbing up the wall by himself.
7 There really is no ______ in continuing this discussion. We will never agree.
8 We were quite happy with the elections. There was no ______ of any cheating.

(16 points)

Vocabulary

3 Match the verbs (1–7) with the phrases (a–g).

1 chat	**a** a social networking site
2 download	**b** a blog
3 use	**c** new products
4 post	**d** online
5 review	**e** photos
6 upload	**f** comments on a forum
7 write	**g** music

(7 points)

4 Complete the sentences with the phrases in the box.

ballpark figures	game plan	in the loop
it's not rocket science	think outside the box	
on the same page	reality check	win-win situation

1 I want to know the results, so please keep me ___________ .

2 You will get some benefits, and so will we. It's a ___________ .

3 You really don't understand what's going on! Take a ___________ !

4 It's difficult to predict, these are just ___________ .

5 Jim's very creative, he always ___________ .

6 Oh, come on, Jim! It's simple! ___________ !

7 What are your strategies? What is the company's ___________ ?

8 Jill and Suzie work together very well. They're really ___________ .

(16 points)

5 Circle the correct option to complete the sentence.

1 The thieves broke *through / up / in* through the kitchen window.

2 He's smoked for years, but now he's finally broken *the habit / the mould / the bank.*

3 We're waiting to break *the ice / the news / even* of our engagement until everyone's here.

4 I'm worried about the company. We really have to break *the bank / up / even* to survive.

5 The house was a real mess, but we've broken *the ice / the back / the mould* of the work now.

6 Yes, we can afford it. It's not very expensive. It won't break *the bank / the back / the ice.*

7 It's not always easy to break *the mould / the ice / the bank* and get people talking at formal dinners.

(7 points)

Functions

6 Complete the speech with the hedging expressions from the box.

arguably	tend to	it seems that
which suggests that	perhaps	

Following recent reports on our work here, [1] ___________ we are not achieving the expected results. That is [2] ___________ understandable in the current economic climate. However, comments from the management team [3] ___________ imply that they think we could be doing much better than we are. They say that there are easy ways to improve productivity, [4] ___________ we need to look carefully at the systems we have in place. Brainstorming some ideas for improved efficiency is [5] ___________ the best way to proceed in the short term.

(10 points)

Writing

7a Read the newspaper story below. Underline examples of the following in the texts.

a verbs for speculating (e.g. *seem*)

b passive reporting verbs

c adverbs of degree or frequency

d adverbs that speculate about a fact

From what has been said, it appears that the company has been in trouble for some time. Despite a policy of so-called 'best practice', it has frequently failed to deliver both in terms of quality and quantity. There have been many complaints over the years, and although the directors are supposed to have made radical changes two years ago, these were probably cosmetic, apart from the replacement of Production Manager George Stone. It is known that this move gave some relief to the troubled company. However, they have generally continued to have a reputation for poor quality. Apparently, a restructuring of the workforce last month has improved things in this area.

(5 points)

7b Write a similar newspaper report about a toy manufacturer which has not been doing well. Explain the reasons for their difficulties and what they have been doing about it. Use examples of all four features listed in 7a.

____

____

____

____

____

____

____

(15 points)

Speaking

8 Talk about a particular aspect of modern technology that you are familiar with, and speculate on its future, using hedging expressions where possible.

(10 points)

Unit 9 Test

Grammar

1 Rewrite these sentences using *just* instead of the words in bold. The word order may be different.

1 She came back from Brazil **very recently**.

____

2 The children **simply** don't like cabbage.

____

3 He thinks the cake is **only** for him, not for everyone!

____

4 I am very interested in blues music. **So** is Thomas.

____

5 He is a **little** bit taller than me.

____

6 The house was **exactly** as he had imagined.

____

7 Do as I tell you, **nothing else**!

____

8 He **only** got back home **a few minutes ago**.

____

(16 points)

2 Complete the sentences using the correct form of the words in brackets.

1 I worked in the factory last summer ______________ . (in order / earn / some extra money)

2 She went to bed early last night ______________ . (so that / get up / at five o'clock)

3 They play tennis ______________ . (keep fit)

4 He works at the school ______________ . (for / enjoy / not payment)

5 They went home another way ______________ . (avoid / meet / their neighbours)

6 They left the window open ______________ . (so as / get / some fresh air)

7 They didn't buy a lottery ticket ______________ . (in order / not / raise / their hopes)

(14 points)

Vocabulary

3 Complete the sentences with these expressions.

music to my ears	changed his tune	struck a chord with
play it by ear	know the score	blow her own trumpet
face the music	make a song and dance about	

1 He wasn't interested at first, but when I mentioned money he soon ______________ .

2 Susan loves talking about her achievements. She always wants to ______________ .

3 The things she said about looking after pets really ______________ me after owning a dog.

4 I thought he understood everything, but he really doesn't ______________ .

5 When they said I looked five years younger, it was ______________ .

6 I'm not really certain about what they expect, so we'll just have to ______________ .

7 I know her comments were quite annoying, but there's no need to ______________ it.

8 If you make a serious mistake, you will have to ______________ at some time.

(16 points)

4 Choose the correct option to complete the sentences.

1 I think it's time I ______ – I need to be home by ten.
a hit and miss **b** hit the road **c** hit the right note

2 When he joined the company, he didn't ______ with his new colleagues.
a hit a nerve **b** take a big hit **c** hit the right note

3 The company ______ when the last recession started.
a hit the road **b** took a big hit **c** hit and miss

4 I can see that the new school is ______ with your son.
a hit and miss **b** hit a nerve **c** a real hit

5 When she joked about his bad driving, she really ______ .
a hit a nerve **b** hit the road **c** hit and miss

6 Their work varies a lot; they're always a bit ______ .
a a real hit **b** hit and miss **c** hit the right note

(6 points)

5 Match the words (1–8) with the definitions (a–h).

1 a ballad	**a** a musician who plays in the street
2 instrumental	**b** someone who performs alone
3 a busker	**c** a form of music, often sad
4 soothing	**d** an Indian stringed instrument
5 a solo artist	**e** a slow, often romantic, song
6 a sitar	**f** the words of a song
7 lyrics	**g** calming and relaxing
8 blues	**h** music with no words

(8 points)

Functions

6 Complete the discussion with these expressions.

That's an interesting question	I really don't know
That's difficult to say	I've never really thought about it

B: Do you think we can pull out of this recession?

A: [1] ______________ in a brief answer. But I think so!

C: Do you think the Prime Minister was right to cut taxes?

A: [2] ______________ . I think we'll have to wait and see what the effects are.

D: Would you like to manage the World Bank?

A: Well, I must admit [3] ______________ . Can I answer that for you some time later?

E: What advice would you give to someone starting a new company today?

A: Thank you. [4] ______________ and one I would like to discuss in detail. First, I'd say …

(10 points)

Writing

7a Look at this description of a concert and underline examples of powerful adjectives and similes.

Last weekend I went to an unusual little music club, hidden away down a dingy back street in a suburb of London. Inside, the dimly-lit room was absolutely packed out. Some friends took me because a band called Blues Train were playing there, and they know I am crazy about blues music. This band were incredible! They really were rocking like a train all night, with lively, rhythmic tunes interspersed with a few slower, heart-rending numbers.

People were jumping around like popcorn over a hot fire, and the stinging guitar solos played by the lead singer were like a waterfall of endless sound. We had a really stupendous night and I will be looking out for the next time Blues Train play.

(5 points)

7b Write a description of a concert you went to using powerful adjectives and similes to recreate the atmosphere of the event.

____

____

____

____

____

____

____

(15 points)

Speaking

8 Talk about a particular musician or group that you like, describing the music they play, the issues and themes they deal with, and what feelings it arouses. Give any other reasons why you like it.

(10 points)

Unit 10 test

Grammar

1 Put the correct tag question onto the end of these statements.

1 They live in Paris, __________ ?
2 She doesn't like fish, __________ ?
3 He went there yesterday, __________ ?
4 You haven't closed the door, __________ ?
5 It will be very nice, __________ ?
6 We must get it finished soon, __________ ?
7 Mum wouldn't like it, __________ ?
8 They hadn't seen it before, __________ ?
9 You were very quiet, __________ ?
10 She can't play tennis, __________ ?
11 I'm late, __________ ?
12 Let's meet at four, __________ ?
13 Nobody told you, __________ ?
14 Somebody said something, __________ ?

(14 points)

2 Complete the sentences with an adverbial form of the words in the box.

quick	careful	fast	hard	live	new	bare	long

1 It was __________ light when Jane left at 6 a.m.
2 She hurried down the road, walking __________ through the sleeping village.
3 It didn't take __________ to reach the port.
4 She had __________ arrived when Paul's boat came into view; it had been __________ painted and cleaned.
5 When Paul pulled alongside the quay, Jane went __________ down the steep, slippy steps.
6 Paul seemed happy and talked __________ as the boat moved __________ over the water.

(16 points)

Vocabulary

3 Match words 1–10 with words a–j to make collocations.

1 ethnic	**a** standing
2 first	**b** knit
3 long	**c** generation
4 extended	**d** rooted
5 deep	**e** heritage
6 close	**f** group
7 social	**g** worker
8 rich	**h** community
9 migrant	**i** family
10 immigrant	**j** gathering

(10 points)

4 Complete the sentences using animal verbs derived from the animals in the box.

monkey	beaver	crow	wolf	duck	hound	parrot

1 Liz didn't want to be involved, so she just __________ out of everything.

2 He's in the kitchen __________ down the sandwiches I made him.

3 I wish those kids would stop __________ around with my wheelbarrow.

4 He hasn't got any ideas of his own. He just __________ what other people say!

5 Listen to Phil __________ about his latest success.

6 The journalists __________ him for weeks after his divorce.

7 Angela's very busy, __________ away in her room.

(14 points)

5 Match each phrase (1–6) with a sentence (a–f).

1 There's no such thing as a free lunch.

2 feel free to do something

3 a free for all

4 to be given a free rein

5 to get off scot-free

6 to be a free spirit

a The boss says we can do whatever we like.

b They say we can help ourselves to tea and coffee.

c She's gone travelling somewhere in the Far East.

d Nobody ever discovered the awful things that Peter had done.

e You might have had a nice time, but you will have to pay him back in the future.

f I'd go into dinner now; it's a self-service buffet and everyone's taking lots.

(6 points)

Functions

6 Complete the conversation with these phrases.

really	yes, do	me neither	I doubt it	I hope so

Lynn: Hi, John. Did you enjoy the lecture?

John: Not much, I'm afraid.

Lynn: [1] __________ . He's not a very good speaker, is he?

John: No, he isn't. And unfortunately he's my uncle.

Lynn: [2] __________ ? Oh, I'm sorry. Do you think his next lecture will be better?

John: [3] __________ . He's always a bit boring.

Lynn: Perhaps next month's speaker will be better.

John: [4] __________ . Listen, I have to go, but can I give you a call later?

Lynn: [5] __________ . Bye.

(10 points)

Writing

7a Read this short essay and write which paragraph contains

a the analysis of the facts paragraph ______

b the writer's conclusions paragraph ______

c the thesis paragraph ______

It has long been known that watching TV can have a negative effect on children, but recent research has highlighted the very serious damage which hours in front of a screen can have on very young children.

Studies carried out by the University of Wessex have clearly shown that children under the age of three suffer from an inability to communicate clearly if they spend an hour or more alone in front of the TV daily. At this stage, children need to spend all their time in direct interaction with parents, eye to eye, not with a screen. The studies seem to show that children develop normally if they watch limited amounts of TV with an adult and communicate about what they see, as they might when reading a story-book together.

It seems imperative that health workers and teachers of young learners get this message across to parents and child-minders urgently. It is crucial that computers and TVs are kept out of young children's bedrooms, and their use of such devices is seriously limited.

(3 points)

7b Write a short essay with three similarly organised paragraphs about the issue of teenagers eating too much junk food and not enough fresh fruit or vegetables, and not drinking enough water. You can invent facts of your own.

(17 points)

Speaking

8 Talk about what you think people's social responsibilities are in a modern democratic society, suggesting the types of behaviour you believe to be desirable and explaining why.

(10 points)

Unit 11 test

Grammar

1 Complete the unreal past sentences using the correct form of the words in brackets.

1 What would you do ________________? (if / you / be / me)
2 ________________ there yourself tomorrow afternoon. (I / rather / you / go)
3 ________________ her the truth. (It / be / high time / he / tell)
4 ________________ with her. What would happen? (Supposing / they / come)
5 ________________ it himself. (I / just as soon / he / buy)
6 ________________ as cheap as in 1980. (If / only / food / be)
7 ________________ you a new dress? (What / if / she / be / make)
8 ________________ a bit more. (I wish / Karl / eat)

(16 points)

2 Complete the inverted conditional sentences with *should*, *were* or *had*.

1 ____________ you told me about it, I would have known.
2 ____________ you ever be in the area, please get in touch.
3 ____________ it not for your courage, we would all be dead.
4 ____________ he come earlier than expected, do not open the door.
5 ____________ I seen it myself, I would have believed you.
6 ____________ she to marry him, she would be very unhappy.
7 ____________ she explained the situation, I would have understood.

(14 points)

Vocabulary

3 Match the adjectives 1–5 with the meanings a–e.

1 petrified	a very unhappy
2 astonished	b really angry
3 ecstatic	c extremely frightened
4 despondent	d totally amazed
5 livid	e very happy indeed

(10 points)

4 Complete the sentences with the idiomatic expressions from the box.

all over the place	a bit down	done in	on edge
hot under the collar	speechless	thrilled to bits	upbeat

1 Pete was ________________ when I told him his work was awful. He just stood there!
2 Jane's a bit ________________ today because she's starting her new job tomorrow.
3 The boys were ________________ when I told them they'd come first in the competition.
4 Colin was not at all well prepared for the meeting. He was ________________.
5 Sue thought her interview went well – she was quite ________________ about it.
6 He was up all night working on the report, and he's ________________ today.
7 He always gets rather ________________ if anyone criticises his work.
8 Anna's old dog died at the weekend, so she's ________________ at the moment.

(10 points)

5 Circle the correct words to complete each sentence.

1 Mike was running with the others, then he moved *around / up / up in* a gear and left everyone else behind.
2 It was such a sad film, everyone was moved *around / to tears / a muscle.*
3 They said we had two weeks to do the report, but now they've moved *the goalposts / around / to tears* and say they want it on Monday.
4 When I was young, my parents moved *into / around / up* from place to place.
5 Jane only stays in the best hotels these days. I think she's moved *around / up / up in* the world.

(10 points)

Functions

6 Complete this extract from a speech with the correct expressions recognising others' feelings from the box.

You look a little puzzled	Did I say something funny?
Please don't think me rude	Sorry, that came out wrong

Now, I would first like to talk about our department's – what shall I say? – little error. (*laughter*)
[1] ________________ This is not intended to be amusing. I don't think making mistakes is funny.
[2] ________________ – of course, they can be quite amusing at times, and the way in which the products we sent to Bristol ended up in Berlin, and the ones for Berlin in Budapest was quite funny, in a strange kind of way.
[3] ________________ – perhaps you have not heard the end of the story. The amazing thing is: the Berlin factory needed the things that should have gone to Bristol, and the Budapest office needed the things that should have gone to Berlin … [4] ________________, but we are all to blame for the goods going to the wrong places, myself included.

(10 points)

Writing

7a Look at the sentences from the emails below and decide which one:

a has a spelling mistake in it
b is not clear
c is rude
d is aggressive or threatening

1 I am sick and tired of your poor quality work, and if you do not improve very quickly, there will be real trouble.
2 Please ensure that our submitions are ready by Monday at the latest.
3 Can you and Joanne collect Pauline and all three of you go to the main entrance, then leave her there while you go off and meet David who will be arriving by car.
4 I really can't understand what you are asking for!! Can't you write in decent English?!

(5 points)

7b Write an email to a colleague explaining the following things without being rude or aggressive. Make sure the writing is clear with no spelling mistakes.

- They got the meeting time wrong: it is ten o'clock not eleven o'clock.
- They got the room wrong: it is room 18 on floor 2, not room 18 on floor 4.
- They need to meet Mr Dancer at the station at nine and bring him to the meeting, offering coffee on the way.
- They should tell Mr Dancer some general information about the company, but nothing personal and no gossip.

____
____
____
____
____
____
____

(15 points)

Speaking

8 Prepare to talk about robots. Include information about the following.

- how real robots compare to those in science fiction books and films
- what sort of things robots can do at present
- what you think they might be able to do in the future
- what you think their main value is
- their advantages and disadvantages over people

(10 points)

Unit 12 test

Grammar

1 Complete the sentences with these words.

brownish	kind of	roughly	ten or so
some	things	stuff	dozens

1 What's all that __________ on the back seat?
2 There are __________ twenty people interested in joining the club.
3 This picture should give you __________ idea of what it's like.
4 She seems quite serious, but she's actually __________ soft.
5 There were __________ of cars parked outside.
6 I don't know how to describe it – it's sort of __________ outside.
7 John put his __________ away in the drawer before he left the office.
8 Not many girls came to the dance – only __________ .

(16 points)

2 Put the words in the correct order in these sentences.

1 find / beach / unusual / it's / shells / the / these / rather / to / on
____
2 to / she / castle / quite / her / enjoyed / the / visit
____
3 get / with / he's / easy / a / to / on / fairly / person
____
4 than / expected / he's / I / slightly / older /
____
5 with / Martin / to / bit / work / little / is / difficult / a
____
6 their / house / further / little / a / is / down
____
7 walkers / said / dangerous/ area / they / for / pretty / was / the
____

(14 points)

Vocabulary

3 Match the adjectives 1–7 with the definitions a–g.

1 bleak	**a** always the same
2 sparse	**b** full of healthy green plants
3 monotonous	**c** empty and unfriendly
4 rustic	**d** perfect, like in a dream
5 rolling	**e** with few plants or trees
6 lush	**f** gently hilly
7 idyllic	**g** rural and traditional

(7 points)

4 Complete the sentences with the words in the box.

pitch	brand	stone	sopping	wide	rock	bone	fast

1 It poured with rain, but the things inside the tent were still __________ dry.

2 Have you seen Jane's camera? It's __________ new – the latest model.

3 Don't worry, he won't wake up. He's __________ asleep.

4 I was worried when I got home and saw the front door was __________ open.

5 When I got inside the cave, it was __________ black and I couldn't see a thing.

6 The fuel had run out long ago, and the heater was __________ cold.

7 After falling into the pool, all my clothes were __________ wet.

8 I forgot to put the cakes away and by morning they were __________ hard.

(16 points)

5 Complete the sentences with *space* or *room*.

1 Have you got any __________ in the drawer for these papers?

2 John drove round the car park looking for a __________ .

3 One has a great sense of __________ standing on the top of this hill.

4 His skiing technique is good, but there's __________ for improvement.

5 Next year I will be famous. Watch this __________ .

6 Stand back, please. I need more __________ to show you this trick.

7 I can't possibly finish by Monday. I need some breathing __________ .

(7 points)

Functions

6 Complete the conversation with these expressions.

Yes, but	a moment, please.
can I just finish what I was saying?	hang on a minute …
can I just interrupt you there?	

A: The situation has got worse in the past six months …

B: [1] Sorry, __________ Because I think that the situation has actually improved …

A: [2] Just __________ . There are signs that the situation has got worse and I don't think it will improve unless we take some pretty serious …

B: [3] No, __________

A: [4] Sorry, __________ Unless we take some pretty serious measures things won't improve.

B: [5] __________ actually, there are signs that things have improved recently …

(10 points)

Writing

7a Read this speculative letter and underline the following points.

a offers something extra for free or at a reduced price

b shows awareness of their financial limitations

c refers to the type of customer it is aimed at

d offers a clear service

Dear Mr Jones

We are a new office cleaning company which specialises in small private companies like yours. We offer a comprehensive cleaning service, including office interiors, desks, etc. as well as communal areas like toilets and kitchens. We also clean windows.

We specialise in giving our clients a quick and efficient daily service at a price that your size of company can afford. As this is our first month of operation we are offering to clean all your office windows inside and outside free of charge, if your company signs up for a one-month trial period of cleaning.

I look forward to hearing from you in due course.

Yours sincerely

Harry Bland

(5 points)

7b Write a similar speculative letter offering painting and decorating services for pensioners' houses. Include the elements listed in 7a.

(15 points)

Speaking

8 Describe a place in the country you would like to visit. Use a full range of descriptive adjectives to add interest and give detail.

(10 points)

Photocopiable tests: answer key

Unit 1 Test

Grammar

1

1 every week
2 While
3 next month
4 since Friday
5 already
6 at the moment
7 last year
8 How long

2

a 7
b 8
c 2
d 1
e 4
f 4
g 3
h 7
i 3
j 6

3

a 3 b 5 c 6 d 1 e 4 f 2

Vocabulary

4

1 odds and ends
2 by and large
3 ifs and buts
4 rough and ready
5 heart and soul
6 in this day and age
7 peace and quiet
8 law and order

5

1 control freak
2 chatterbox
3 free spirit
4 doer
5 outgoing type
6 joker
7 go-getter
8 drifter

6

1 b 2 d 3 f 4 e 5 g 6 a 7 c

Functions

7

1 as I was saying
2 just look at my notes
3 I'll begin again
4 I'll just have a sip of water
5 I lost the thread

Writing

8a

a 3 b 2 c 1 d 2 e 3

Unit 2 Test

Grammar

1

1 will (still) be working
2 are living
3 had been studying
4 were eating
5 have been trying

2

1 Not paying
2 Having lived
3 Working
4 Not having met
5 Having watched
6 hoping
7 not wanting

Vocabulary

3

1 footed the bill
2 shot herself in the foot
3 following in his father's footsteps
4 will get your foot in the door
5 putting / going to put my foot down
6 put my foot in it

4

1 by
2 down to
3 on with
4 ahead
5 at
6 through

5

a 4 b 5 c 1 d 2 e 8 f 3 g 6 h 7

6

1 Monday
2 documents
3 university
4 per week
5 something
6 first
7 plus / and
8 students
9 including
10 for example

Functions

7

1 I'd just like to say one thing
2 how many of you actually
3 I remember when I first
4 So what does this tell us
5 That's the key thing.

Writing

8a

1 bright
2 sheer
3 daring
4 slick
5 confident

Unit 3 Test

Grammar

1

1 really
2 an absolutely
3 really
4 extremely
5 so
6 totally
7 entirely
8 quite

2

1 What attracts you is the colour of the flowers.
2 It's the height of the trees you notice first.
3 Rarely do you see so many different plants together.
4 Never has a garden like this been created before. / Never has anyone created a garden like this before.
5 He really does like exotic plants.
6 The thing that is noticeable is the care he has taken.

3

1 but
2 Although
3 Indeed
4 So
5 However

Vocabulary

4

1 e 2 g 3 a 4 h 5 b 6 d 7 f 8 c

5

1 veranda
2 conservatory
3 courtyard
4 gym
5 sauna

6

1 go to the wall
2 driving me up the wall
3 banging my head against a brick wall
4 a fly on the wall
5 are off the wall
6 the writing is on the wall

Functions

7

1 I have to say
2 It seems
3 Also, the fact that
4 I think this is important, given
5 What I mean is

Writing

8a

1 b 2 a 3 d 4 c

Unit 4 Test

Grammar

1

1 ought to have made
2 might have enjoyed
3 couldn't have got (or couldn't get)
4 had to run
5 shouldn't have told
6 must have noticed

2

1 This may well revolutionise work in the kitchen.
2 The likelihood is that they will win the match on Saturday.
3 The chances are that it will snow tomorrow.
4 Travel to the Moon will almost certainly be open to everyone by 2050.
5 There is a good chance that solar power will save the planet.
6 It is unlikely that people will live on Mars. / People are unlikely to live on Mars.
7 Perhaps everyone will have robots in their homes in 50 years' time.
8 It is likely that we will soon stop using petrol cars.
9 These cells might be the answer to the problem.

Vocabulary

3

1 across
2 about
3 up against
4 off
5 down to
6 up with

4

1 take it one stage further
2 spot a trend
3 have a bright idea
4 reinvent the wheel
5 fill a need
6 make a breakthrough

5

1 flash
2 scrap
3 hint
4 stroke
5 drop
6 shred

Functions

6

1 What is it?
2 So what, I hear you say?
3 How does it work?
4 Isn't it going to be expensive?
5 So, how do we achieve this?

Writing

7a

1 , (comma)
2 ? (question mark)
3 : (colon)
4 ! (exclamation mark)
5 – (dash)

Unit 5 Test

Grammar

1

1 don't
2 it
3 one
4 a lot
5 others

2

1 influences was Henry Moore's sculptures
2 a special interest in French impressionism
3 the silence of the hills
4 the very bright colours of her paintings, most of her works are small and delicate
5 Maria's success as a painter

3

1 subject
2 description
3 setting
4 attraction
5 comment

Vocabulary

4

1 path
2 way
3 trail
4 motorway
5 street
6 route
7 track
8 ascent

5

1 nitty-gritty
2 ill will
3 no-go
4 tell-tale
5 real deal
6 fine line
7 hot spot
8 wishy-washy

6

1 c 2 f 3 e 4 b 5 a 6 d

Functions

7

1 extract
2 technique
3 enunciate
4 Stress
5 character

Writing

8a

1 fast-moving
2 strong-willed
3 well-written
4 thought-provoking
5 heart-wrenching

Unit 6 Test

Grammar

1

1 taking it up
2 came across it
3 get out of it
4 put you off
5 puts it down to
6 came up with it
7 has fallen back on it
8 set it up

2

1 d 2 g 3 a 4 e 5 c 6 b 7 f

Vocabulary

3

1 grazed
2 bump
3 sprained
4 stubbed
5 chipped
6 pulled

4

1 to face the music
2 put on a brave face
3 let's face it
4 to lose face
5 do you have a long face
6 On the face of it
7 keep a straight face
8 at face value

5

1 d 2 h 3 a 4 e 5 c 6 g 7 f 8 b

Functions

6

1 It's not a particularly
2 I know that
3 I haven't thought through
4 Admittedly
5 I'm just thinking off the top of my head

7a

1 Therefore
2 On the whole
3 at first
4 It seems that
5 To be exact

Unit 7 Test

Grammar

1

1 Although
2 In spite of
3 on account of
4 as well as
5 However
6 After
7 Following / After

2

1 Considering (that) he is
2 Supposing the boss finds out
3 compared to studying
4 As far as Liz was concerned,
5 thinking about it
6 in case the door was locked
7 assuming they like it
8 regardless of their quality

Vocabulary

3

1 hit the jackpot / struck gold
2 get a break
3 missed the boat
4 not gone (been going) my way
5 blew his chance
6 strike gold / hit the jackpot

4

1 b 2 c 3 a 4 b 5 c 6 a

5

1 d 2 f 3 b 4 a 5 c 6 e

Functions

6

1 d 2 c 3 e 4 a 5 b

Writing

7a

1 d 2 a 3 e 4 c 5 b

Unit 8 Test

Grammar

1

1 Some jaguars are still believed to live there.
2 A big cat is known to be killing animals in the area.
3 Footprints were not reported to have been seen.
4 The locals are said to have feared going out at night.
5 The mystery isn't expected to be solved soon.
6 No one was thought to have been attacked.
7 The damage is estimated to be around £ 2,000.

2

1 choice
2 question
3 intention
4 matter
5 mention
6 difficulty
7 point
8 suggestion

Vocabulary

3

1 d 2 g 3 a 4 f 5 c 6 e 7 b

4

1 in the loop
2 win-win situation
3 reality check
4 ballpark figures
5 thinks outside the box
6 It's not rocket science
7 game plan
8 on the same page

5

1 in
2 the habit
3 the news
4 even
5 the back
6 the bank
7 the ice

Functions

6

1 it seems that
2 perhaps
3 tend to
4 which suggests that
5 arguably

Writing

7a

a it appears; are supposed
b has been said; are supposed to have made; it is known that
c frequently; generally
d probably; apparently

Unit 9 Test

Grammar

1

1 She just came back from Brazil.
2 The children just don't like cabbage.
3 I think he thinks the cake is just for him, not for everyone!
4 I am just as interested in blues music as Thomas (is).
5 He's just a bit taller than me.
6 The house was just as he had imagined.
7 Just do as I tell you!
8 He just got back home.

2

1 in order to earn some extra money
2 so that she could get up at five o'clock
3 to keep fit
4 for enjoyment, not payment
5 to avoid meeting their neighbours
6 so as to get some fresh air.
7 in order not to raise their hopes

Vocabulary

3

1 changed his tune
2 blow her own trumpet
3 struck a chord with
4 know the score
5 music to my ears
6 play it by ear
7 make a song and dance about
8 face the music

4

1 b 2 c 3 b 4 c 5 a 6 b

5

1 e 2 h 3 a 4 g 5 b 6 d 7 f 8 c

Functions

6

1 That's difficult to say
2 I really don't know
3 I've never really thought about it
4 That's an interesting question

Writing

7a

powerful adjectives: *dingy, dimly-lit, crazy, incredible, stupendous, heart-rending, stinging, endless*

similes: *rocking like a train, jumping around like popcorn over a hot fire, like a waterfall of endless sound*

Unit 10 Test

Grammar

1

1 don't they
2 does she
3 didn't he
4 have you
5 won't it
6 mustn't we
7 would she
8 had they
9 weren't you
10 can she
11 aren't I
12 shall we
13 did they
14 didn't they

2

1 barely
2 quickly
3 long
4 hardly, newly
5 carefully
6 in a lively way, fast

Vocabulary

3

1 f
2 c
3 a
4 i
5 d
6 b
7 j
8 e
9 g
10 h

4

1 ducked
2 wolfing
3 monkeying
4 parrots
5 crowing
6 hounded
7 beavering

5

1 e 2 b 3 f 4 a 5 d 6 c

Functions

6

1 Me neither
2 Really
3 I doubt it
4 I hope so
5 Yes, do

Writing

7a

Paragraph 1: c
Paragraph 2: a
Paragraph 3: b

Unit 11 Test

Grammar

1

1 if you were me
2 I'd rather you went
3 It's high time he told
4 Supposing they came
5 I'd just as soon he bought
6 If only food were (was)
7 What if she were to make
8 I wish Karl would eat

2

1 Had
2 Should
3 Were
4 Should
5 Had
6 Were
7 Had

Vocabulary

3

1 c 2 d 3 e 4 a 5 b

4

1 speechless
2 on edge
3 thrilled to bits
4 all over the place
5 upbeat
6 done in
7 hot under the collar
8 a bit down

5

1 up
2 to tears
3 the goalposts
4 around
5 up in

Functions

6

1 Did I say something funny?
2 Sorry, that came out wrong
3 You look a little puzzled
4 Please don't think me rude

Writing

7a

a 2 (submissions)
b 3 (is 'her' Pauline or Joanne?)
c 4
d 1

Unit 12 Test

Grammar

1

1 stuff
2 roughly
3 some
4 kind of
5 dozens
6 brownish
7 things
8 ten or so

2

1 It's rather unusual to find these shells on the beach.
2 She quite enjoyed her visit to the castle.
3 He's a fairly easy person to get on with.
4 He's slightly older than I expected.
5 Martin is a little bit difficult to work with.
6 Their house is a little further down.
7 They said the area was pretty dangerous for walkers.

Vocabulary

3

1 c 2 e 3 a 4 g 5 f 6 b 7 d

4

1 bone
2 brand
3 fast
4 wide
5 pitch
6 stone
7 sopping
8 rock

5

1 room / space
2 space
3 space
4 room
5 space
6 room / space
7 space

Functions

6

1 can I just interrupt you there?
2 a moment, please.
3 hang on a minute …
4 can I just finish what I was saying?
5 Yes, but

Writing

7a

a to clean all your office windows inside and outside free of charge
b a price that your size of company can afford
c small private companies like yours
d a comprehensive cleaning service, … a quick and efficient daily service …

Unit 1 Communicative activity

Lessons for life

Think about the things that you believe are important for satisfaction in life. What are they? What lessons have you learnt? How did you learn these things? You might think about people who have been an example to you, advice you have been given, good and bad experiences, professional training, books. Make notes and then answer your partner's questions. Ask your partner questions about their ideas and where they came from, and complete the table with the information you are given. Then compare your views. What is similar and what is different?

	Me	**My partner**
What is important for me for satisfaction in life?		
What I have learnt from different sources: Family		
Friends		
Books		
Training		
Experiences		
Other (what?)		

Unit 2 Communicative activity

Your first day

Student A

It is your first day at university. You and your partner have both met your personal tutors. You both took notes about the important things you have to do tomorrow, but you haven't written the same information. Ask and answer questions to check all the details with your partner, and complete the information.

First talk: where	*Great Hall*
when	
Registration: where	*Next to the Student Union building*
when	*11.00-13.00*
who	*Mrs Johnstone*
what	*Take exam certificates*
Lunch: where	*Student Canteen*
when	*13.00-14.00*
Dinner: when	*19.30 be there*
clothes	*Formal*
Evening: what	*Film about student life*
where	*Student Union*
when	

Student B

It is your first day at university. You and your partner have both met your personal tutors. You both took notes about the important things you have to do tomorrow, but you haven't written the same information. Ask and answer questions to check all the details with your partner, and complete the information.

First talk: where	
when	*09.30-11.00*
Registration: where	
when	
who	*The Registrar*
what	*Take birth certificate*
Lunch: where	*Student Canteen, first floor New Building*
when	*13.00 onwards*
Dinner: when	*20.00 dinner starts*
clothes	*Evening dress*
Evening: what	*Film / talk from president of Student Union*
where	
when	*22.00 onwards*

Unit 3 Communicative activity

A building that I like

Use the headings in the table below to prepare information about a building you particularly like. Then interview two people about the building they have chosen. Make notes on their answers.

	Student 1: ________________	**Student 2:** ________________
Name or brief description of building		
Location		
Architect / builder		
When built		
What the building is used for		
Construction materials		
Condition of the building		
Immediate surroundings		
What the person likes about the building		

Unit 4 Communicative activity

Describing a company

Choose a company that you know something about, either from working for it, from using it or from reading about it (e.g. a high-street shopping chain, a bank, an insurance company, a small shop, a local company, a food manufacturer). Write down details in the *My company* column. Then tell your partner about your company. Ask about your partner's company and complete the *My partner's company* column. Afterwards, compare your two companies and see what is similar and different about them.

	My company: ______	**My partner's company:** ______
What does the company do? (products, services)		
Where is it based?		
How does it advertise itself?		
How successful is it?		
What relationship does it have with staff (working hours, terms of employment, pensions, etc.)?		
Why did you choose this company and what is your relationship with it?		
Other		

Unit 5 Communicative activity

Describing a journey

Complete the table with information about an interesting journey you once made. Ask your partner questions and complete the right-hand column of the table with their information. Answer their questions. Then discuss the similarities and differences in the two journeys.

	My journey	My partner's journey
Month / year		
Travel companions		
Starting from:		
Finishing at:		
Route		
Places visited (how long for?)		
Food and drink		
Things of interest		
People		
Weather		
Best aspect		
Worst aspect		
Other		

Unit 6 Communicative activity

A health, exercise and sports survey

Complete the *Me* column in the table. Then ask questions to three other students and complete the columns for them. Answer their questions about yourself. Use the information to write a short report about health, exercise and sporting activity in your class.

	Me	**1** ______	**2** ______	**3** ______
Health: what is your health like in general?				
Health problems at present				
Health problems in the past				
Diet now				
Diet in the past				
Exercise now				
Exercise in the past				
Sports now				
Sports in the past				
Plans and intentions for the future				

Unit 7 Communicative activity

Talking about an event in history

Work in a group of four. Decide on a particular historical event, from the recent or distant past, which you all know something about. Talk about it in a group, and make notes about it on the table in the *My event* column. Then find a partner from another group which has discussed a different event, exchange information about your respective events and make notes in the *My partner's event* column.

	My event	My partner's event
Event		
Duration		
People involved		
Where it happened		
Why it happened		
Outcome		
Other information		

Unit 8 Communicative activity

Making a report on technology use

Complete the details about your use of technology in the *Me* column. Then work with a partner. Each of you should interview three different people in the class and record their responses carefully. When you have finished get back together with your partner and compare the answers. Write your results up as a survey of the way people use technology.

	Me ________	1 ________	2 ________	3 ________
1 Mobile phone: how many?				
camera?				
Internet?				
number of apps?				
music?				
other				
2 Own computer: PC?				
laptop?				
tablet?				
other?				
4 MP3 player: model				
other information				
5 Internet: social networking sites				
live chat				
other Internet sites used				
6 Email: personal				
work				
7 Favourite TV channel				
Favourite TV programmes				
watch online or on TV set?				
8 Films: buy DVDs				
rent DVDs				
online / downloads				
9 Music: buy CDs				
downloads				
10 News: TV				
radio				
podcasts				
newspapers				
other				

Unit 9 Communicative activity

Discussing music

Complete this table about music with your notes. Say what you like and don't like, and why. Then work in a group of four to ask and answer questions, and discuss the answers.

My favourite kind of music	
My favourite musician / group	
My favourite piece of music	
The kind of music I most dislike	
The musician / group I most dislike	
The piece of music I most dislike	

Unit 10 Communicative activity

An ideal society

Imagine that you could plan an ideal society. How would it work? How would people live together? How would industry and agriculture be managed? Would there be a government? Would there be elections of some kind? What about education and health care? Work in a group of four and discuss the issues, then use the table below to make notes on your ideas. Then each member of your group should join three people from three other groups to share and discuss ideas. What was similar and different?

Government / management of society
Health care
Education
Agriculture
Industry
Religion / beliefs
Entertainment
Other

Unit 11 Communicative activity

Discussing emotions

Think about your emotions; what arouses emotions for you and how do you express them? Complete the table below. Work with a partner and ask and answer questions in order to complete your partner's side of the table.

Emotion		Me	My partner
Happiness	How you show it		
	What makes you feel it		
	Your happiest moment		
Sadness	How you show it		
	What makes you feel it		
	Your saddest moment		
Anger	How you show it		
	What makes you feel it		
	Your angriest moment		
Fear	How you show it		
	What makes you feel it		
	Your most frightened moment		
Other: ___________	How you show it		
	What makes you feel it		
	Your ___________ moment		

Unit 12 Communicative activity

How much do you remember? Do the quiz.

1 What is a Tuareg? ____________________

2 Who said: *Consideration for others is the basis of a good life, a good society?* ____________________

3 Who was Ben Jonson? ____________________

4 What bird do the nomads of western Mongolia use for hunting? ____________________

5 Where do the Moken people live? ____________________

6 What dangerous activity does Alex Honnold do? ____________________

7 What is Gary Chang's profession? ____________________

8 What is Poundbury and whose idea was it? ____________________

9 What was Zaha Hadid known as for a long time? ____________________

10 What is Shweeb? ____________________

11 What is 'the mother of invention' ? ____________________

12 What is Japanese paper folding called? ____________________

13 Who is Blake Mycoskie? ____________________

14 What did Dervla Murphy do on a bicycle? ____________________

15 Who is Hergé and where is he from? ____________________

16 Who wrote the book *In Patagonia*? ____________________

17 What are calisthenics? ____________________

18 What is the Ultra-Trail and where is it? ____________________

19 When did Ghengis Khan live? ____________________

20 Who is 'the father of history' ? ____________________

21 Which city had a large sinkhole in it in 2007? ____________________

22 What is a sitar? ____________________

23 Who wrote *I Shot the Sheriff, Trenchtown Rock* and *Redemption Song*? ____________________

24 What are there more than 20,000 species of worldwide? ____________________

25 Who are the Hadza people? ____________________

26 What did George M Pullman do, where and when? ____________________

27 What does EI stand for? ____________________

28 What is a heteronym? ____________________

29 What does William Albert Allard do? ____________________

30 What is Basho famous for writing? ____________________

Photocopiable communicative activities: Teacher's notes

Unit 1

AIM: To practise talking about the things that are important in life

MATERIALS: A copy of the worksheet for each student

METHODOLOGY: Ask students to read through the instructions, and give them time to make notes about their ideas individually. (Because it might require some thought, they might do this as homework, so their notes are ready to use in class.) Stress that not all the sources will be relevant to everyone, and there may be other sources which are not listed which they should add. Ask them to work in pairs, to ask and answer questions and complete notes about their partner's views. They can then discuss what is similar and different about how they see life.

Unit 2

AIM: To exchange information about dates, times, places, etc.

MATERIALS: One photocopy for each pair of A and B students (cut in half). Each student should only see their own half of the worksheet.

METHODOLOGY: Ask students to look through their worksheet, to see what the timetable of events for the day is, and the details they have about each item. The pairs should then ask and answer questions about everything, checking what they know, and adding information as necessary. When they have finished, they can compare their worksheets to see if they missed anything.

Unit 3

AIM: To practise talking about buildings

MATERIALS: one copy of the worksheet for each student

METHODOLOGY: Give out the worksheets, and ask students to think of a building they like, and make notes on a separate piece of paper about the information listed in the table. Then ask the students to get up and move around the class, asking two people about their building, and making notes about their answers. Finally, students can tell a partner about what the two students said. If there is no time to do this in class, they could write a paragraph for homework describing the similarities and differences in what they liked.

Unit 4

AIM: To practise asking and answering questions about a company and its business

MATERIALS: A copy of the worksheet for each student

METHODOLOGY: Ask students to complete the *My company* column, as far as they can. Ask them to think of a company that they know most about in relation to the worksheet (e.g. a company they or a friend or family member have worked for). Make sure they realise that they do not have to complete everything, and that some things can be subjective. They can complete the worksheet for homework to save time, and could also do some internet research to find additional information, if you or they wish. They should then do an information exchange with their partner, asking and answering questions in pairs before comparing their results together.

Unit 5

AIM: To exchange information about a journey made in the past

MATERIALS: A copy of the worksheet for each student

METHODOLOGY: Ask students to prepare the task individually by completing the information in the *My journey* side of the table. (You could give this as a homework task the previous lesson.) Ask them to work in pairs, and ask and answer each other's questions about their journey to complete the *My partner's journey* column. They should then compare their journeys and see what was the same and different. You can elicit information about the journeys from the whole class.

Unit 6

AIM: To get students actively asking and answering questions about health, sport and exercise

MATERIALS: A copy of the worksheet for each student

METHODOLOGY: Ask students to complete the *Me* column details first. They should then ask questions of three other students and complete the chart with the answers they receive. They should also answer questions when they are asked. They should then use the information to write a short report on the health, exercise and sports habits of the class.

Unit 7

AIM: To collect and exchange information about a historical event

MATERIALS: One copy of the worksheet for each student

METHODOLOGY: First ask students to work in groups of four. They should choose an event that all of them know something about; it can be a big event (e.g. World War II) or a smaller event (e.g. the last general election in their country). They should pool their knowledge to complete the first column of the table. They should then get together with one person from a group that has discussed a different event, and ask and answer questions to complete the second column of the table.

Unit 8

AIM: To encourage multiple interactions on the topic of digital media

MATERIALS: A copy of the worksheet for each student

METHODOLOGY: Give out the worksheets to students and ask them to complete the *Me* column. They should then work with a partner. They should not interview each other, but choose three different classmates each to interview, and complete the table with their information. There is space for other answers, as necessary. They should then get back with their partner, and compare their results. They should work together to write a short report about trends in digital media use.

Unit 9

AIM: To discuss musical likes and dislikes, giving reasons

MATERIALS: A copy of the worksheet for each student

METHODOLOGY: Ask students to make notes about the music they like best and least. You could ask them to do this for homework. They should then get together in groups of four, and ask and answer questions to discuss their opinions with the others, giving reasons for their choices.

Unit 10

AIM: To discuss society and systems of social living

MATERIALS: A copy of the worksheet for each student

METHODOLOGY: Ask students to think through their own ideas about this 'utopian' society first. They might do this for homework. Then ask them to get into groups of four to discuss their ideas and come to a compromise solution. They should all make notes on the different areas on their worksheets. Then label the members of each group A, B, C and D, and ask all the A students in the class to work together, all the B students, and so on. (If it is a large class you might want to have two groups for each letter.) They should share and compare their ideas and find what was similar and different about them.

Unit 11

AIM: To think about and discuss personal emotions

MATERIALS: A copy of the worksheet for each student

METHODOLOGY: Ask students to complete the *Me* column about their own emotions and responses, with examples. They might do this as homework. Ask them to work in pairs and ask and answer questions in order to complete the chart about their partner.

Unit 12

AIM: To remember / revise information from the Student's Book in a quiz

MATERIALS: A copy of the quiz questions for each student, pair of students, or group of four (see below)

METHODOLOGY: You could do this in several ways:

- Individuals answer as many questions as they can within a 20-minute time-limit. They exchange papers and mark each other's.
- Students work in pairs to do the quiz.
- Students work in teams of four to do the quiz.

If the quiz is done in teams or pairs you can decide whether to set a time limit and make the quiz competitive, or keep it more relaxed.

ANSWERS

1 a member of an ethnic group living in Libya and around the Sahara.
2 the Chinese philosopher, Confucius
3 a 16th-century British dramatist, rival to Shakespeare
4 an eagle
5 Myanmar – the Mergui Archipelago in the Andaman Sea
6 free climbing
7 architect
8 a new town in Britain; Prince Charles
9 'the paper architect'
10 a transport system using bicycle power on a monorail
11 necessity
12 origami
13 an American businessman – founder of TOMS – one-for-one shoes.
14 cycled from Ireland to India
15 a cartoonist, creator of Tintin; Belgium
16 Bruce Chatwin
17 gentle warm-up exercises
18 a high mountain race of 161 km on Mont Blanc in France
19 13th century (1162–1227)
20 Herodotus
21 Guatemala City
22 an Indian stringed instrument
23 Bob Marley
24 ants
25 hunter gatherers living in Tanzania
26 set up a model society in Chicago in the 1880s
27 Emotional Intelligence
28 a word which is spelt the same but pronounced differently
29 He is a photographer.
30 haikus (17-syllable, 3-line poems)

Workbook answer key

Unit 1

1a (pages 4 and 5)

1 1 his book about scientific inventions
2 some rules of life (that he read about 15 years ago in a book by Charles Sykes)

2 1 unjust
2 can't expect
3 more strict
4 a beginning
5 your
6 have to be done by everyone
7 seldom
8 technical expertise

3 1 Currently
2 about 15 years ago
3 Before that
4 next year
5 Many years ago
6 at the time
7 Over the last 20 years
8 rarely
9 Sooner or later

4 1 am taking
2 attended
3 had never been
4 seem
5 have been wondering
6 will have

5 1 said (than) done
2 valuable
3 guiding
4 point
5 stead
6 thumb

6 One of the problems with advice is that people tend to interpret it to suit their own purposes. An example of this is the wisdom of the 18th-century economist, Adam Smith. One of his main ideas was that if you allow people to seek wealth for themselves, they will naturally create jobs and wealth for others. He called this 'the invisible hand'. People, trying to improve their own situation, also help their neighbour to improve theirs, but without meaning to, as if with an invisible hand. Unfortunately, a lot of people took Smith to mean that it was all right to be greedy and selfish and not to help others directly, which is not at all what he meant.

1b (pages 6 and 7)

1 b

2 1 T 2 T 3 T 4 T 5 T 6 F

3 1 not much difference, but (a) the past perfect emphasises that one thing happened before another
2 a = looking back from the present to an indefinite time in the past; b = referring to a specific point in the past
3 a = describing the future; b = looking back from a point in the future
4 a = assumes it was still the family profession; b = looking back to what the profession was at a earlier time (but probably was not then)
5 a = I have left university; b = looking back from the present, i.e. I'm still at university

4 1 Had you been waiting
2 Has someone been smoking
3 had been playing, had fallen
4 will probably have finished
5 have been living / have lived
6 have heard

5 1 f 2 c 3 b 4 e 5 d 6 a

6 1 foremost 2 large 3 age 4 pieces 5 when 6 quiet

8 1 d 2 b 3 f 4 e 5 a 6 c

1c (page 8)

1 1 T 2 T 3 F 4 F 5 T 6 F

2 1 b 2 a 3 a 4 a 5 b 6 a

3 1 b 2 a 3 b 4 a 5 b

4 1 story
2 fact
3 walks
4 time
5 saver
6 larger than life
7 lifelike
8 life

1d (page 9)

1 1 qualities
2 passion
3 achievements
4 yourself
5 image

2 1 infrastructure projects
2 He spent one year working on a transport and metro hub in Osaka, where he helped to design the programme for planning work schedules for staff.

3 1 good planning and organisation, up-to-date IT skills
2 interested in different cultures / approaches to life and travel
3 a first degree in Town Planning, a master's degree in Business Administration, a commendation for his work in Osaka

4 a sip b as c thread d was e let f again

5 He used phrase b. He uses it to keep talking about the programme he designed.

6b I spent one year in Japan working on a metro and transport hub in the city of Osaka – it's a major city on Honshu island. It was for work experience and I received a commendation when I left the project.

7 Students' own answers.

1e (page 10)

1a **a** attracts *or* attracted
b available
c response
d Currently
e As, suitable
f enclosed
g considering
h requirements

1b 1 c 2 f 3 d 4 e 5 a 6 h 7 g 8 b

2 The missing elements are:
1 when it was advertised
3 your present situation
4 why you are suited to the job
and 9 (possibly) give a personal touch

3 … in response to your advertisement on the Jobsonline website (1) this week … and relevant experience. …
(3) I am currently working in a temporary position for a local charity making calls to potential donors. (9) It is interesting and worthwhile work but desk-based and I am someone who likes to get out and meet people.
The job attracted me because … world of work again.
(4) As someone who understands the education sector and has experience of fundraising, I think I am a suitable candidate.

Wordbuilding / Learning skills / Check! (page 11)

1 1 is more awareness of/about
2 showed us great kindness
3 Nervousness
4 the usefulness of
5 Baldness is
6 showed (a) willingness
7 selfishness (in people)
8 Forgetfulness increases/gets worse

2 1 You can sound more natural, impress your audience and create more vivid images to support your arguments.
2 It can sound ridiculous.
3 a T
b F Putting a correct idiom in an otherwise incorrect sentence could sound odd.
c T
d F Use idioms that have widespread and established use.
e F Slang is very informal language that is usually spoken rather than written.

3 1 no 2 yes

5 1 a sit b work c yourself d blind
2 dreamer b joker c outgoing
3 a nowadays, generally
b so far, recently
c sooner or later
d prior to that

Unit 2

2a (pages 12 and 13)

1 1 In Tibet
2 a small fungus (called *yartsa gunbu*), because it is highly valued
3 herding yaks and/or sheep

2 1 searching 2 fungus 3 medicinal 4 caterpillar 5 stalk 6 energy 7 soared 8 herding 9 overpicking

3 1 get by 2 Getting ahead in 3 get down to 4 get through 5 gets on with 6 getting at

4 1 has dropped 2 are looking for 3 fetches 4 had been searching 5 have prescribed 6 was herding 7 started 8 has been growing 9 are thriving 10 will be searching
Note that 5 *have been prescribing*, 6 *herded* and 9 *thrive* are also possible.

5 1 generally do, are always trying
2 is becoming, are now moving *or* has become, have now moved
3 are studying *or* have been studying, won't recommend

6 1 way 2 livelihood 3 task 4 trade 5 vocation 6 living

7 1 I will = I'll
2 She has been = She's been
3 We are = We're
4 She was hoping to get a new job. (no contraction)
5 I had been = I'd been

8 1 I've been travelling in this region for many years and I'd seen this phenomenon before but never paid it much attention.
2 Well, often you'll visit a place with a particular story in mind. Then, while you're researching it, you find something else catches your interest.
3 I was very struck by how well off people in the village seemed compared to when I'd last visited.
4 So I decided to investigate and got this amazing story of the golden worm.

2b (pages 14 and 15)

1 1 they are difficult to find (because of overfishing and the use of seine nets which has reduced the numbers by 80 per cent); they weigh in excess of 300 kilos and are difficult to land
2 (deep-sea) line fishing

2 1 T 2 F 3 T 4 N 5 F 6 N

3 1 Because I hadn't done any line finishing at sea before,
2 after they have spent many hours and hundreds of dollars.
3 with the result that it has been reduced by over 80 per cent.
4 while we were waiting *or* while we waited for something to happen.

4 1 Having found them,
2 Having nothing else to do,
3 using these to keep our prey interested.
4 knowing that the fish can swim towards the boat.

5 1 Having got the fish on the hook, you then manoeuvre the boat carefully to keep it on the line.
2 In the last 15 years, quotas have been introduced for bluefin tuna, helping to stabilise their numbers.
3 Often trapping other large sea creatures like dolphins, purse seine fishing is considered environmentally unfriendly.
4 Having been overfished for so long, bluefin tuna now weigh on average half what they did in the 1970s.

6 1 d 2 f 3 a 4 h 5 b 6 g 7 e 8 c

7 1 be on the safe side
2 wrap (your children) in cotton wool
3 second nature
4 cut corners
5 take precautions

2c (page 16)

1 c

2 1 a missing cat
2 a geography teacher
3 memorising dots on a map
4 outdoor
5 adventures
6 reality of the city
7 by walking
8 think at a high level
9 how friendly the community is
10 creative and innovative

3 1 a 2 b 3 b 4 a

4 1 a 2 c 3 d 4 b

5 1 She got off on the wrong foot, but relations with her colleagues are much better now.
2 I hope I didn't put my foot in it when I told her how like her sister she was.
3 Most people supported either one candidate or the other, but he had a foot in both camps.
4 She really shot herself in the foot by not taking the promotion when she was offered it.
5 People often ask me why I didn't follow in my father's footsteps and become a doctor.
6 Hannah found her feet very quickly at university and made some good friends.
7 I thought the company would pay for my hotel, but in the end I had to foot the bill.
8 She was going to jump from the ten metre board but she got cold feet.

2d (page 17)

1 1 simple 2 remind 3 rhetorical 4 end 5 pace

2 1 It's an opportunity to get new experiences that can help you to grow as a person and as an employee.
2 Think about the kind of project you would like to volunteer on and how it's going to improve you directly. Then go and sell the idea to your employer.
3 He gets people to take a minute and tell each other what personal skill they'd like to improve or they think needs improving.

3 1 here to
2 key thing
3 what (is a sabbatical) for
4 just give
5 really (my) message
6 could ask

5 Students' own answers.

2e (page 18)

1 1 pay grade 6 2 line manager 3 18 months

2 1 weeks
2 that is *or* that is to say
3 months
4 years
5 to be confirmed
6 for example

3 1 approx
2 e.g.
3 incl
4 etc.
5 10 a.m.
6 hrs
7 NB
8 i.e.
9 2nd *or* sec (time)
10 pw

4 Jeff rang at eleven o'clock. He wants you to go to London to discuss the contract details, i.e. commission, quantities, etc. The time of the meeting is to be confirmed. Note that he isn't in the office until Thursday.
Note that *i.e.* and *etc.* are perfectly acceptable in writing.

5 New policy
no limits on how much / little holiday staff can take try policy out for limited period, i.e. 6 mths not entirely sure if going to work, but pretty confident

Reasons for policy
much better to be adult and responsible – all have busy working lives + busy lives outside work given a little freedom, organise time better

Employee responsibilities
NB not an excuse to take as much time off work as possible can't organise completely independently – negotiate with colleagues to avoid disruptions also still have work targets to reach

Details
start date tbc – 2nd half of this year policy applies to every employee incl part-time staff reviewed after approx 4 mths

Wordbuilding / Learning skills / Check! (page 19)

1 1 g 2 f 3 a 4 c 5 b 6 d 7 e 8 h

3 Example answers:
1 a to inform
b specific information
c When will it be available to buy? How much will it cost?
2 a to inform, to persuade
b gist
c What is different about this book? Have attitudes to childhood changed?
3 a to inform, to give opinions
b gist and specific information
c What is the film? Would they recommend it?

4 1 a eagle hunter b gypsy c smokejumper
2 a wait a long time b see well c keep fit and healthy
3 a aspect, progress b conjunction
4 a foot b down c put d your
Phrase: put your foot down

Unit 3

3a (pages 20 and 21)

1 1 Geography: Mustang, a former kingdom in north-central Nepal; Climate: the climate is incredibly inhospitable; wind-savaged
2 10,000 (conservatively estimated)
3 It was a centre of scholarship and art, and a key place on the salt trade route from Tibet to India.
4 most showed signs of domestic habitation; in others there were stunning treasures: in one cave, a 26-foot-long mural; in another, 8,000 calligraphed manuscripts; many seemed to be elaborate tombs full of absolutely amazing riches
5 burial chambers
6 Because the territory was frequently fought over, they placed safety over convenience and took refuge in the caves.

2 1 ~~absolutely~~
2 ~~extremely / utterly~~
3 ~~so~~
4 ~~really~~
5 ~~absolutely~~
6 ~~so~~
7 ~~absolutely / really~~
8 ~~incredibly~~

3 1 incredibly *or* really *or* very
2 absolutely *or* completely *or* totally
3 absolutely *or* quite
4 incredibly *or* really *or* so *or* very
5 absolutely *or* really
6 incredibly *or* really *or* so *or* very
7 completely *or* totally
8 quite

4a 1 I'm utterly exhausted.
2 I'd really appreciate that.
3 It's so hot today.
4 It's OK. I quite understand.
5 You're absolutely right.
6 It's very difficult to say.

5 1 f 2 i 3 j 4 a 5 g 6 c 7 e 8 h 9 b 10 d

6 1 wildly optimistic
2 vaguely familiar
3 desperately unlucky
4 perfectly reasonable
5 deadly serious
6 painfully slow

7 I: conservatory, games room, garage/workshop, gym, home cinema, sauna, walk-in wardrobe
O: courtyard, garage / workshop roof garden, veranda

3b (pages 22 and 23)

1 1 A 2 D 3 A

2 1 metropolis 2 garden 3 gardens 4 centre 5 walk 6 outskirts 7 greenbelt 8 32,000

3 1 seventy per cent
2 a sign of an urban vitality
3 opportunity
4 less energy per capita
5 a quiet dormitory town

4 1 in the human body
2 squalid = dirty, cramped = lacking space
3 positive
4 the sea
5 giving an example
6 to limit

5 1 town 2 city 3 estate 4 suburb 5 town 6 metropolis 7 village 8 city

6 1 What he was referring to were the appalling slums that a booming city had spawned.
2 What he proposed was drawing people away from the metropolis.
3 In 1907, his vision actually did become reality when the garden city of Letchworth was built.
4 It is large cities that have spread around the world, not small garden cities.
5 Not only has urbanisation spread, but expert opinion now sees this as a positive trend.
6 In his book *Triumph of the City* – which, incidentally, I do recommend you read – Ed Glaeser …
7 The thing that we often ignore is that poor people are attracted to cities because they offer opportunity.
8 Very seldom do cities themselves make people poor.

7 1 What I love about Berlin is the feeling of space. *or* It is the feeling of space in Berlin that I love. *or* I do love the feeling of space in Berlin.
2 What really strikes you about Istanbul is the friendliness of the people. *or* It is the friendliness of the people in Istanbul that really strikes you.
3 I did like Los Angeles, but I found it very polluted. *or* I liked Los Angeles but I did find it very polluted.
4 What you won't find anywhere else in the world are such dramatic buildings as in Dubai.
5 What is amazing about Jerusalem is the sense of history. *or* It is the sense of history in Jerusalem that is amazing.
6 Rarely is a place found where nature and man-made structures blend so well together. *or* Rarely do you find a place where nature and man-made structures blend so well together.

8 **A:** What did you think of Moscow?
B: I loved it. I'm glad I chose to get around by metro though. The traffic is terrible.
A: And how did it compare to St Petersburg?
B: Very different. The thing about St Petersburg is that it feels much more European somehow. It's also incredibly grand and gracious.
A: Well, that's not so surprising. It is much further west.
B: Yeah, that's the thing about Russia. What you don't realise before you go there is what an enormous country it is.
A: Did you go anywhere else, then?
B: Well, we went up to a city just north of Moscow – I can't remember the name immediately – and took a boat trip along the Volga River.
A: How was that?
B: Amazing. It was in April, but there were still huge chunks of ice floating in the river.

3c (page 24)

1 1 It means copying good design from nature and applying it to things that are man-made.
2 biomimetrics has been used in the design of the Swiss Re Tower; the architect Gaudi took inspiration from nature in his design of the Sagrada Familia; the chimneys in the Eastgate Centre in Harare imitate the heating and cooling system in a termite mound

2 1 a 2 c 3 b 4 b 5 b 6 c

3 1 a 2 b 3 b 4 b 5 a

4 1 head 2 off 3 fly 4 hole 5 up 6 to 7 writing

3d (page 25)

1 For: 1) people won't have to waste time going down to the canteen to get their coffee; 2) it will encourage employee interaction
Against: staff might spend too much time there away from productive work

2 1 all 2 recommend 3 have 4 appeals 5 underestimate 6 mean 7 given 8 touch

3a 1 d 2 y 3 r 4 t 5 w 6 w

3b 1 first‿of‿all
2 with‿a bit‿of luck
3 as‿a matter‿of‿fact
4 as far‿as‿I'm‿aware
5 between you‿and me /w/
6 let's be‿honest /j/
7 at the‿end‿of the day /j/
8 I've no‿idea, I'm‿afraid /w/

4 Students' own answers.

3e (page 26)

1 a 4 b 3

2 against
the benefits of high-rise building to the wider environment are great; it's not possible to keep expanding our cities outwards

3 1 b 2 e 3 d 4 f 5 a 6 c

Wordbuilding / Learning skills / Check! (page 27)

1 1 affordable 2 walkable 3 likeable 4 moveable 5 contactable 6 doable 7 watchable, forgettable 8 retrievable

4 1 There are only two interesting buildings in the area around Newport.
2 The green belt should definitely be protected from developers.

6 Across: 1 drives 5 stair 6 concrete 7 leafy 8 fly
Down: 1 distinctly 2 vibrant 3 sprawl 4 shack

Unit 4

4a (pages 28 and 29)

1 1 d 2 b 3 a 4 c

2 1 scientists 2 day 3 problem 4 money 5 afford 6 tests

3 1 a 2 b 3 b 4 b 5 a 6 b

4 1 d 2 a 3/4 e/f 5 c 6 b

5 1 I must have ridden
2 I should have taken
3 I didn't need to
4 I could have wheeled
5 I had to be
6 I had to find
7 I needn't have worried
8 Someone might have dropped

6a 1 have 2 have 3 have 4 to 5 have 6 to

7 1 about 2 across 3 up 4 down 5 up

4b (pages 30 and 31)

1

Speaker	Type of foldable device	Main advantages	Probability of success
1	electric car	very compact no carbon emissions	low (with private individual buyers)
2	smartphone screen	don't break or shatter	high
3	audio speakers	beautiful design	high
4	sofa	cheaper and more energy-efficient	high

2 1 a a child's buggy
b it can only go for about 100 kilometres before it needs recharging
2 c smartphones d the perfection of the technology
3 e your portable music player f origami
4 g as small as a regular size metre-cubed box
h the furniture industry

3 1 consortium 2 fleet 3 norm 4 perfected 5 slip 6 must 7 compromising 8 efficient

4 1 likelihood 2 certainly 3 should 4 may 5 likely
strongest: statement 2

5 1 I think the chances of it catching on with private individual buyers is pretty low.
2 I think they're almost bound to become the norm in the next few years.
3 The days of broken or shattered screens will probably be over.
4 I think what is likely to determine the success of foldable products is their design.
5 I think we may well see more and more of this kind of solution as energy prices rise.

6 1 Yes, we're bound to find a good alternative to petrol-driven cars in the near future.
2 But the chances are that they won't be electric cars.
3 Because the lithium needed for batteries will definitely become scarcer.
4 It's likely to be natural sources: wind or solar or water.
5 It should have a positive effect on pollution.
6 They're unlikely to welcome such a development.

7 1 a small amount 2 a small amount 3 a small amount 4 a small piece

8 1 scrap 2 stroke 3 dash 4 shred 5 hint 6 sliver 7 stroke 8 glimmer

9 The problem with electricity is that you cannot store it. If you could, then wind and solar energy would be much more attractive options.
But now a garage inventor from England thinks he might have found the answer.
Peter Dearman has developed a system that uses electricity to turn air into liquid at very low temperatures.
When energy is needed, the air can be warmed to drive a turbine and generate electricity.
Mr Dearman has already successfully used this method to power a car. But it seems that, with this flash of inspiration, he could have hit upon something really big.

4c (page 32)

1 1 internet and mobile communications
2 they are actively involved in spending their money (more 'hands on') whereas past philanthropists set up long-term foundations and scholarships for future generations; they want to see a quick return on investment as they would in business

2 1 T 2 T 3 F 4 T 5 F 6 F

3 1 self-made 2 counterparts 3 return 4 seed 5 bring about 6 no strings 7 self-confessed 8 ethos

4 1 ethos 2 seed (money) 3 return 4 bring about 5 self-made 6 counterpart 7 self-confessed 8 no strings

5 1 all *or* best 2 thought 3 break 4 go 5 ahead 6 time

4d (page 33)

1 1 (school) children
2 not all children have a desk at school or even a table at home
3 it's a bag that also functions as a desk; it has compartments for notebooks, pens and a water holder
4 the price will be a little higher in Europe than in developing countries

2 1 so, original, ask
2 would, want, that
3 how, people, be, able

3 1 The bag also functions as a desk.
2 Not all children have a desk at school or even a table at home.
3 The price is a little higher in Europe to help lower the cost of a bag for a family in a developing country.

4 Example answers:
1 So how does it work?
2 Isn't that rather expensive, you ask?
3 So why would I need one?
4 So, what's our ambition for this?

5a 1 s<u>o</u> /əʊ/
2 f<u>o</u>ld /əʊ/
w<u>o</u>rk /ɜː/
3 sch<u>oo</u>l /uː/
4 –
5 n<u>u</u>merous /juː/, comp<u>ar</u>tments /ɑː/
6 hydr<u>a</u>tion /aɪ/eɪ/, imp<u>or</u>tant /ɔː/

6 Students' own answers.

4e (page 34)

1 1 – *or*: 2 – 3 – 4 : 5 ; 6 :

2 The Solidarity Bag

Overview

The Solidarity Bag is a totally new concept in school bag design. It functions both as a school bag and as a portable desk so that children can work anywhere anytime. A low-cost version will be available to children in poor countries where finding a good space to work can be more difficult.

Features

The bag has the following elements and compartments:

- a water bottle
- two notebooks
- a pencil case
- a solar powered flashlight
- a compartment for books and a compartment for small objects like coins or keys.

The low-cost version

The low-cost version will work like this. Each time a full-cost version is sold in Europe, 50 per cent of the profit will be allocated to the production of another lower-cost version of the same product. This will be sold in developing countries for 5€. A further donation of 5€ can be made by buyers if they wish to provide a free bag to a child in need.

3 Example answer:

The Electronic T-shirt

Overview

The Electronic T-shirt is a totally new concept in clothes design. It functions both as a T-shirt and as a digital screen – the logo on the T-shirt is programmable. The T-shirt is also: a fair trade product made in India – the manufacturer gets their fair share of the profits; and completely washable. It is priced at $30.

How the Electronic T-shirt works

- The T-shirt contains a small digital screen that displays up to 28 characters.
- The background colour is changeable.
- The logo is programmed from your computer.

Wordbuilding / Learning skills / Check! (page 35)

1 1 forecasted 2 known 3 mown 4 spilt 5 boiled, burnt 6 shaven 7 forgotten 8 infected 9 proven 10 used

2 2 money or assets that are or can be invested

5 1 necessity 2 wheel 3 origami 4 profit 5 seated

6 1 shred 2 hint 3 with 4 extra 5 entrepreneur 6 breakthrough

Transport system: Shweeb

Unit 5

5a (pages 36 and 37)

1 1 to educate the rest of the world about Africa
2 the football World Cup in South Africa in 2010
3 They aim to reveal Africa as seen by Africans themselves rather than through the eyes of an outsider.
4 presenting a one-dimensional, stereotyped view of Africa

2 a haphazardly b seize c conspicuous d turbulent e (her) portrait f stereotyped g decree

3 1 a Chinua Achebe Centre for African Writers and Artists b writer
2 a (The fact that) many things are already familiar to them b observing the details
3 a series of travel books b travel books
4 a be b authors / writers

4 1 one 2 to 3 do (so) 4 others *or* other ones 5 This *or* That 6 one 7 former, latter 8 it is

5a 1 B: Yes, I'd love to.
2 B: No, I've got one, thanks.
3 B: No, I'm afraid not.
4 B: Oh, I'm sorry to hear that.
5 B: I hope so.
6 B: Oh, yes. I love a good thriller.
7 B: Catching up on emails.

6 1 wary 2 affable 3 track 4 ascent 5 setting 6 cosy

5b (pages 38 and 39)

1 1 A 2 A 3 D 4 A 5 D

2 1 non-fiction 2 dumbing down 3 misconception 4 genre 5 complementary 6 implication

3 1 b 2 d 3 f 4 e 5 a 6 c

4 1 a 2 a 3 b 4 a

5 1 share 2 will 3 line 4 washy 5 go 6 gritty

6 1 has greatly increased 2 choose that 3 understand 4 more attractive 5 implies (that)

7 1 the reason is mainly that
2 is *or* makes an attempt to
3 whose preference is for
4 is the claim of

8 1 of marrying 2 to trick 3 for wearing 4 to do 5 for wanting 6 in getting

9 The idea of comic strips as a useful teaching tool has been around for some time.
There is a belief among educators that comic books can act as a gateway to other literature.
The result is a number of textbooks for younger learners in comic form, helping bring subjects like history to life.
Now this trend has been taken a step further with the appearance of computer software tools with which you can create your own comic strips.
Educators say these offer learners a new and stimulating way to present their ideas and findings about a subject.

5c (page 40)

1 1 He dreamed about exploring.
2 The glamour had gone. *or* It had ceased to be a mystery. *or* It had become a place of darkness.
3 He got a job as a ship's captain aboard a steamboat.

2 1 blank spaces
2 rivers, lakes and names
3 an immense, uncoiled snake
4 It was used for trading.
5 a captain
6 It was featureless, monotonous and grim.

3 1 positive
2 No, they haven't.
3 It is curled up/asleep.
4 b
5 a
6 cannot speak *or* not speaking

4 1 mind 2 doubt 3 shadow 4 vote 5 an eye 6 net

5d (page 41)

1 1 background
2 Enunciate
3 Pause
4 pace, volume
5 expression

2 1 The Congo, Africa.
2 The author narrates the story from his own experience as a steamboat captain in the Congo.
3 To illustrate how alien / strange the world is that he has entered.

3 1 extract 2 works 3 set 4 tells 5 narrates 6 illustrates

4a The broadening waters flowed through a mob of wooded islands; / you lost your way on that river / as you would in a desert, / trying to find the channel, / till you thought yourself cut off / for ever / from everything you had ever known.

4b In the first version, the reader reads more slowly, with longer pauses, more expression, and her words are enunciated more clearly.

5 Students' own answers.

5e (page 42)

1 [3] It is 1857 and the British Empire in India is facing severe unrest from the indigenous population. For the ruling British class in the northern town of Krishnapur, life is calm and polite until the sepoys at a nearby military fort rise in mutiny and the British are forced to retreat into the British Residency. Food and other supplies become short, disease sets in and the inhabitants' resources are tested to the limit.
This is the first part of J.G. Farrell's empire trilogy, [1] an examination of the British Empire in its decline. *The Siege of Krishnapur* serves as a metaphor for this decline as each character is forced to examine their own view of the world. Although the situation is desperate, [4] Farrell describes it with great elegance and humour, conveying the ridiculousness of the British position. Some would argue that in not describing the hardship and injustice suffered by the local Indian population, Farrell has done them a great injustice. But I do not think that was his aim. [2] What he has done is to write both a gripping story and a thought-provoking study of colonial life.

2 d

3 1 provoking
2 going
3 uneventful
4 fetched
5 convincing
6 wrenching
7 uninspiring
8 poorly

Wordbuilding / Learning skills / Check! (page 43)

1 1 e 2 h 3 c 4 j 5 i 6 b 7 g 8 a 9 f 10 d

4 1 officious
2 rocky, horseback
3 comic, graphic
4 poet
5 density
6 aloud
7 thought-provoking
8 transformative

Unit 6

6a (pages 44 and 45)

1 1 Rishikesh, India
2 chronic back pain
3 yes – because he's given up worrying about his bad back

2 1 the Beatles turned up in Rishikesh to study transcendental meditation at Maharishi Mahesh Yogi's ashram
2 songs the Beatles wrote in Rishikesh
3 foreign visitors who go to Rishikesh each year
4 disadvantaged boys that the Parmarth Niketan Ashram supports
5 the man started his exercise regime on the first day
6 the table from which they had lunch
7 the man's visit to the ashram
8 the man could sit cross-legged through a meal

3 1 a 2 b 3 b 4 a 5 a 6 a

4 1 intransitive
2 intransitive
3 chronic back pain
4 the day
5 mental and physical healing
6 hundreds of thousands of foreign visitors
7 them
8 a breathing technique
9 intransitive
10 it
11 worrying

5 1 put up
2 put up with
3 separable: pull in, put off
inseparable: get over, look for, work on, carry on, give up

6 1 The pain is quite bad, but I've learned to put up with it.
2 I got the injury playing football and it took me a long time to get over it.
3 If you think going to yoga classes will help, then there's no point putting it off.
4 I used to ski a lot, but I gave it up.
5 Reducing the cost of the course for students really pulled them in.
6 Can you put me up for the night on Tuesday when I'm in town?
7 I'm not as supple as I used to be, but I put that down to my age.
8 I can't touch my toes yet, but I'm working on it.

7 1 come across
2 set aside
3 take up
4 put someone off
5 go in for
6 takes off
7 get out of
8 carry out
9 comes about
10 fall back on

8 1 keep
2 do
3 out
4 shape
5 on
6 am *or* keep
7 watch
8 for

9 **A:** The other day I looked up what fitness classes there were available locally and I couldn't believe how many there were.
B: Did you come across any that you liked the look of?
A: Not really. I didn't know what half of them were: Boxercise, Boot camp, Aqua aerobics … and loads based on dance.
B: You mean like Zumba.
A: Yes. I knew Zumba was a craze that had taken off, but there were others: Jazzercise, Bodyjam. I mean, if you go in for dancing, why don't you just sign up for a dance class?
B: And do you? Go in for dancing, that is?
A: Yes, I do. I think that's what I'll do … take up samba or something.

6b (pages 46 and 47)

1 1 Simply put, cross-training means practising other sports or forms of exercise to improve, indirectly, your abilities in your main or target sport. (para 1)
2 Finally, and most importantly, it prevents athletes from getting the kind of repetitive strain injuries that they often suffer if they only practise the same activities day in day out. (para 2)
3 The lesson of cross-training is that the body reacts well to new experiences. (para 4)

2 1 c 2 c 3 a 4 b 5 a 6 c

3 1 help (more generally) to increase, tend(s) to be, learn to deal with
2 require(s) you to control, enable them to continue (playing)
3 let(s) you build
4 mean(s) practising, recommend (to everyone) incorporating
5 succeed(ing) in performing
6 prevent(s) athletes from getting

4 1 to warm up
2 to do
3 doing
4 exercise, (to) see
5 playing
6 about getting
7 for getting
8 to be
9 playing *or* to play
10 playing, training

5 1 grazed
2 stubbed
3 bumped
4 chipped
5 bruised
6 lost
7 sprained
8 pulled

6 1 passed out
2 on the mend
3 run down
4 shaken up
5 off colour
6 in a bad way

7a 1 Is he in‿a bad way?
2 She was pretty shaken‿up.
3 I almost passed‿out.
4 He looks‿a bit‿off colour.
5 She's‿on the mend.
6 I feel‿under the weather.

6c (page 48)

1 b

2 1 a is worth around $200 billion
b spend over a billion each year on their fingernails alone
2 Male grooming (now)
3 regular washing with soap could help to turn a dark skin whiter
4 McDonald's alters its menu to suit the tastes of each local market
5 a black soap in Africa
b in South America as an ingredient in hair dye

3 1 similar 2 selling 3 idea 4 changes 5 shine

4 1 long 2 straight 3 brave 4 it 5 lose 6 music

6d (page 49)

1 1 b 2 d 3 e 4 f

2 1 lift
2 air conditioning
3 staff canteen
4 staff to do sports together

3 1 wheelchair access
2 fresh air wouldn't always be cool
3 who should be responsible for making the list
4 not everyone will want to join in in doing sports with other staff

4 1 realise, around
2 Admittedly, but
3 really, through, do
4 know, everyone

5a 1 I'm not very much in favour of the proposal.
2 It's not exactly what I had in mind.
3 It's not a particularly cheap option.
4 It hasn't proved to be so successful.
5 I'm not entirely convinced.

6 Students' own answers.

6e (page 50)

1 1 There is concern that children in the school are not eating healthily enough, and this is affecting both their general health and their academic performance.
2 Most children are not getting a balanced diet.
3 That school meals should be compulsory for all pupils and that they are given the choice of different meals, but not a choice of different elements within each meal.

2a 1 Evidently
2 apparently
3 As might be expected
4 Specifically
5 In view of this

2b 1 Overall 2 on the face of it 3 ultimately 4 Conversely

3 Students' own answers.

Wordbuilding / Learning skills / Check! (page 51)

1 1 finished off
2 fill up
3 shaved off
4 messed up
5 pay off
6 gave up
7 use up
8 wrote off
9 Eat up
10 called off

2 1 cancel 2 wreck 3 stop

4 1 a, c, d 2 a, b 3 b, c 4 c, d

5 1 jogging, swimming
2 Japan
3 India
4 very long
5 necks
6 wealth, well-being
7 calories
8 health insurance

Unit 7

7a (pages 52 and 53)

1 c

2 1 c 2 a 3 b 4 b 5 a 6 a

3 1 revolts 2 defeated 3 punishment 4 accepting 5 accumulate 6 rebel 7 rob 8 run away

4 1 Following the conquest of a territory, how do you make the inhabitants of that land loyal to you?
2 Although they oppose your rule, they are so afraid of vengeance that they don't dare to do anything.
3 They see that they have a better standard of living when there is a change of regime.
4 He rewarded them and (he) also kept them afraid.
5 He was merciless to those who opposed him, but this was not always the case.
6 Since the local people disliked him, Kuchlug found that he had little support.

5 1 Although the Mongols seemed like a united force, they were made up of a group of warring tribes.
2 After Genghis Khan died in 1227, his empire continued to grow.
3 Because the Mongols had a nomadic lifestyle, they depended on their horses.
4 As well as relying on great force, Genghis Khan also used spies to discover an enemy's weakness.
5 Although most armies are made up of cavalry and infantry, all of Genghis Khan's army were on horseback.
6 Because Genghis Khan was often cruel, he has a reputation in history as a merciless warrior.

6 1 sides 2 outlaw 3 sacrifices 4 pioneers 5 inside 6 feats 7 notoriety 8 jinxed 9 story

7 Archaeologists working outside Vienna, Austria, believe they have discovered a huge school for ancient Roman gladiators, rivalling in size the training grounds outside Rome's Colosseum.
The facility includes features never before seen at a Roman gladiators' school, such as a wooden training dummy and outside its gates, the first known gladiators' cemetery.
In addition to a walled field for wild animals, it includes a mini-amphitheatre. Here gladiators, who were mostly foreign slaves, could practise their moves and perform in front of potential purchasers.

7b (pages 54 and 55)

1 1 broken sleep may be a natural pattern/better for you
2 diaries, literary sources, medical books
3 at the beginning of the 18th century
4 because of industrialisation, improvements in lighting and an increase in business activity at night
5 You shouldn't worry about waking up in the night.

2 a uninterrupted b chunks c dusk d coincided with e entirely smooth f bears (this) out

3 a compared to a single period of sleep,
b As far as the beds themselves are concerned,
c Given that this disappearance coincided with industrialisation in these countries,

4 1 Assuming that Ekirch is right, we shouldn't think there is something wrong with us if we wake in the night.
2 You should never sleep on a mattress that is too hard in case it gives you back pain.
3 Regardless of how many hours I sleep, I always feel tired.
4 In spite of (always) wearing earplugs in bed, I still wake up if I hear a noise.
5 Having said that history can be fascinating, I don't think I'd have the patience to be an historian. *or* History can be fascinating. Having said that, I don't think I'd have the patience to be an historian.
6 Considering people in the past had few ways to amuse themselves during hours of darkness, I am amazed they didn't complain about insomnia.
7 As far as I'm concerned, power naps don't work.
8 Contrary to the popular belief that you need at least six hours sleep a night, it is possible to manage on less.

6 1 got 2 missed 3 struck 4 gone 5 blew 6 hit

7c (page 56)

1 1 28 April 1789, off Tofua (in the Pacific Ocean)
2 Christian and his mates were attracted by the idea of living on an island paradise and had had enough of Captain Bligh's strictness and cruelty.
3 for Captain Bligh, yes (he sailed to Timor and then returned to England)
for Fletcher Christian and the other mutineers, no (only one mutineer was still alive ten years after they arrived at Pitcairn Island)

2 1 to transport breadfruit from Tahiti to the West Indies
2 They were tied up, forced into the launch (a small boat) and cast adrift in the open ocean. They then sailed to Timor and then returned to England.
3 eight other crew members, six native men and twelve Tahitian women
4 They were captured a year and a half later when the frigate *Pandora* arrived in Tahiti.
5 He stripped her, ran her ashore and burned her. (Note that ships are sometimes referred to as *she*.)
6 One the mutineers, John Williams, took the wife of one of the Tahitians.
7 He was shot to death as he worked in his field.

3 1 appalling
2 loaded
3 everything that could be used
4 that the English Admiralty would find him

4 1 sailed 2 breadfruit 3 mutiny 4 commander *or* captain 5 launch *or* boat 6 ocean 7 returned 8 women *or* natives 9 Pitcairn 10 uninhabited 11 stripped *or* burned 12 mutineers 13 Tahitians 14 one

5 1 resemblance 2 fruit 3 mind 4 brunt 5 grudge 6 witness

7d (page 57)

1 a Hammurabi's code of laws in Babylon
Hammurabi was the sixth king of Babylon 1792 BC to 1750 BC. He is known for the set of laws called Hammurabi's code, one of the first written codes of law in recorded history. These laws were inscribed on stone tablets standing over eight feet tall (2.4 metres), found in Persia in 1901. Owing to his reputation in modern times as an ancient law-giver, Hammurabi's portrait is in many government buildings throughout the world.

2 **1** a pick, on b case, then, possible
2 a understood b expand, more
3 a mentioned b right, thinking
4 a conclusion, seems b that, what
5 a missed b fit, with

3 **1** 2a, 3b, 4a, 4b
2 1a, 1b, 2b, 5a, 5b

4a 1 R 2 F 3 F 4 R 5 F

5 Students' own answers.

7e (page 58)

1 **1** 400 British cavalrymen were killed
2 by quoting Bosquet who said it was madness

2 **a** some hours earlier
b The following day

3 **1** at the time
2 At the time
3 a few days earlier
4 Up to / till then
5 the following day
6 The previous year

4 Example answer:
On the morning of 6 May 1937, the Hindenburg airship passed over Boston, having left Germany three days earlier. Bad weather had delayed its landing at Lakehurst, New Jersey.
Cabin boy Werner Franz was working in the kitchen on board the Hindenburg. He planned to visit New York before the Hindenburg returned to Germany the following day.
The captain was trying to steer the airship next to a docking tower when there was a loud bang and Werner saw a big ball of flame. The skin of the ship had broken and the hydrogen inside had ignited.
The ship crashed to the ground. Horrified onlookers ran for their lives. Franz opened the kitchen hatch where food was pulled up into the kitchen, jumped and then ran to safety. Ten minutes after the fire had started, there was nothing left of the airship.

Wordbuilding / Learning skills / Check! (page 59)

1 **1** defeat **2** invasion **3** resistance **4** amendment **5** command **6** imprisonment **7** disturbance **8** guidance **9** enforcement **10** expansion

4 Across: 2 Roman 5 wreck 7 father 9 Thames 10 ago 12 story 13 BC 14 ship
Down: 1 arrow 2 ruthless 3 micro 4 narrow 6 Krakatoa 8 Namib 9 toys 11 drop

Unit 8

8a (pages 60 and 61)

1 using 3D glasses

2 **1** an archaeologist; he does archaeology in a virtual reality way by using technologies such as satellite imagery and radar
2 a totally immersive virtual reality room

3 **1** a **2** b **3** a **4** b, c **5** c

4 **1** bits of brick, concrete block, glass, etc.
b repair
2 shirts
3 a knife
4 holy
5 a burglars
b only bad luck
6 process

5 **1** Technology is generally thought to be a positive thing.
2 Plastic debris in our oceans is believed to be changing marine ecosystems irreparably as we speak.
3 The quest is known to have frustrated scientists and historians for centuries.
4 The tomb is considered to be an extremely sacred place.
5 Lin learns from an ancient text where a particular mountain was supposed to have been in the past.
6 These new approaches are expected to benefit all kinds of projects in future.

6 **1** Lin is thought to be unusual because of his varied interests.
2 Lin is said to have been inspired by an art historian who uses digital imaging.
3 Genghis Khan is known to have died far from his homeland.
4 It is also known that he wanted to be buried in some mountains in the north.
5 He was reported at the time to have asked to be buried in an unmarked tomb.
6 His tomb isn't expected to be found any time soon.

7 **1** ~~upload~~ **2** ~~blog~~ **3** ~~network~~ **4** ~~tweet~~ **5** ~~posted~~ **6** ~~uploading~~

8 I was very aware on my travels across Europe, posting my blog and photos, that Paris was going to present a particular challenge. I didn't want to photograph the obvious sites, like the Eiffel Tower, even though I was keen to visit them all. But as Paris is said to be one of the world's most photogenic cities, instead I decided to take as few images as possible and come away with some really memorable compositions.
So here they are. They're not supposed to be anything more than a small collection of my memories of this wonderful place: more like postcards than photos. I'll let you decide how successful they are.

8b (pages 62 and 63)

1 1 F You might be forgiven for thinking there was no chance of anyone wanting to follow a company on Twitter or Facebook. But that's where you'd be wrong.
2 T Poor use of social media can actually dissuade customers from coming.
3 F Within 18 months of joining Twitter, he had 1,000 followers and had generated £150,000 of new business.
4 F It has to engage customers and be interesting. 'One of the keys to Lloyd's success is engaging his followers in subjects they find interesting: … new items on the menu, bits of local news and a "Did you know … ?" post with fun facts.'
5 T Using a tool called 'Klout', Lloyd can measure the effect of his efforts – not just the number of people who look at the messages, but how they react to them – and adapt them accordingly.

2 1 thinking there was no chance of anyone wanting to follow a hotel on Twitter or Facebook
2 by poor use of social media on a website
3 started using social media (when it was a relatively new phenomenon)
4 trying to market his hotel through social media
5 an example of a fun tweet which should make you want to read more
6 his tweets which are aimed at engaging his followers in subjects they find interesting

3 1 no harm (in) trying
2 no guarantee of getting
3 no chance of anyone wanting
4 no doubt that
5 no choice but to include
6 No matter what you do

4 1 (in) waiting
2 of it being
3 who you ask
4 complaining
5 of getting
6 but to do

5 1 difficulty (in) finding
2 point in arguing
3 doubt that he's
4 chance / hope of us winning
5 choice / alternative but to / except to
6 matter what anyone says

6a There is an intrusive /w/ which links the expressions. In number 5, there is also an intrusive /r/.
1 no‿/w/‿intention
2 no‿/w/‿idea
3 no‿/w/‿alternative
4 no‿/w/‿use
5 no‿/w/‿other‿/r/‿option

7 1 ballpark
2 loop
3 game
4 rocket
5 practice
6 page
7 box
8 reality

8 1 problems
2 contact *or* talk to
3 exploit / use to one's advantage
4 so simple/obvious that it doesn't require thinking about

8c (page 64)

1 and 2
A hackathon is an event where computer programmers and web experts come together to design new software or new apps.
The focus was on applying technology – web, mobile, social media technology – to the task of conserving resources, minimising pollution, creating cleaner fuels, reducing waste, and so on.

3 1 hack-day, hackfest
2 a day or a weekend
3 web, mobile, social media
4 conserving resources, minimising pollution, creating cleaner fuels, reducing waste
5 less ownership
6 a tool, e.g. an electric drill

4 1 start innovating now
2 dynamic and positive
3 to make comparisons between the energy efficiency of different electrical appliances
4 some of the sponsors and other companies that were present were clearly very interested in their app
5 a movement

5 1 bank
2 news
3 habit
4 in
5 ice
6 mould
7 back
8 even

8d (page 65)

1

What is it?	a flesh-ripping dinosaur
Where was it found?	south-eastern Morocco
Who found it?	a team of scientists led by Andrea Cau of the Bologna Geological Museum
What does the discovery tell us?	this area of North Africa seems to have been particularly popular with predatory dinosaurs

2 1 is believed
2 conclude, probably
3 perhaps
4 suggests that
5 appears that
6 seems to
7 tended to
8 Arguably

3 **2-syllable words**
detect
species
fossil
conclude
dozen
gather
climate

words of 3 or more syllables
previously
terrorise
identify
scientist
dinosaur
popular
predatory

4 Students' own answers.

8e (page 66)

1 1 David Attenborough and German zoologists
2 German zoologists believe they have found an even smaller species, *Brookesia micra*
3 on one of the smaller Madagascan islands
4 The German team used a different method to find *Brookesia*: searching with torches at night when the tiny chameleons climb into the trees and are said to be easier to spot.
5 recently (Now German scientists …)
6 The discovery is significant because it seems to suggest that in certain circumstances, such as being confined to an island, some animals grow smaller in order to adapt to a restricted habitat.

2a **a** it seems to suggest
b are said to be easier to spot
c almost
d generally
e likely (para 1), certainly (para 3)

2b 1 David Attenborough is probably one of the world's best-known nature documentary makers.
2 Attenborough seems to have found his pygmy chameleon by looking on the forest floor.
3 Apparently, German zoologists believe they have found an even smaller species.
4 The German team appear to have used a different method to find *Brookesia*.
5 Some animals are believed to grow smaller in order to adapt to a restricted habitat.

3 Example answer:
We already know that some species of snake can fly and it is believed that some can glide up to 100 metres. But up to now no one has been able to understand how they are able to do this. Now a new study from Virginia Tech shows that scientists may have found the answer.
It seems that snakes can flatten their bodies to make a wing shape. In flight, they usually hold their heads up and their tails down, enabling them to glide.
It is not thought likely that this discovery will have any significance for aeroplane or military technology, but it is certainly true that it will change our view of what snakes are capable of.

Wordbuilding / Learning skills / Check! (page 67)

1 1 clothesbrush 2 Rainfall 3 onlooker 4 breakdown 5 toolbox 6 fireplace 7 footnote 8 letterbox *or* postbox 9 Sunburn 10 Wallpaper

2 all three

3 1 main verb = implies, subject = the evidence, object = an increase
2 subject = the evidence that Jenkins has supplied, object = an increase in the number of people under 50 suffering from memory loss
3 extra information = whether you agree with Jenkins's methods of collecting data or not; an increase rather than a decrease, i.e. as some people think

5 1 social 2 invisible 3 No 4 keep 5 hackers 6 outside 7 light 8 even
Phenomenon: sinkhole

Unit 9

9a (pages 68 and 69)

1 1 in school
2 They're from Hawaii.
3 traditional music
4 a variety of styles; cover songs of more popular music
5 Because music can give great pleasure; you can feel more connected to things around you; it can be relaxing.

2 1 hooked 2 synonymous with Hawaii 3 cliques 4 created his own technique 5 freaked out 6 raw human emotion 7 have a blast 8 contemplative time

3 1 age 2 up 3 stressful 4 picking 5 yoga 6 silly

4 1 d 2 e 3 a 4 c 5 b

5 1 We just got back from holiday.
2 The new museum is just stunning.
3 That's just what I think.
4 We just use bicycles; we don't own a car.
5 There are just under three million people living in the city.
6 Can you just wait a moment?

6 1 b *or* f 2 b 3 f 4 b *or* c 5 a 6 b

7 One of the song titles on Shimabukuro's album *Peace, Love and Ukelele* consists of just three numbers: 143. Shimabukuro says that the song was written for his fiancée at the time and that the significance is that in those days they just had pagers, not mobile phones. 143 means 'I love you' in numeric code.
So he used to page her with that code, in just the same way that some people now text the letters *ILY*. Even after pagers were replaced with mobile phones, they still used the code, because it was just something they both understood. So the song is just a piece of nostalgia, really.

8a 1 d 2 e 3 f 4 a 5 b 6 c

9 and 10
Genres of music: folk, classical
Adjectives that describe music: soothing, uplifting
Musicians: busker, composer
Adjectives describing taste: eclectic, conservative
Compositions: ballad, pieces

9b (pages 70 and 71)

1 The article mentions neurological disorders such as: Alzheimer's, dementia, multiple sclerosis and Parkinson's.

2 1 F 2 T 3 T 4 F 5 T 6 T

3 1 for the alleviation of boredom
2 so as to use
3 to prevent the subject feeling
4 to improve
5 so that we can lift our spirits *or* so that our spirits are lifted
6 so as not to be

4 1 d He left his job at the bank to concentrate on playing music.
2 a We perform live sometimes, but just for fun.
3 e Please turn any phones or music devices off so as not to disturb other passengers.
4 c You have to practise to / in order to / so as to get better.
5 b Singers drink a lot of water to avoid getting throat problems.

5 1 play 2 dance 3 tune 4 ears 5 trumpet 6 chord 7 score 8 face

6 Is there a way to learn an instrument fast? What do you think? The answer is almost certainly not, if you want to do it properly. To do anything well takes time and patience. You can take shortcuts to avoid learning each step, but in the end this will catch up with you. You may reach a certain destination faster, but it won't be the one that you're ultimately aiming for. I always advise people to bear in mind the three 'P's: pay attention to your instructor; practice – to improve you need to practise as often as possible; and patience. Progress is always slower at first and ninety per cent of people give up within the first year of taking up an instrument.

9c (page 72)

1 1 the harmonica *or* blues harp
2 He was charismatic and moody.
3 as a legend

2 1 a 2 c 3 b 4 a 5 c 6 a

3 1 star
2 radio *or* midday
3 hard
4 five *or* young
5 hands
6 wandering *or* drifting *or* travelling
7 jamming *or* playing
8 simple
9 negativity
10 charisma
11 Europe
12 influenced
13 respect
14 legend

4 1 road 2 miss 3 nerve 4 note 5 record

9d (page 73)

1 1 musical: father a musician, aunt a singer
2 a singer
3 They wanted her to be a doctor or lawyer initially, but in the end let her find her own way.

2 1 really thought about it like
2 good question
3 honestly don't
4 that's difficult to
5 tell you really

3a Sentences 1, 3, 4 and 6 use wavering intonation.

4 Students' own answers.

9e (page 74)

1 1 Indian pop stars, in Bollywood films; everywhere
2 Yes. The music is joyous, infectious and feel-good.

2 1 vibrant, deafening
2 like a throng of happy voices
3 the already hectic nature of Indian city life, an environment which threatens to overwhelm your senses
4 The music is joyous and infectious. You can't help tapping your foot along to the rhythm.
5 I'd be surprised if you weren't carried along in its happy wake.
6 match the prettiest faces on screen with the best voices around; It's not great music, it's feel-good music.

3 Example answers:
1 friendly faces
2 in modern styles *or* in western styles
3 are infectious dance songs
4 and its modern side
5 performing dance routines; acting
6 Bollywood focuses almost entirely on musicals

Wordbuilding / Learning skills / Check! (page 75)

1 1 discontinue
2 discomfort
3 atypical
4 nonsense
5 disoriented
6 non-payment
7 dysfunctional
8 asymmetrical
9 non-attendance
10 disability

3 1 reggae
2 country
3 calypso
4 experimental
5 fusion
6 opera

4 1 instrument; instrumental
2 solo
3 hit
4 Fado; folk
5 electric; eclectic
6 love

Unit 10

10a (pages 76 and 77)

1 1 John Byrne, a homeless man, jumped into the river to save a rabbit.
2 He challenged anti-social behaviour; he saved a vulnerable animal.

2 1 T 2 T 3 F 4 NI 5 NI 6 T

3 Possible answers:
1 film actors, directors, producers
2 you might give them money or food
3 a coin
4 a floor, a chimney
5 after 11 p.m.

4 1 are they
2 don't they
3 was it *or* wasn't it
4 can it
5 did they *or* didn't they
6 did he

5 1 go, shall we
2 right to say that, aren't I
3 tell anyone, will you
4 have asked me first, couldn't you
5 the first time this has happened, is it
6 accepted the money, did you
7 had expected her to win, had they
8 offend you, did I

6a 1 rises 2 falls 3 rises 4 falls 5 rises

7 1 groups, minorities
2 values, culture
3 immigrant community, friends
4 family, community
5 extended, nuclear
6 first-generation, economic
7 social, family
8 rich, cultural

10b (pages 78 and 79)

1 The adjectives that match the description of female elephant behaviour are: considerate, intelligent, protective, cooperative.

2 1 b 2 c 3 b 4 a 5 c 6 a

3 1 socially aware (b)
2 in a considerate way (e)
3 (leaves) voluntarily (a)
4 long (c)
5 barely (d)

4 1 What makes them socially intelligent?
2 This is well documented.
3 She was wandering around in a disoriented way.
4 This group rejected her – literally pushed her away.
5 She marched straight over to the other herd.
6 You'd hardly think that was possible.
7 If they pulled simultaneously on their rope, a table with corn on it appeared.
8 The elephants very fast / quickly learned to coordinate their pulling.

5 1 parroting 2 wolf 3 duck 4 beavering 5 hound 6 swanning

6 1 b 2 e 3 a 4 c 5 d

7 1 Research suggests that crows are able to tell the difference between one human being and another from their faces.
2 If one dolphin is ill, another will stay by it and help it to breathe.
3 Meerkats can be very selfless: one will often stand watch while the others are playing or eating.
4 Young Emperor penguins often group together and play together in a kind of nursery.
5 Killer whales in the Northern Pacific live with their mothers all their lives.

10c (page 80)

1 1 For bringing peace to Liberia.
2 She appealed to women to play their part in bringing an end to the war.
3 She spreads her message around the world and continues to campaign for social change.

2 1 female president in Africa
2 civil war
3 women's peace
4 counsellor
5 forgive
6 hope
7 public places or markets
8 the end of the civil war

3 1 hurt 2 chained 3 offends 4 skips 5 dream of 6 move forward

4 1 d 2 a 3 e 4 f 5 b 6 c

5 1 spirit 2 lunch 3 scot 4 feel 5 rein

10d (page 81)

1 1 It was about success and failure.
2 He criticised the idea of meritocracy, because it suggests that those who are at the bottom deserve to be there.
3 He suggests that we change our attitudes about people who don't suceed; that we don't make judgements about them.

2 a, c, d

3 1 Watching 2 isn't he 3 too 4 suppose so 5 neither 6 see 7 do 8 doubt it

4a 1 I doubt it.
2 I expect so.
3 I couldn't tell you, I'm afraid.
4 I'm afraid not.
5 I suppose so.
6 It's a good idea, isn't it?

5 Students' own answers.

10e (page 82)

1 Possible answers:
He worked hard; he was very ambitious; he'd already had a good educational foundation; his parents were high achievers; he came from a comfortable background; he was intelligent/gifted; he had a natural business instinct; he had the skills and knowledge required to start his own business.

2a Example answers:
I agree: you can't expect to be able to achieve anything in life; it depends on your abilities.
I disagree: I think you can achieve anything in life if you want it enough.

2b The main argument is that the writer doesn't believe that anyone can achieve anything.

2c 1 not everyone has access to a good education
2 you might not have a natural talent or ability to do something

2d The final paragraph is the conclusion, where the writer repeats the main argument, i.e. that we can't all achieve whatever we want.

3 Students' own answers.

Wordbuilding / Learning skills / Check! (page 83)

1 1 handed 2 boiled 3 sounding 4 spirited 5 willed 6 faced 7 standing 8 minded 9 talking 10 cut

2 Possible answers:
1 Never mind. Thanks anyway.
2 Chocolates? That's very kind of you, but you shouldn't have!
3 Do say 'hello' from me. *or* Give them my best wishes.
4 I'm so sorry, I didn't realise.
5 Have you come far? *or* Have you seen this speaker before?
6 I'd love to, but I can't. *or* I'm afraid I've got too much work on.

3 Possible situations:
You've arrived late at a meeting or lecture; you've met someone and you can't remember their name; someone sneezes; someone's just had their hair cut; you need to interrupt someone who's working to ask them a question; someone tells you they can't join you for dinner; someone offers to help you with a heavy bag; someone asks if you mind if they smoke.

4 1 b, j 2 e, g 3 a, d 4 c, i 5 f, h

Unit 11

11a (pages 84 and 85)

1 1 Young people in Japan who have withdrawn from society.
2 uncertain economic prospects in Japan; high achieving parents
3 Japan could be left with a whole generation that has never worked or been integrated into society.

2 1 regained control of their emotions
2 being alone *or* apart from others
3 a situation where teenagers don't grow up/mature
4 caused this *or* made this happen
5 less willing
6 a life of isolation *or* living apart from others

3 1 c 2 b 3 e 4 a 5 d

4 1 were, would you do
2 had left, wouldn't have got
3 tell, told
4 lived, would be
5 treated
6 would find *or* had found

5a 1 If <u>only</u> you had <u>waited</u>.
2 I <u>wish</u> you were <u>here</u>.
3 If <u>only</u> it was that <u>easy</u>.
4 I <u>wish</u> they would <u>stop</u> making that <u>noise</u>.
5 I <u>wish</u> I hadn't <u>said</u> anything.

6 1 e 2 a 3 b 4 c 5 d

7 1 confused and disorganised
2 miserable
3 exhausted
4 cross
5 nervous
6 taken aback *or* astonished
7 ecstatic
8 optimistic

8 Possible answers:
1 cross *or* a bit down *or* miserable
2 optimistic *or* upbeat
3 taken aback *or* astonished
4 done in *or* exhausted
5 livid *or* cross
6 content
7 scared *or* on edge *or* petrified
8 all over the place

11b (pages 86 and 87)

1 Students' own answers.

2 Statement 2

3 1 T 2 T 3 F 4 F 5 F 6 T

4

1 through	3 objective	5 account
2 regrets	4 distort	6 justify

5

1 Were	3 Had	5 to, would
2 didn't, would	4 Should	6 would have

6 Sentences 1, 3, 4, 5 and 6 are examples of inversion in conditionals.

7 1 Were the owner to lower the price, our client would consider making an offer.
2 Had we been told earlier, we could have done something about it.
3 Should anyone ask, I'll be back in the office on 23rd September.
4 Were the pipes to freeze, it could result in them bursting.
5 Had customers just put the money in the bank, they would be a lot better off.
6 Should it rain, please bring in any furniture from outside.

8 1 If I hadn't rushed into buying the latest phone, I would have got it for half the price a month later.
2 Should you need help finding your way around, please ask any of the staff.
3 If shelters hadn't been available after the storm, many people would have been left homeless. *or* Had shelters not been available after the storm, many people would have been left homeless.
4 If you were faced with the same situation again, would you do the same thing?

9a

1a <u>ob</u>ject (n)	b ob<u>ject</u> (v)
2a con<u>test</u> (v)	b <u>con</u>test (n)
3a in<u>crease</u> (v)	b <u>in</u>crease (n)
4a <u>ref</u>use (n)	b re<u>fuse</u> (v)
5a <u>proj</u>ect (n)	b pro<u>ject</u> (v)
6a im<u>port</u> (v)	b <u>im</u>port (n)

Rule: for the noun form, the stress falls on the first syllable. For the verb form it falls on the second syllable.

10 OK, so here's my dilemma. I've been offered a fantastic job in Australia, 6,000 miles away from where I live now. The problem is that my parents are in their eighties and I'm the only one in the family who lives near them still. If I took the job, I wouldn't be able to see them more than once or twice a year. Should anything happen to them while I was in Australia, I'd feel terrible. But at the same time, I don't know if I will ever get an opportunity like this again. Were I to tell them, they'd of course say that I must go, but it's not that simple.

11c (page 88)

1 1 flying properly; powering the robot / using an appropriate fuel source which isn't too heavy
2 Examples given in the text: pollinating crops; search and rescue missions following natural disasters; traffic monitoring; weather mapping; evaluating or exploring areas which are dangerous for humans to enter; military surveillance

2 1 robot dogs and cats
2 a TV programme about the decline of the honey bee population
3 to pollinate crops where there is a shortage of honey bees
4 They would like to create colonies of Robobees who will work cooperatively and collectively.
5 artificial sensors

3 1 nervous system
2 crashes a lot
3 refuelling station
4 honey, pollinate crops
5 eyes and antennae

4

1 inspired	3 nature	5 Science
2 lobsters	4 principles	6 $2 million

5

1 perform	3 face	5 determine
2 adapt to	4 flap	6 take

6 1 move(d) to tears
2 move(d) up in the world
3 move up a gear
4 on the move
5 move(d) the goalposts

11d (page 89)

1 Speaker 1: c Speaker 2: a Speaker 3: d

2 1 Because the first speaker hadn't been clear about their opinion before the meeting.
2 That she moans (complains) about routine paperwork.
3 No, because he's thick-skinned.

3 1 look, little, offend
2 came out
3 think
4 seem
5 say, upset
6 so funny
7 sounded

4a 1 /t/
2 /d/
3 /d/
4 /d/
5 /d/
6 /ɪd/
7 /d/
8 /t/
9 /ɪd/
10 /t/

4c /aɪd/

5 Students' own answers.

11e (page 90)

1 1 <u>I'm joking of course!</u>
2 <u>Many thanks for getting back to me so quickly.</u>
3 <u>Please don't take this the wrong way. We do really appreciate your offer.</u>
4 <u>I'm not offended in any way. It just took me rather by surprise.</u>

2 1 D 2 A 3 C 4 B

3 Example answers:
A
<u>Thank you for your long and thoughtful answer</u>. I <u>do appreciate all your work on this</u>. I will reply to you when I have time to read it properly.
B
Great to hear from you! Your spelling hasn't improved much since we were at school. I had to re-read your email three times before I could understand it. <u>I'm joking, of course!</u> Your idea of meeting up on 8th December sounds perfect. Let me know where you'd like to meet.
C
I sent you a quotation as promised a week ago, but you have not replied. <u>I don't want to pressure you, but</u> are we to suppose that you are not interested?
D
I received your email saying that you don't want to take up my offer of advice about the design of your website. <u>It took me rather by surprise, but I'm not offended in any way</u>. I hope the person you have found to help you with this does a good job.

Wordbuilding / Learning skills / Check! (page 91)

1 1 f 2 b 3 h 4 g 5 d 6 e 7 a 8 c

2 1 wound (v) /waʊnd/ wrapped around
2 tear (v) /teə(r)/ rip or split
3 row (n) /raʊ/ argument or dispute
4 minute (adj) /maɪˈnjuːt/ very small, tiny
5 alternate (adj) /ɔːlˈtɜːnət/ one of every two
6 sewers (n pl) /ˈsuːə(r)z/ pipes which take away waste water
7 refuse (n) /ˈrefjuːs/ rubbish or waste
8 delegate (v) /ˈdeləgeɪt/ pass on or give responsibility to someone below you

5 Across: 3 emotional 4 bits 5 livid 9 irrational
Down: 1 android 2 slow 5 if 6 tears 8 only

Unit 12

12a (pages 92 and 93)

1 North America: fields of grass photo 3
South America: mountain, jungle, prairie and shanty towns photos 1, 2, 4
She also mentions the coastal desert and islands.

2 1 snow-covered 2 lush, jungle 3 fields 4 shanty

3 1 b 2 c 3 b 4 b 5 c 6 a

4 1 a 2 a 3 b 4 a 5 a 6 b

5 1 over fifteen
2 hundreds of miles
3 a kind of desert
4 close-ish
5 30 years or so
6 around 1,500 metres
7 some (small airplane)
8 stuff

6 1 120-odd years
2 roughly 300
3 kind of small
4 in the next year or two
5 some ambition
6 dozens of ideas
7 help out with stuff

7 1 rolling
2 cloudless
3 rich
4 open
5 lush
6 sparse
7 rustic
8 idyllic
9 night-time
10 snow-capped

8 1 We've moved to a city in Jordan called Irbid, about 100 kilometres north of the capital.
2 It's close-ish. The journey to work at the university takes me 30 minutes or so.
3 It's farmland mostly, but not very rich. Some people would call it sparse, but I kind of like it.
4 The desert is to the east, some distance away, but we haven't visited it yet. I'd love to go some time, but there's so much other stuff to see that we haven't got round to it.

12b (pages 94 and 95)

1 Students' own answers.

2 1 red tides
2 aurora borealis
3 red tides, ice circles
4 sailing stones
5 aurora borealis, ice circles
6 aurora borealis, red tides, ice circles

3 1 dew 2 the poles 3 toxic 4 scorched 5 spinning

4 1 fairly
2 rather
3 quite
4 a little *or* rather
5 pretty *or* fairly
6 rather
7 fairly
8 quite

5 1 quite *or* fairly *or* pretty *or* rather
2 quite
3 quite *or* rather
4 rather *or* quite *or* slightly *or* a bit *or* a little
5 rather
6 rather *or* a little *or* a bit
7 rather *or* pretty *or* quite
8 rather *or* quite *or* a bit of

6a 1 I 2 D 3 I 4 I 5 I 6 D

7 1 sopping
2 brand
3 fast
4 rock
5 pitch
6 freezing
7 lightning
8 sick
9 wide
10 stiff

8 a bored stiff b dirt cheap, bored stiff, filthy rich

12c (page 96)

1 landscape, rural, spring, scene

2 1 T 2 F 3 T 4 F 5 F 6 T

3 1 tired 2 depicting 3 changes 4 paint *or* draw 5 photo 6 freezes *or* captures 7 masters 8 air 9 iPad

4 1 negative (overdone)
2 slightly negative/neutral (surprised)
3 negative (repetitive)
4 neutral (mixed feelings)
5 neutral (basic)
6 positive (friendly)

5 1 room *or* space 2 room 3 space 4 space 5 room 6 space

12d (page 97)

1a 1 just 3 finish 4 there 5 in 6 on 7 moment 8 make

1b Interrupting: 1, 2, 4, 5, 6
Preventing interruptions: 3, 7, 8

2 a golf courses are attractive, they provide a facility to play sport, the land will be better looked after, it protects against other development
b golf courses are exclusive, they are not environmentally friendly

3 Phrases 1, 2, 3, 4, 5, 6 and 8 are used.

4a They are all said with a polite and firm intonation, except number 3.

5 Students' own answers.

12e (page 98)

1 1 a piece of marketing computer software
2 a small business retailer

2 It will increase your business; help you understand customers better; it's not expensive; it's an easy way to do market research; it doesn't take a lot of time to do; there's a discount available.

3 I am taking this opportunity to write to you [1] <u>with an idea that will help you understand your customers better and significantly increase business</u>.

[2] <u>Smaller retailers like you do not</u>. This means you often lose out by being unable to adapt to changing customer needs.
[4] <u>We know how difficult it is for a small business to keep up with everything</u>: dealing with suppliers, staffing issues, etc.
[3] <u>You would love to do more marketing</u>, but it is often the last thing on the list.

[5] <u>If you call us in the next week quoting the reference number at the top of this letter, we will give you a first year discount of 20 per cent.</u>

We look forward to helping you.

4 1 b (strong claim)
2 b (clear, short sentences)
3 a (empathising)
4 a (understanding what the customer wants)

5 Students' own answers.

Wordbuilding / Learning skills / Check! (page 99)

1 1 celebrated 2 simple 3 humid 4 eternal 5 clear 6 dignified 7 familiar 8 anonymous 9 vain 10 monstrous
The two which are regular are *humid* and *familiar*.

2 1 eternity 2 dignity 3 monstrosity 4 anonymity 5 celebrity 6 clarity 7 simplicity 8 familiarity

5 1 Allard (A)
2 obscura (O)
3 speculative (S)
4 haiku (H)
5 blot on the landscape (B)
Name: BASHO

IELTS practice test

Listening

1 A a number of local companies are involved in that
2 B I did have to take photo ID with me
3 C they wanted to check that we didn't hold strong views about shopping malls
4 6/six (hours) I'm not supposed to work more than six hours in any one twenty-four hour period
5 (a/your) badge As long as you've got your badge on, you can wear what you like.
6 60/sixty But at least sixty per cent are meant to be in the first group (A)
7 35/thirty-five I've got a target of thirty-five interviews over the seven days
8 text (message) you're sent a text message each morning
9 12/twelve hours You've got twelve hours from the time of the interview to do that.
10 Survey Host We're using Survey Host actually
11 C Very few reserves in Africa have the biodiversity that Phinda offers.
12 A although the area was at one time somewhat depleted in major mammal species
13 A worldwide significance, and the recent release of black rhino into the reserve is evidence of this
14 B Most probably, however, you'll spend some time monitoring the white rhino
15 database Volunteers assist in the building up of a database
16 eye(s) individuals, which are identified through their eye markings
17 leopard leopard research project, keeping a note of where they are seen
18 B volunteers are provided with a weekly food kitty to do their own shopping
19 C The house is equipped with a fridge, freezer, stove, oven and microwave.
20 F there is also a DVD player
21 B spores which form on fallen leaves and then infect the leaves of a healthy tree
22 B It seems to be less of a serious problem on Far Eastern ashes.
23 C it migrated from its Japanese home and took up residence somewhere in Eastern Europe
24 A Diana: Are there different subtypes? Dennis: Well, no.
25 A Probably more than one generation, actually
26 A nobody knows exactly how many there are in reality
27 C still less exactly how evenly they're spread across the country
28 D we need to find out if it's affecting old and young trees equally
29 F whether it's spread to all regions
30 G whether there are populations of ash trees in areas that can be isolated from the spread of the disease
31 electronic commerce an internship is an integral part of your degree programme in electronic commerce
32 unpaid working for a company as an unpaid member of staff
33 faculty guide following the specifications outlined in the Faculty guide
34 job (description) secondly it should outline your job description there
35 critical analysis on the third component, the critical analysis of a specific internship-related topic
36 routine tasks you'll be asked to do routine tasks most of the time
37 logical thinking and demonstrate your ability in logical thinking
38 B acronyms used in your work place? If in doubt, leave them out
39 E If your report includes typos and spelling mistakes, then your readers are likely to be distracted and you risk losing credibility.
40 F A fellow intern or workmate will tell you if what you've written is understandable.

Reading

1 Texas moving North Dakota into second place among US states, ahead of Alaska … output could eventually close in on that of Texas – at two million barrels.
2 14 million barrels By the time the frenzy ends, perhaps 20 years from now, as many as 14 billion barrels
3 pipelines Until more pipelines are built … most of the oil and water will be transported by truck
4 farms/farming But how does a region of farms weather the human onslaught?
5 sand fracking, by which large amounts of fresh water combine with sand and smaller amounts of other substances
6 dirty water How will the dirty water that's pumped out be prevented from contaminating groundwater …?
7 TRUE The extraction technology refined in the Bakken is in effect a skeleton key that can be used to open other fossil fuel treasure chests.
8 FALSE North Dakota has boomed before, in the 1950s and 1980s.
9 FALSE in southwestern Montana, where they still live
10 FALSE Earlier in her career, the Delaware native had driven a commercial bus … also an airport transit bus.
11 NOT GIVEN (We only know that she did the special training course – not how she found it.)
12 TRUE 'It was a big gamble,' she says, referring less to the likely availability of work than to the reception she would almost certainly get in such a male-dominated environment.
13 FALSE waiting out the 'umpteenth blizzard' of the season … the owner of a small water-hauling company … he cold-called and offered her a job next day.
14 iv The overwhelming evidence is that the wildcat is going to be extinct very soon.
15 x That is certainly a more encouraging figure, but the future of this … animal is worryingly uncertain
16 v the answer stems from recent studies into the origins of wildcats
17 viii Soon the cats adapted to life with humans, who in turn came to rely on them as a means of pest control. As farming spread westwards, the cats came too.
18 ii Its population had already been drastically reduced by loss of habitat in historic times. Wildcats disappeared in low-land England around 1800. Then they vanished … 1860.
19 vii it is not the loss of habitat that is causing the imminent extinction of the species. It is the spread of the domestic cat.
20 ix domestic cats can survive there in such numbers … their ever growing population
21 B *Felis silvestris lybica* is the Middle Eastern wildcat, which has now become feral in Scotland.
22 A *Felis silvestris silvestris* is the Scottish wildcat, which disappeared from England in the 19th century.
23 B *Felis silvestris lybica* is the Middle Eastern wildcat, which was domesticated about ten thousand years ago.
24 C *Felis silvestris cafra* is not mentioned in relation to Scotland.
25 neutering almost certainly involves the widescale neutering … of feral cats.

26 rescue project its prospects have been transformed by a rescue project
27 snares persuaded local hunters … to stop … laying down snares in lynx territory
28 relocating conservationists have since been capturing animals and relocating young adult lynxes in protected territory
29 captive breeding Captive breeding centres have also been established … thanks to those programmes.
30 disproportionate Some would consider that disproportionate, whilst others would think it money well spent.
31 B not even published in a peer-reviewed journal
32 C 'epidemic' 'zombies' 'retailer of style' all reflect journalistic rather than academic style
33 FALSE the *British Medical Journal* reported that Crichton-Browne had testified to the British parliament (quoting from this)
34 TRUE resulting from enforced evening study in the case of young children … He clearly saw homework as the culprit.
35 FALSE His words were ignored.
36 TRUE Terman and Hocking … reported similar sleep durations among US school children.
37 TRUE compared to earlier studies, the younger children … slept for a shorter period.
38 NOT GIVEN (there is no mention of this in the text)
39 TRUE This suggests that sleep recommendations start with the assumption that children don't get enough sleep, rather than an empirical assessment of how much they actually need.
40 FALSE If short sleep does cause obesity, then the effect is moderate at best

How to mark the Writing Test

Task 1

There are four criteria for marking the Part One tasks, which are equally weighted.

Task achievement

This is an assessment of how well the student has fulfilled the task.

A successful task will:

- include at least the minimum number of words
- have a text structure appropriate to a letter
- be relevant to the context established in the input material
- achieve the writer's intended purpose
- cover the functions indicated in the bullet points

Coherence and cohesion

This is an assessment of how clear and fluent the writing is.

A successful task will:

- be appropriately organised
- successfully link information and ideas
- contain logical sequencing
- make effective use of cohesive devices

Lexical resource

This is an assessment of the use of vocabulary.

A successful task will:

- include a range of relevant vocabulary
- use vocabulary accurately
- use vocabulary in an appropriate way

Grammatical resource

This is an assessment of the use of grammar.

A successful task will:

- use an appropriate range of grammatical forms at sentence level
- use grammatical forms accurately

Task 2

There are four criteria for marking the Part Two tasks, which are equally weighted.

Task response

This is an assessment of how well the student has responded to the task.

A successful task will:

- make clear the writer's position on the issues raised in a question or statement
- develop arguments to support that position
- support the arguments with evidence and examples
- include at least the minimum number of words

Coherence and cohesion

This is an assessment of how clear and fluent the writing is.

A successful task will:

- be appropriately organised
- successfully link information and ideas
- contain logical sequencing
- make effective use of cohesive devices

Lexical resource

This is an assessment of the use of vocabulary.

A successful task will:

- include a range of relevant vocabulary
- use vocabulary accurately
- use vocabulary in an appropriate way

Grammatical resource

This is an assessment of the use of grammar.

A successful task will:

- use an appropriate range of grammatical forms at sentence level
- use grammatical forms accurately

How to mark the Speaking Test

The speaking test is an assessment of how effectively students can communicate in English.

There are four criteria for marking the Speaking Test, which are equally weighted.

Fluency and coherence

This is the ability to:

- talk at a consistently normal speed
- link ideas and language together in logical sequences
- use the language features which create coherent, connected speech

Lexical resource

This is the ability to:

- use a range of relevant vocabulary
- use words appropriately to convey meaning
- use paraphrase strategies when required

Grammatical range and accuracy

This is the ability to:

- use a range of grammatical forms appropriately
- use grammatical forms accurately

Pronunciation

This is the ability to:

- use a range of phonological features to convey meaning
- produce intelligible individual sounds
- use stress, rhythm and intonation effectively

IELTS practice test [3.37]

PRESENTER: In this test you'll hear a number of different recordings and you'll have to answer questions on what you hear. There will be time for you to read the instructions and questions and you will have a chance to check your answers. The recording will be played once only. The test is in four sections.

Now turn to Section 1 on page 100 of your book. You will hear a student called Fiona telling her friend about a research project she is taking part in. First you have some time to look at questions 1 to 3. You will see that there is also an example which has been done for you.

Now we shall begin. You should answer the questions as you listen because you will not hear the recording a second time. Listen carefully and answer questions 1 to 3.

MAN: Hi, Fiona. How did the meeting about the research project go?

FIONA: Hi. It was interesting. The project's doing a survey into the attitudes of people who use the downtown shopping district as opposed to suburban shopping centres. I picked up a leaflet about it in the college library, but the meeting was held at the head office building of a big retail chain that's based locally.

MAN: So is that where the money for the project's coming from?

FIONA: Well, a number of local companies are involved in that, although the funds are being administered by the local council, which is working in partnership with a large educational charity that's organising the actual survey I'll be working on. They were running the meeting.

MAN: So was it a bit like an interview?

FIONA: No, I'd already applied online and provided a character reference – I got my college tutor to do that – this was more of a briefing meeting. But I did have to take photo ID with me to prove that I was the same person who'd made the application.

MAN: Wow – serious stuff then. But you're not getting paid, are you?

FIONA: No, it's voluntary – but because our task is to conduct face-to-face interviews with members of the public, they wanted to check that we didn't hold strong views about shopping malls. You had to declare that in the application, and my tutor told me he was asked to comment on that in the reference. I mean, most of the volunteers are students, and it is useful in terms of seeing how a big public survey is set up.

PRESENTER: Before you listen to the rest of the conversation, you have some time to read questions 4 to 10.

Now listen and answer questions 4 to 10.

MAN: So what exactly will you be doing?

FIONA: A week of interviewing people in the city centre.

MAN: And is it like, all day every day?

FIONA: Well, that's up to me. Each interview takes twenty minutes, but I'm not supposed to work more than six hours in any one twenty-four hour period.

MAN: Right. Will you have to dress up smart?

FIONA: No, there's no dress code. As long as you've got your badge on, you can wear what you like.

MAN: And have they told you what sort of people to target?

FIONA: There are three groups. Group A is like people of working age, group B is retired people and group C is students. But at least sixty per cent are meant to be in the first group, and the other forty per cent roughly divided between B and C.

MAN: So how many do you have to do in a day?

FIONA: I've got a target of thirty-five interviews over the seven days, which works out at five a day, but I can choose which days I work and how many I do each day.

MAN: So how do you know where to stand?

FIONA: I go where I'm told. So that you don't have to go into the office or phone up, you're sent a text message each morning. Where they send you depends on how interviews have gone the previous day.

MAN: How do they know?

FIONA: 'Cos you have to send in your data online each evening. You've got twelve hours from the time of the interview to do that. There's a secure site you log into.

MAN: Is it called Survey Monkey? I used that one once.

FIONA: We're using Survey Host actually – though I have used that one for other things.

PRESENTER: Now turn to Section 2 on page 101 of your book. You will hear someone giving a talk about opportunities to do voluntary work on a game reserve in southern Africa. First you have some time to look at questions 11 to 14.

Now listen and answer questions 11 to 14.

WOMAN: Hi there. I've come along today to give you some information about opportunities to work as a volunteer at the Phinda Game Reserve in southern Africa.

The reserve is located between the Indian Ocean and the Lebombo Mountains. Very few reserves in Africa have the biodiversity that Phinda offers. This vast tract of bush, river valley and forest is home to dynamic populations of African mammals, and this is where the help of volunteers proves invaluable. As a volunteer, you can join the research team at Phinda dedicated to the management of this ecosystem. Indeed, the people managing the reserve rely on volunteers to support the research taking place at Phinda.

This research aims to ensure that the various wildlife populations remain in balance and well managed within the reserve. Because although the area was at one time somewhat depleted in major mammal species, large-scale reintroduction programmes have allowed for the development of this stunning reserve, which now has viable populations of elephants, big cats and antelope, as well as both black and white rhino species.

What's more, regular and dedicated research has allowed Phinda to become a partner in essential conservation initiatives of worldwide significance, and the recent release of black rhino into the reserve is evidence of this.

A volunteer joining an experienced research team could well be involved in one of a number of research components. Big cat monitoring is a possibility, and this could even include the chance to record the movements and sightings of lions. Most probably, however, you'll spend some time monitoring the white rhino as over one hundred are now in residence, although there is also research into small mammals for those more interested in those species.

PRESENTER: Before you hear the rest of the talk, you have some time to look at questions 15 to 20.

Now listen and answer questions 15 to 20.

WOMAN: So what would a volunteer on one of the research programmes at Phinda expect to do? Firstly, let's talk about white rhino monitoring. Over one hundred rhino now roam the reserve, following the reintroduction of a handful some years ago. Volunteers assist in the building up of a database that has been created to record details of gender, age, territorial information and movements. By putting what are called 'notches' in the animals' ears it is possible to collect this information.

Then there's big cat and predator research. For example, there's cheetah monitoring. This involves finding out about the territory and movements of individuals, which are identified through their eye markings. A unique hunting substrate of the forest is also being investigated as part of this research programme. Alternatively, a volunteer might join the active leopard research project, keeping a note of where they are seen. Or if you're very lucky, you might even get to record movements and sightings of two lion prides. In any case, as a volunteer, you are likely to gain useful experience and acquire key skills, such as tracking and the use of telemetry equipment.

Finally, a word about the facilities for volunteers who come to work at Phinda. In terms of accommodation, a rustic farmhouse on the reserve is set aside for both research staff and volunteers. Running water and electricity can occasionally be intermittent due to the remoteness of the reserve, but volunteers are provided with a weekly food kitty to do their own shopping and cooking is on a rotational basis with the other volunteers. The house is equipped with a fridge, freezer, stove, oven and microwave.

Volunteers generally work a six-day week, with Sundays free, when there might be the chance to go to the beach if you can get a lift with someone. Any excursions, whether to the coast or nearby towns, are at the volunteers' own cost, so bringing some spending money is recommended.

The daily work schedule varies heavily depending on the research objectives at the time. But volunteers do get some time to relax. There is a TV in the house, though only local channels are available, but there is also a DVD player. Volunteers are encouraged to bring some films to watch, as there is not much available to buy locally.

So I hope I've covered everything – does anyone have any questions?

PRESENTER: Now turn to Section 3 on page 103 of your book. You will hear part of a radio programme about a disease which is affecting a species of tree called the European ash. First you have some time to look at questions 21 to 25.

Now listen and answer questions 21 to 25.

DIANA: Hi, I'm Diana Wherry and on today's programme we're talking about trees. A major news story in the UK recently has been the discovery of ash dieback disease, a fungal infection that destroys members of the ash species of trees. To find out more about this threat I'm talking to plant pathologist, Dennis Walkern. First of all, what is this disease that we're calling colloquially 'ash dieback'?

DENNIS: It's a fungus which spreads by spores which form on fallen leaves and then infect the leaves of a healthy tree. Once established, it spreads from there into the bark and the other parts of the tree. Eventually, it will kill small trees. In older trees, it kills shoots and maybe branches, and weakens the tree so that it becomes vulnerable to other diseases.

DIANA: Is it just ash trees that are vulnerable to this particular infection or can it hop on to other trees and species too?

DENNIS: As far as we're aware, it only affects ash trees – and here that means the common European ash, which is the one we have in the UK. It seems to be less of a serious problem on Far Eastern ashes. It seems to exist in a benign form, co-existing fairly happily with certain types of ash tree in Japan and presumably other parts of East Asia.

DIANA: So how come it's only relatively recently arrived in the UK?

DENNIS: It's happened because sometime in the early 1990s, it migrated from its Japanese home and took up residence somewhere in Eastern Europe, and it's been spreading from there ever since. It moved to Scandinavia, where by 2009, I think, ninety per cent of Danish ash trees had some signs of infection. Then it turned up in France, so this is a big spreading wave of infection. How it got to Europe in the first place, we don't know.

DIANA: We're hearing this number of ninety per cent of European ash trees being vulnerable. Is this a reflection on the fact that not all European ashes are made equally? Are there different subtypes?

DENNIS: Well, no. It's more that ash trees are quite variable. In studying trees which appear to have been less badly affected in Scandinavia, it's been found that some trees appear to have survived because they're genuinely more resistant to the infection. In looking at the seeds that arise from those trees, there are estimates that maybe one per cent of the population will be able to survive.

DIANA: So, is the long-term prospect that we'll end up selecting out the trees that are vulnerable to this, and breed a new strain of trees just naturally, which are naturally resistant to it? So we just have to wait for one generation of ash trees – then we'll have trees that aren't vulnerable and the problem will go away.

DENNIS: Probably more than one generation, actually, because you'd have a sort of sputtering epidemic – in other words you'd have some trees which survive the first waves anyway. Otherwise, I think that you're probably correct. The only catch there is to think what the generation time of an ash tree is, because some of the more attractive landscape trees may be over a century old.

PRESENTER: Before you hear the rest of the programme, you have some time to look at questions 26 to 30.

Now listen and answer questions 26 to 30.

DIANA: So we're saying that, for the next decade or two, we'd see perhaps a third of the trees around us disappearing – because ash is an extremely common species in the UK.

DENNIS: So much so, actually, that nobody knows exactly how many there are in reality, still less exactly how evenly they're spread across the country. As a mathematical modeller, I'd be interested in establishing such facts and other details about the spread of this disease. We know that immunisation of trees isn't possible because they don't have adaptive immune systems, but some management of the disease may be possible. So we need to find out if it's affecting old and young trees equally, whether it's spread to all regions, and whether there are populations of ash trees in areas that can be isolated from the spread of the disease. We also know that the use of fungicides isn't feasible on a large scale because of the sheer number of ash trees out there, and the need for regular re-application. One much loved ash tree in an urban setting might be saved in that way, but not the species at large. But if those other facts can be established then the prospects of managing the disease might be greater.

PRESENTER: Now turn to Section 4 on page 104 of your book. You will hear a university teacher giving his students some information about internships, and the report that interns have to write as part of the course. First you have some time to look at questions 31 to 37.

Now listen and answer questions 31 to 37.

MAN: Hi, there. Today I want to talk about your internship and the report you have to write after you've done it. As you know, as in other subjects like medicine and law, an internship is an integral part of your degree programme in electronic commerce. Put simply, an internship is a period spent working for a company as an unpaid member of staff. But it should provide you with valuable insights into the practical aspects of the subject.

To fulfil the academic requirements of the internship, you have to submit an internship report following the specifications outlined in the Faculty guide. Please consult the programme website for the latest version of this document.

In a nutshell, your internship report must include a number of specific features: Firstly, it should outline the specific business of the company or department in which you perform your internship; secondly it should outline your job description there. These first two components can be brief, and they can be included in the introduction of the report. The major focus of the report should be on the third component, the critical analysis of a specific internship-related topic, which relates academic knowledge to practical experience.

However, note that sadly many aspects of your daily work can be practice-oriented rather than academically-oriented and you'll be asked to do routine tasks most of the time. It is, of course, important that you do as you are asked. However, to pass the academic requirements of the internship you must go, if necessary, beyond the following of instructions and demonstrate your ability in logical thinking. Ideally, the report will be of practical benefit to your employer and go beyond your usual duties.

PRESENTER: Before you hear the rest of the talk, you have some time to look at questions 38 to 40.

Now listen and answer questions 38 to 40.

MAN: So, now I'll give you some recommendations for the actual writing of your reports. Once you have gathered your information and planned an outline, you can begin writing. Your report needs to be serious and academic, but bear in mind that your tutors are unlikely to be impressed by the excessive use of technical terms. So don't worry about fancy beginnings or profound ideas – just write! As you work, keep your target audience in mind. Are they going to be familiar with the acronyms used in your work place? If in doubt, leave them out and write the words out in full.

Once you have completed your first draft, put it away and give your mind a rest. When you take it out again, begin revising. Substitute accurate words for ambiguous ones; substitute clear simple sentences for complicated grammatical structures. You may want to rewrite paragraphs or entire sections.

The bottom line is to produce a smoothly written, logical report. Having someone else read your revised draft is a sure test of effective communication. A fellow intern or workmate will tell you if what you've written is understandable. Revise a second time on the basis of this criticism. Your final version should be flawless. If your report includes typos and spelling mistakes, then your readers are likely to be distracted and you risk losing credibility.

Although the internship report should conform to the overall structure I've described, there's no strict rule when it comes to length and specific formatting of text. You should be able to present your report in the style most appropriate for your studies. However, a typical internship report consists of three main sections: the preliminaries, the main text and the reference material, all of which are required.